THE OFFICIAL®
1990
BLACKBOOK
PRICE GUIDE OF
UNITED STATES
POSTAGE
STAMPS

TWELFTH EDITION

BY MARC HUDGEONS, N.L.G.

HOUSE OF COLLECTIBLES • NEW YORK

©1989 by Random House, Inc.

All rights reserved under International and Pan-American Copyright Conventions.

Published by: The House of Collectibles
201 East 50th Street
New York, New York 10022

Distributed by Ballantine Books, a division of Random House, Inc., New York, and simultaneously in Canada by Random House of Canada Limited, Toronto.

Manufactured in the United States of America

Library of Congress Catalog Card Number: 80-644087

ISBN: 0-876-37099-7

Twelfth edition: July 1989

10 9 8 7 6 5 4 3 2 1

TABLE OF CONTENTS

The publisher also wishes to express special thanks to Mr. Armin R. Crowe at the Collectors Institute, Ltd., Omaha, Nebraska 68144, the United States Postal System for photographs and illustrations, and for the special help provided by *Linn's Stamp News*.

MARKET REVIEW

Even though the growth in last year's stamp market remained relatively flat, the trend now seems to be a slow, gradual increase indicated for the upcoming year. The demand for higher grade stamps (very fine condition and better) by both investors and collectors, who seem to be upgrading their collections, seems to be dominating the market and at least partially responsible for the increase in prices. This activity has also stimulated the fine to very fine market in rarer stamps, so much so as to create a shortage in available inventory, which should continue to drive prices up. Single Issue U.S. stamps continue to show a slow recovery.

The influx of new collectors in the stamp market has influenced the increase in the demand for Modern Singles and Plate Blocks, 1980 to date, in mint condition. Also popular among first-time collectors are the inexpensive topicals, errors, and oddities. There are many opportunities available with these affordable stamps.

Nineteenth-century General Issue stamps have declined slightly. On the average, prices have fallen about 5%, depending on the specimen. Twentieth-century stamp market prices for lower grade and highest grade stamps have not changed much, and neither has the supply. However, when you look closely at the fine to very fine level, there appears to be much more activity. Specific examples of this would be stamps from the 1950s and 1960s. The dramatic slowdown by the government issuing fewer new stamps may be the beginning of what will become a remedy for sagging prices in the coming decade. Airmails from 1918 to around 1950 have also been off about 5% but, similar to the General Issues, the Post 1950s Issues in fine and very fine stamps have modestly increased.

The slight decline in market values of some stamps over the past year may be regarded as a market correction long overdue, compensating for past surges that pushed prices up unrealistically high—up to 1000–2000% in some extreme cases—before buyers began to slow down. One might also consider that many of the stamps now being offered on the market are relative bargains and should be considered for purchase.

Almost without exception, Classic Issues of 1847–1869, which are supposed to weather any sort of economic storm, suffered value declines.

The early "perfs" showed declines averaging around 10% for unused and used condition. The 1861–1862 second designs were almost uniformly down, as were the various Grills issued shortly after the Civil war.

Confederate stamps seem to always hold their popularity; hence their movement in the market has been slightly above normal. Duck stamps are also favorites year after year. They have recorded increases across the board of about 3% to 5%. Mint Sheets and Plate Blocks have posted modest gains on relatively moderate trading. There are still several bargains remaining in the Mint Sheet area.

As we reflect over the market for the last year, most of the action comes from collectors trying to upgrade their collections. Most are looking for never-hinged stamps of the early 20th-century variety. A hint would be to avoid any stamp that was reperforated or regummed. Be a smart buyer; look only to a dealer who has a good reputation.

THE STORY OF U.S. STAMPS

The world's first postage stamps were issued by Great Britain in 1840 and pictured its new queen, Victoria, then 21 years old. It was not until 1847 that the U.S. released postage stamps, but prior to that time some city postmasters issued stamps of their own. These very valuable stamps, known as "postmaster provisionals," were used in St. Louis, New York, Annapolis and a number of other cities.

The first federally released postage stamps comprised a 5¢ denomination picturing Benjamin Franklin and a 10¢ showing George Washington. Their size was very similar to that of modern non-commemoratives and they had gummed backs, just like our stamps. The chief difference was that they carried no little holes or perforations between each specimen on a sheet, to aid in separation. Instead they had to be cut apart with scissors or creased and torn by hand. These stamps were called "imperforates," or "without perforations." All stamps in those days, including Europe's, were made in this way. The U.S. did not start perforating its stamps until 1857, ten years later.

Imperforates rank today as the hobby's aristocrats, its elder statesmen and foremost classics. They have long been dear to the hearts of collectors, and not merely on grounds of their antiquity. Some specialists maintain that these issues, every one of them bearing a statesman's portrait, are more elegantly engraved than any of their descendants. In addition, they can be found (with luck and the necessary cash) in super specimens that put ordinary perforated stamps to shame. When a stamp is perforated, every one on the sheet is of identical size. Some sheets may be better centered than others, depending on how the paper is fed, but no specimens will be physically larger than any others. With imperforates, it's quite another matter. The cutting was never done very evenly. Some specimens were cropped or cut into by scissor wielders and left with margins so immense that portions of all the surrounding stamps are visible. These are called jumbo margin copies and the prices collectors will give for them is often astronomic, provided the condition is otherwise good. It is not at all unusual for one of these oversized beauties to command three or four times the normal sum. Collectors must take care though, because in philately as in most other things, all that sparkles is not necessarily diamonds. Larcenous persons have been known to take very ordinary average stamps and add fake margins.

Not all imperforates are equally easy (or hard) to get with four full margins. This is all a matter of how closely together they were printed on the sheet. The cutter is less apt to make a mistake if the stamps are further apart on the sheet. Scott's #11, the 3¢ 1851, is by far the most difficult to find with full margins. It also happens to be the least expensive imperforate, thanks to the enormous quantities printed. While the usual specimen will fetch only $4–$6 used, a jumbo margin #11 has no trouble selling for $20, $30 or more.

The second series of imperforates, issued from 1851 to 1856, comprised values from 1¢ to 12¢. There were five stamps, with Washington appearing on three of them; the other two used portraits of Franklin and Jefferson. In 1857 the same group of stamps was released again, this time with perforations and three high values: a 24¢ and 90¢ pictured Washington, and a 30¢ portrayed Franklin. The 90¢ stamp was not exceeded in face value until the Columbian Exposition series in 1893. Because very little mail required the paying of so much postage, most specimens of the 90¢ 1857-1861 that went to private hands never got on letters. Consequently this stamp is much more difficult to find used than unused, a rare circumstance for a U.S. issue. Needless to say, counterfeit cancels exist.

There was no question that by this time postage stamps had scored a big success. Any doubts or complaints that some users may have had about them at the beginning had long since vanished. Certain persons became so fond of stamps that they began saving them, used as well as unused, and thus the hobby of philately was born. For the government, stamps brought greater economy to the postal service than anticipated. They also allowed mail to travel faster. There was just one problem: some people were abusing the system. During the Civil War, and shortly thereafter, it became apparent that many stamps were going through the mails twice or more. People were cleaning off the cancels and using them again. This may have been done by individuals but, more likely, it was a large scale operation in which used stamps were cleaned in wholesale quantities and sold to business houses and other volume mailers at a discount. The government was being bilked out of thousands of dollars but there seemed no solution until a plan was devised to use "grills" on the faces of stamps in 1867. These were networks of tiny embossed dots which weakened the paper and would, presumably, cause it to break apart if any attempt was made at erasing the cancel. After just two years the grill was dropped but it had appeared on enough stamps in that short time to provide philatelists with an intriguing subspecialty. Not all the grills were alike. They differed in size and style and collecting them is quite a sport.

The year 1869 marked the first year of U.S. pictorial stamps that portrayed things or events rather than portraits. They cannot really be termed commemoratives in the modern sense but they were extremely pictorial. Subjects included a pony express rider, a rail locomotive, panoramas of the landing of Columbus, the signing of the Declaration of Independence, and others. This series also presented the first stamps to be printed in more than one color. Multicolor printing was no small operation in those days. It required two separate plates; one consisting of frames to be printed in one color, and the other central designs to be printed in a different color. The sheets were fed through one press, allowed to dry, then fed into the next to receive the final printing. As the feeding was done by hand, human error occasionally occurred. A few sheets were fed upside down the second time around, resulting in the first, but not the most famous, U.S. inverts, or stamps with upside down centers. These are very valuable and seldom offered on the market. The king of all United States inverts is a twentieth century stamp, the 24¢ airmail of 1918. This small stamp has a central design of a Curtiss Jenny single engine plane. It was printed 100 to a sheet. On the day it was issued, a Washington, D.C. collector, William T. Robey, took a few minutes from his lunch hour to go into the local post office and buy a sheet. He had no intention of using the stamps but merely wanted them for his collection. After putting down his $24 he received what appeared to be a normal sheet, but after looking closer, Mr. Robey found that on every stamp the airplane was upside down. This incident stirred a furor of considerable proportion. The government was embarrassed since it had claimed that the old 1869 inverts could not happen again with its new machinery and rigid controls. It tried, without success, to buy the sheet back from Robey. Meanwhile it notified postmasters around the country to check their stocks for further error sheets. No more were found, and when it became evident that Robey's sheet was the only one in existence he began receiving substantial offers from collectors and dealers. The offers seemed tempting and he finally sold his treasure for $15,000 to Eugene Klein of Philadelphia, a prominent dealer. Klein immediately resold the sheet to Col. Edward H. R. Green of New York, the legendary collector who also owned the only five known specimens of the 1913 Liberty nickel. It is believed Green paid at least $17,500 for this philatelic morsel, a huge sum in those days but only about one third as much as each of the 100 stamps are now individually worth. Green broke up the sheet into blocks, selling most of them and recovering his entire cost. Several single specimens were subsequently lost, one was supposed to have disappeared into a vacuum cleaner while Green's housekeeper was tidying up.

FACTORS BEHIND STAMP PRICES

The collector value (or "market value") of any stamp rests with a variety of factors. Philately becomes a bit less mysterious when one understands the forces at work in the stamp marketplace.

A beginner will normally presume that expensive stamps are expensive because of rarity. Certainly there is a great deal of talk about stamp rarities within the hobby, and so it is natural enough to ascribe high prices to the phenomenon of rarity. In fact rarity is only one of several factors that influence stamp prices, and the influence it carries is not particularly clear-cut.

In this book you will note some stamps (mostly among the early regular issues) with values of $1,000, $2,000, and even higher. Obviously these stamps are rarer than those selling for $10 or $15. But once having said that, we have virtually summed up our useful knowledge of rarity and its effect on prices. A comparison of prices, between stamps in roughly similar ranges of value, does not indicate which is the rarer. A stamp selling for $1,000 is not necessarily rarer than one selling for $500. A $10,000 stamp may actually be more abundant than one which commands $5,000. This hard-to-comprehend fact of philatelic life prevails because of the other factors involved in determining a stamp's price. If rarity were the only factor, one could, of course, easily see which stamps are the rarest by the prices they fetch.

The word "rare" is an elixir to many collectors, not only of stamps but other collector's items. Sellers are well aware of this, and seldom fail to sprinkle the word liberally in their sales literature. There is no law against calling a stamp rare, as this represents a personal opinion more than anything else and opinions are allowable in advertising. Unfortunately there is no standard definition for rarity. Does "rare" mean just a handful of specimens in existence, with one reaching the sales portals once in five years? Does it mean 100 in existence, or 1,000, or some other number? Since stamps are—today, at any rate—printed in the multimillions, a thousand surviving specimens might seem a very tiny total to some people. Further complicating this situation is the fact that the specific rarity of most stamps cannot be determined, or even estimated with any hope of accuracy. The quantities printed are recorded for most of our stamps, going back even into the nineteenth century, but the quantity *surviving* of any particular stamp is anyone's guess. It is obvious that a stamp that goes through the auction rooms once a year is fairly rare, but this provides no sound basis for guessing the number of specimens in existence. That could only be accomplished if some sort of grand census could be taken, and all specimens tallied. This of course is nothing but a pipe dream. Some collectors would not participate in such a census; some might be unaware that it was being conducted. Then, too, there are many scarce or rare stamps in hands other than those of collectors, such as dealers and museums. Additionally, there could be (and probably are) existing specimens of rare stamps yet to be discovered, as fresh discoveries are made periodically in the hobby through attic cleaning and the like.

In terms of influence on price, rarity is outdistanced somewhat by *popularity*. Some stamps, for one reason or other, are simply more popular than others. They have a sort of innate appeal for hobbyists, either through reputation, exquisite designing, circumstances of issue, oddity, or various other potential reasons. These stamps sell out rapidly from the stocks of dealers, while some stamps that are supposedly scarcer will linger in stock albums for ages and ages waiting to tempt a customer. It is no wonder, then, that the prices of popular stamps rise more quickly than those that are scarce but not in brisk demand. The Columbian series typifies the effect of popularity on stamp values. If stamp prices were fixed by scarcity alone, none of the Columbians would be selling for nearly as much. Much of their value derives from their overwhelming popularity with collectors of U.S. stamps. It would be safe to say, in fact, that *all* of the Columbians, from the lowest face value to the $5, are more plentiful than other U.S. stamps selling for precisely the same sums. Every dealer has Columbians in stock, and quite a few dealers have the high values of the set, too. They are not "hard to get." But they *are* very costly.

Popularity, of course, does not remain constant forever. There are shifts in philatelic popularity, usually slight but occasionally extreme. The popularity of commemoratives as a whole versus regular issues as a whole can change from time to time. Then, too, there are swings of popularity for airmails, first day covers, blocks, coil pairs, mint sheets, and all other philatelic material. A climb or decline in the price of any philatelic item is often an indication of the forces of popularity at work. Then there are activities of investors to consider, whose buying habits seldom reflect those of the pure collector. A great deal of buying by investors in any short period of time (such as occurred during 1979 and 1980, and to less extent in 1981) can make prices seem well out of balance.

Also on the subject of prices, it is important for the beginner to realize that arithmetic is usually futile when dealing with stamp values. You cannot determine the price of one philatelic item by knowing the value of a similar one. This can best be shown by the relative values of singles and blocks of four. A block of four is, as one would expect, worth *more* than four times as much as single specimens of that stamp. It is not just four specimens of the stamp, but four of them *attached,* which lends added scarcity and appeal. The difficulty lies in trying to use mathematics to determine a block's value. Some blocks are worth five times as much as the single stamp; some six times; some ten times as much or even more. Almost all blocks—except very common ones—will vary somewhat in value, in relation to the value of the individual stamp. There is no satisfactory explanation for this, other than the presumption that some blocks are scarcer than others or just in greater demand than others.

In the case of common philatelic items, the value hinges greatly on the method of sale. If you want to buy one specimen of a common cover, you may have to pay $1.50. But if you were willing to buy a hundred common first day covers *of the dealer's choice,* you could very likely get them for $75 or 75¢ each. Buying in quantity, and allowing the dealer to make the selections, can save a great deal of money. Of course one may then ask: What is the real value of those covers? Is it $1.50 or 75¢? The only answer is that it depends on how you buy!

If this article seems to raise a great many questions without supplying many answers, it will, hopefully, serve to show that stamp collecting is not bound to rigid formulas. What happens in the stamp market is largely beyond prediction, or precise explanation. This, indeed, is one of the exciting aspects of the hobby.

STAMP COLLECTORS' TERMINOLOGY

Adhesives—A term given to stamps that have gummed backs and are intended to be pasted on articles and items that are to be mailed.

Aerophilately—The collecting of airmail or any form of stamps related to mail carried by air.

Airmail—Any mail carried by air.

Albino—An uncolored embossed impression of a stamp generally found on envelopes.

Approvals—Stamps sent to collectors. They are examined by the collector, who selects stamps to purchase and returns balance with payment for the stamps he retained.

Arrow Block—An arrow-like mark found on blocks of stamps in the selvage. This mark is used as a guide for cutting or perforating stamps.

As-Is—A term used when selling a stamp. It means no representation is given as to its condition or authenticity. Buyers should beware.

Backprint—Any printing that may appear on reverse of stamp.

Backstamp—The postmark on the back of a letter indicating what time or date the letter arrived at the post office.

Bantams—A miniature stamp given to a war economy issue of stamps from South Africa.

Batonne—Watermarked paper used in printing stamps.

Bicolored—A two-color printed stamp.

Bisect—A stamp that could be used by cutting in half and at half the face value.

Block—A term used for a series of four or more stamps attached at least two high and two across.

Bourse—A meeting or convention of stamp collectors and dealers where stamps are bought, sold and traded.

Cachet—A design printed on the face of an envelope generally celebrating the commemoration of a new postage stamp issue. Generally called a first day cover.

Cancelled to Order—A stamp cancelled by the government without being used. Generally remainder stamps or special issues. Common practice of Soviet nations.

Cancellation—A marking placed on the face of a stamp to show that it has been used.

Centering—The manner in which the design of a stamp is printed and centered upon the stamp blank. A perfectly centered stamp would have equal margins on all sides.

Classic—A popular, unique, highly desired or very artistic stamp. Not necessarily a rare stamp, but one sought after by the collector. Generally used only of nineteenth-century issues.

Coils—Stamps sold in rolls for use in vending machines.

Commemorative—A stamp issued to commemorate or celebrate a special event.

Crease—A fold or wrinkle in a stamp.

Cut square—An embossed staple removed from the envelope by cutting.

Dead Country—A country no longer issuing stamps.

Demonetized—A stamp no longer valid for use.

Error—A stamp printed or produced with a major design or color defect.

Essay—Preliminary design for a postage stamp.

Face Value—The value of a stamp indicated on the face or surface of the stamp.

Frank—A marking on the face of an envelope indicating the free and legal use of postage. Generally for government use.

Fugitive Inks—A special ink used to print stamps, which can be rubbed or washed off easily, to eliminate erasures and forgeries.

General Collector—One who collects all kinds of issues and all types of stamps from different countries.

Granite Paper—A type of paper containing colored fibers to prevent forgery.

Gum—The adhesive coating on the back of a stamp.

Handstamped—A stamp that has been handcancelled.

Hinge—A specially gummed piece of glassine paper used to attach a stamp to the album page.

Imperforate—A stamp without perforations.

Inverted—Where one portion of a stamp's design is inverted or upside down from the remainder of the design.

Local Stamps—Stamps that are only valid in a limited area.

Margin—The unprinted area around a stamp.

Miniature Sheet—A smaller than usual sheet of stamps.

Mint Condition—A stamp in original condition as it left the postal printing office.

Mirror Print—A stamp error printed in reverse as though looking at a regular stamp reflected in a mirror.

Multicolored—A stamp printed in three or more colors.

Never Hinged—A stamp in original mint condition never hinged in an album.

Off Paper—A used stamp that has been removed from the envelope to which it was attached.

On Paper—A used stamp still attached to the envelope.

Original Gum—A stamp with the same or original adhesive that was applied in the manufacturing process.

Pair—Two stamps unseparated.

Pen Cancellation—A stamp cancelled by pen or pencil.

Perforation Gauge—A printed chart containing various sizes of perforation holes used in determining the type or size of perforation of a stamp.

Perforations—Holes punched along stamp designs allowing stamps to be easily separated.

Philatelist—One who collects stamps.

Pictorial Stamps—Stamps that bear large pictures of animals, birds, flowers, etc.

Plate Block Number—The printing plate number used to identify a block of four or more stamps taken from a sheet of stamps.

Postally Used—A stamp that has been properly used and cancelled.

Precancels—A stamp that has been cancelled in advance. Generally used on bulk mail.

Reissue—A new printing of an old stamp that has been out of circulation.

Revenue Stamp—A label or stamp affixed to an item as evidence of tax payment.

Se-tenant—Two or more stamps joined together each having a different design or value.

Seals—An adhesive label that looks like a stamp, used for various fund raising campaigns.

Sheet—A page of stamps as they are printed usually separated before distribution to post offices.

Soaking—Removing used stamps from paper to which they are attached by soaking in water. *(NOTE: Colored cancels may cause staining to other stamps.)*

Souvenir Sheet—One or more specially designed stamps printed by the government in celebration of a special stamp.

Splice—The splice made between rolls of paper in the printing operation. Stamps printed on this splice are generally discarded.

Tete-Bechs—A pair of stamps printed together so that the images point in opposite vertical directions.

Transit Mark—A mark made by an intermediate post office between the originating and final destination post office.

Typeset Stamp—A stamp printed with regular printer's type, as opposed to engraved, lithographed, etc.

Ungummed—Stamps printed without an adhesive back.

Unperforated—A stamp produced without perforations.

Unhinged—A stamp that has never been mounted with the use of a hinge.

Vignette—The central design portion of a stamp.

Want List—A list of stamps a collector needs to fill gaps in his collection.

Watermark—A mark put into paper by the manufacturer, not readily seen by the naked eye.

Wrapper—A strip of paper with adhesive on one end, used for wrapping bundles of mail. Especially in Britain, it refers to any bit of paper to which a used stamp is still attached.

HOW TO GRADE STAMPS

A person need not be an expert to judge the quality or grade of a stamp. All he needs is a discerning eye, possibly a small linear measuring device, and the grading instructions listed below.

The major catalogs traditionally list stamps simply as "Unused" or "Used." Auction houses, however, will describe the stamps for sale in a more informative manner. The greater the value of the stamp, the more thoroughly it is described.

There is no officially accepted system of grading stamps. What we have done in this book is essentially to set up a system of grading stamps using the suggestions and practices of stamp dealers from all over the country. Total agreement was made to the following categories and grades of stamps that are most frequently traded.

CATEGORIES

Mint—The perfect stamp with superb centering, no faults and usually with original gum (if issued with gum).

Unused—Although unused this stamp may have a hinge mark or may have suffered some change in its gum since it was issued.

Used—Basically this will be the normal stamp that passed through the government postal system and will bear an appropriate cancellation.

Cancelled to Order—These are stamps that have not passed through the postal system but have been carefully cancelled by the government usually for a commemoration. These are generally considered undesirable by collectors.

GRADE—STAMP CENTERING

Average—The perforations cut slightly into the design.

Fine—The perforations do not touch the design at all, but the design will be off center by 50% or more of a superb centered stamp.

Very Fine—The design will be off center by less than 50% of a superb stamp. The off centered design will be visibly noticeable.

Extra Fine—The design will be almost perfectly centered. The margin will be off by less than 25% of a superb stamp.

Superb—This design will be perfectly centered with all four margins exactly the same. On early imperforate issues, superb specimens will have four clear margins that do not touch the design at any point.

Average
Centering

Fine
Centering

Very Fine
Centering

Extra Fine
Centering

Superb
Centering

GRADE—STAMP GUM

Original Gum—This stamp will have the same gum on it that it had the day it was issued.

Regummed—This stamp will have new gum applied to it as compared to an original gummed stamp. Regummed stamps are worth no more than those with gum missing.

No Gum—This stamp will have had its gum removed or it may have not been issued with gum.

Never Hinged—This stamp has never been hinged so the gum should not have been disturbed in any way.

Lightly Hinged—This stamp has had a hinge applied. A lightly wetted or peelable hinge would do very little damage to the gum when removed.

Heavily Hinged—This stamp has had a hinge applied in such a manner as to secure it to the stamp extremely well. Removal of this hinge usually proves to be disastrous, in most cases, since either part of the hinge remains on the stamp or part of the stamp comes off on the hinge, causing thin spots on the stamp.

GRADE—STAMP FAULTS

Any fault in a stamp such as thin paper, bad perforations, creases, tears, stains, ink marks, pin holes, etc., and depending upon the seriousness of the fault, usually results in grading the stamp to a lower condition.

OTHER STAMP CONSIDERATIONS

CANCELLATIONS

Light Cancel—This stamp has been postally cancelled but the wording and lines are very light and almost unreadable.

Normal Cancel—This stamp has been postally cancelled with just the right amount of pressure. Usually the wording and lines are not distorted and can be made out.

Heavy Cancel—This stamp has been postally cancelled. In the process excessive pressure was used, and the wording and lines are extremely dark and sometimes smeared and in most cases unreadable.

PERFORATIONS

Not to be overlooked in the appearance of a stamp are its perforations. The philatelist might examine these "tear apart" holes with a magnifying glass or microscope to determine the cleanliness of the separations. One must also consider that the different types of paper, upon which the stamp was printed, will sometimes make a difference in the cleanliness of the separations. The term "pulled perf" is used to denote a badly separated stamp in which the perforations are torn or ragged.

COLOR

Other important factors such as color affect the appearance and value of stamps. An expert will have a chart of stamp colors. Chemical changes often occur in inks. Modern printing sometimes uses metallic inks. These "printings" will oxidize upon contact with the natural secretions from animal skin.

The color of certain stamps has been deliberately altered by chemicals to produce a rare shade. Overprints can be eliminated. Postmarks may be eradicated. Replacing gum is a simple process. Some stamps have been found to bear forged watermarks. The back of the paper was cut away and then the stamps rebacked with appropriately watermarked paper.

There are stamp experts who earn a living in the business of stamp repairing. They are craftsmen of the first order. A thin spot on a stamp can be repaired by gluing it on a new layer of paper. Missing perforations can be added. Torn stamps can be put back together. Pieces of stamps may be joined.

In some countries it is accepted practice for an expert, upon examination of a stamp, to certify the authenticity by affixing his signature to the back of the stamp. If the stamp is not genuine, it is his right and duty to so designate on the stamp; but these signatures can also be faked.

REPAIRS, FAKES, AND OTHER UNDESIRABLES

Philately, like most hobbies, is not without its pitfalls. The collector who buys from reputable dealers runs very little risk, as today's stamp pros have high principles and are hard to fool. Buying from auction sales and small dealers, who may not have expert knowledge, is another matter. Here the collector must call into play his own expertise and learn to distinguish the bad from the good.

In the early years of philately, stamps provided a playground for fakers and swindlers. They took advantage of the public's gullibility and the general lack of published information about stamps. Copies were printed of rare stamps, as well as of stamps that never existed in the first place. Cancels were bleached from used specimens to make them appear unused. Fake margins were added to imperforates, to allow ordinary copies to be sold as "superb with jumbo margins." Perforated stamps were reperforated to make them better centered. Thin spots in the paper were filled in, tears closed, missing portions of paper replaced. Stamps were doctored and manipulated in more ways than could be imagined, all in the hope of fooling collectors and making anywhere from a few extra cents to thousands of dollars on them. One of the favorite tricks of fakers was to apply bogus overprints or surcharges. By merely using a rubber handstamp and a pad of ink, they could stamp out a hundred or more "rarities" in a few minutes, turning ordinary British or other issues into varieties not found in any catalogue. It was all a great game and proved very profitable, until collectors and the philatelic public at large became wary of such practices. Even though most of these fakes from the hobby's pioneer years have disappeared out of circulation, a few still turn up and must be guarded against.

United States stamps have not been faked nearly so extensively as those of many other nations, notably South America and Japan. Still the collector should learn to watch for fakes and also repaired specimens.

Total Fake. The counterfeit stamp always varies somewhat from a genuine specimen, though the difference may be very slight. Detection can usually be made if the suspect stamp is examined alongside one known to be genuine. By using a magnifier, the lines of engraving and paper quality can be compared. The ink on a fake is likely to have a fresher appearance and will lie on the surface as a result of being printed at a later date and on less sophisticated equipment; however, this is not always the case. Experts say that when a stamp appears to be a fake, or a reprint, the odds are very good that it is. Some experience is necessary before anyone can get a first glance reaction to a stamp. The presence or absence of a cancel has no bearing on the likelihood of a stamp being a fake, as cancels can be faked too.

Faked Cancel. Faked cancels are very rare on U.S. stamps as nearly all are worth more unused than used. One notable exception is the 90¢ 1857–1861. These are applied either with a fake handstamp or simply drawn with pen and ink. Skillfully drawn faked cancels can be very deceptive. Faked cancels are *much more numerous* on covers than loose stamps.

Removed Cancels. So-called cleaned copies of used stamps, sold as unused, were once very plentiful and are still encountered from time to time. The faker of course chooses lightly canceled specimens from which the obliteration can be removed without leaving telltale evidence. In the case of imperforates he may trim down the margins to remove part of the cancel. Rarely will he attempt to clean a stamp whose cancel falls across the face or any important portion of the stamp. Holding the stamp to a strong light may reveal the cancel lines. X-ray examination provides positive proof.

Added Margin(s). When margins have been added to an imperforate stamp, the paper fibers are woven together (after moistening) along the back and at the front where the margin extends beyond the stamp's design. They can usually be detected by looking closely for a seam or joint at the point where the design ends and the margin begins. A magnifying glass will be necessary for this. When held against a light, the reverse side will probably show evidence of the weaving operation. Sometimes the added margins are of a slightly different grade of paper.

Reperforated. A stamp that has been reperforated to improve its centering will usually be slightly smaller than a normal specimen, and this can be revealed by placing it atop an untampered copy.

Filled In Thin Spots. If held to a light and examined with a good magnifier, filled in thin spots will normally appear darker than the remainder of the stamp. Such spots are often mistaken for discoloration by beginners. Thin spots are filled in by making a paste of paper pulp and glue and applying it gradually to the injured area. After drying, the stamp is placed in a vise so that no telltale hills or valleys are left. This is not really considered forgery but repair work; it becomes forgery only if done with the intent of selling the stamp as undamaged.

Closed Tears. These are almost visible against a light with a magnifier, even if small. A routine examination of any rare stamp should include a check of its margins for possible closed or open tears.

HOW TO USE THIS BOOK

The main section of this book lists all U.S. stamps with the exception of special issues such as airmail, revenues, etc. Special issues are grouped separately in sections of their own. Please refer to the Table of Contents.

Before pricing your stamps, be sure they are correctly identified. Use the photo section as an aid. In some cases, two or more stamp issues are very similar in appearance and can be distinguished only by minor details. These are always noted in the text. Sometimes the evidence is obvious. If a stamp has perforations, it cannot be earlier than 1857.

Prices are given in columns for used and unused specimens, usually in two grades of condition. You need only refer to the column that applies to your stamp and its condition grade.

Prices shown in this book are actual selling prices, so one should not necessarily expect to receive a discount when buying from dealers.

When a dash (—) appears in place of a price, this indicates that the item is either unavailable in that condition grade or is so seldom available that its price is open to question. It should not be assumed, however, that such items are invariably more valuable than those for which prices are shown.

Prices are given for hinged stamps that have been in collections. In today's stamp market a premium value is placed on stamps that have never been hinged. To determine the premium on any stamp, refer to the premium percentages shown on every page.

The stated values are general guides only and cannot reflect the price of occasional superb specimens, such as imperforates with four wide margins, which may sell considerably higher.

A small box has been provided to the left of each listing for keeping a record of the stamps in your collection.

IMPORTANT

Because of the space limitation on each page we have not been able to include very fine, extra fine, never hinged, or lightly hinged pricing on each stamp. To determine these prices please use the following procedure.

Very Fine Pricing—Prior to 1941: *Double the average price quoted.*

Very Fine Pricing—After 1941: *Add 25% to the fine price.*

Extra Fine Pricing—Prior to 1941: *Triple the average price quoted.*

Never Hinged Pricing—Prior to 1941: *Add the percentage indicated at the right of the issue to any price listed. Example: (N-H add 5%).*

Never Hinged Pricing—After 1941: *Add 15% to any price listed.*

Lightly Hinged Pricing—*Add one half of the N-H percentage indicated for each issue to any price listed.*

DEALER BUYING PRICES

Buying prices will vary greatly depending upon condition, rarity, and existing dealers' stock of a particular stamp. With these facts in mind, a dealer can be expected to buy stamps between 40 percent and 50 percent of their quoted prices; but this will depend upon supply and demand.

EQUIPMENT

To collect stamps properly a collector will need some "tools of the trade." These need not be expensive and need not all be bought at the very outset. That might in fact be the worst thing to do. Many a beginning collector has spent his budget on equipment, only to have little or nothing left for stamps and then loses interest in the hobby.

It may be economical in the long run to buy the finest quality accessories but few collectors, just starting out, have a clear idea of what they will and will not be needing. It is just as easy to make impulse purchases of accessories as of stamps and just as unwise. Equipment must be purchased on the basis of what sort of collection is being built *now,* rather than on what the collection may be in the future. There is no shame in working up from an elementary album.

Starter Kits. Starter or beginner outfits are sold in just about every variety shop, drugstore, etc. These come in attractive boxes and contain a juvenile or beginner's album, some stamps, which may be on paper and in need of removal, a packet of gummed hinges, tongs, a pocket stockbook or file; and often other items such as a perforation gauge, booklet on stamp collecting, magnifier, and watermark detector. These kits are specially suited to young collectors and can provide a good philatelic education.

Albums. When the hobby began, more than a century ago, collectors mounted their stamps in whatever albums were at hand. Scrapbooks, school exercise tablets and diaries all were used, as well as homemade albums. Today a number of firms specialize in printing albums of all kinds for philatelists, ranging from softbounds for the cautious type to huge multi-volume sets that cost hundreds of dollars. There are general worldwide albums, country albums, U.N. albums, and albums for mint sheets, covers, and every other conceivable variety of philatelic material. Choose your album according to the specialty you intend to pursue. It is not necessary, however, to buy a printed album at all. Many collectors feel there is not enough room for creativity in a printed album and prefer to use a binder with unprinted sheets. This allows items to be arranged at will on the page, rather than following the publisher's format, and for a personal write-up to be added. Rod-type binders will prove more durable and satisfactory than ring binders for heavy collections. The pages of an album should not be too thin, unless only one side is used. The presence of tiny crisscrossing lines (quadrilled sheets) is intended as an aid to correct alignment. Once items have been mounted and written up, these lines are scarcely visible and do not interfere with the attractiveness of the page.

Hinges. These are small rectangular pieces of lightweight paper, usually clear or semiopaque, gummed and folded. One side is moistened and affixed to the back of the stamp and the other to the album page. Hinges are sold in packets of 1,000 and are very inexpensive. Though by far the most popular device for mounting stamps, the hobbyist has his choice of a number of other products if hinges are not satisfactory to him. These include cello mounts which encase the stamp in clear sheeting and have a black background to provide a kind of frame. These are self-sticking. Their cost is much higher than hinges. The chief advantage of cello mounts is that they prevent injuries to the stamp and eliminate the moistening necessary in using hinges; however, they add considerably to the weight of each page, making flipping through an album less convenient, and become detached from the page more readily than hinges.

Glassine Interleaving. These are sheets made of thin semitransparent glassine paper, the same used to make envelopes in which stamps are stored. They come punched to fit albums of standard size and are designed to be placed between each set of sheets, to prevent stamps on one page from becoming entangled with those on the facing page. Glassine interleaving is not necessary if cello mounts are used, but any collection mounted with conventional hinges should be interleaved. The cost is small. Glassine interleaving is sold in packets of 100 sheets.

Magnifier. A magnifier is a necessary tool for *most* stamp collectors, excepting those who specialize in first day covers or other items that would not likely require study by magnification. There are numerous types and grades on the market, ranging in price from about $1 to more than $20. The quality of magnifier to buy should be governed by the extent to which it is likely to be used, and the collector's dependence upon it for identification and study. A collector of plate varieties ought to have the best magnifier he can afford, and carry it whenever visiting dealers, shows or anywhere that he may wish to examine specimens. A good magnifier is also necessary for a specialist in grilled stamps and for collectors of Civil War and other nineteenth-century covers. Those with built-in illumination are best in these circumstances.

Tongs. Beginners have a habit of picking up stamps with their fingers, which can cause injuries, smudges and grease stains. Efficient handling of tongs is not difficult to learn, and the sooner the better. Do not resort to ordinary tweezers, but get a pair of philatelic tongs which are specially shaped and of sufficiently large size to be easily manipulated.

Perforation Gauge. A very necessary inexpensive article, as the identification of many stamps depends upon a correct measuring of their perforations.

TIPS ON STAMP BUYING

There are many ways to buy stamps: packets, poundage mixtures, approvals, new issue services, auctions and a number of others. To buy wisely a collector must get to know the language of philately and the techniques used by dealers and auctioneers in selling stamps.

Packets of all different worldwide stamps are sold in graduated sizes from 1,000 up to 50,000. True to their word, they contain no duplicates. The stamps come from all parts of the world and date from the 1800s to the present. Both mint and used are included. When you buy larger quantities of most things, a discount is offered; with stamp packets, it works in reverse. The larger the packet, the higher its price per stamp. This is because the smaller packets are filled almost exclusively with low grade material.

Packets are suitable only as a collection base. A collector should never count on them to build his entire collection. The contents of one worldwide packet are much like that of another. Country packets are sold in smaller sizes, but there are certain drawbacks with packets.

1. Most packets contain some canceled-to-order stamps, which are not very desirable for a collection. These are stamps released with postmarks already on them, and are classified as used but have never gone through the mail. Eastern Europe and Russia are responsible for many C.T.O.'s.

2. The advertised value of packets bears little relation to the actual value. Packet makers call attention to the catalog values of their stamps, based on prices listed in standard reference works. The lowest sum at which a stamp can be listed in these books is 2¢, therefore, a packet of 1,000 automatically has a minimum catalog value of $20. If the retail price is $3 this seems like a terrific buy when in fact most of those thousand stamps are so common they are almost worthless.

Poundage mixtures are very different than packets. Here the stamps are all postally used (no C.T.O.'s) and still attached to small fragments of envelopes or parcel wrappings. Rather than sold by count, poundage mixtures are priced by the pound or ounce and quite often by kilos. Price varies depending on the grade, and the grade depends on where the mixture was assembled. Bank mixtures are considered the best as banks receive a steady flow of foreign registered mail. Mission mixtures are also highly rated. Of course the mixture should be sealed and unpicked. Unless a mixture is advertised as unpicked the high values have been removed. The best poundage mixtures are sold only by mail. Those available in shops are of medium or low quality. Whatever the grade, poundage mixtures can be counted on to contain duplicates.

If you want to collect the stamps of a certain country you can leave a standing order for its new releases with a new issue service. Whenever that government puts out stamps, they will be sent to the collector along with a bill. Usually the service will supply only mint copies. The price charged is not the face value, but the face value with a surcharge added to meet the costs of importing, handling and the like. New issue services are satisfactory only if the collector is positive he wants all the country's stamps, no matter what. Remember that its issues could include semipostals, long and maybe expensive sets, and extra high values.

By far the most popular way to buy stamps is via approvals. There is nothing new about approvals, as they go back to the Victorian era. Not all services are alike, though. Some offer sets, while others sell penny approvals. Then there are remainder approvals, advanced approvals, and seconds on approval. Penny approvals are really a thing of the past, though the term is still used. Before inflation, dealers would send a stockbook containing several thousand stamps, all priced at a penny each. If all the stamps were kept, the collector got a discount plus the book! Today the same sort of service can be found but instead of 1¢ per stamp, the price is anywhere from 3¢ to 10¢. Remainder approvals are made up from collection remainders. Rather than dismount and sort stamps from incoming collections, the approval merchant saves himself time by sending them out right on the album pages. The collector receives leaves from someone else's collection with stamps mounted just as he arranged them. Seconds on approval are slightly defective specimens of scarce stamps, which would cost more if perfect. Advanced approvals are designed for specialized collectors who know exactly what they want and have a fairly substantial stamp budget.

In choosing an approval service you should know the ground rules of approval buying and not be unduly influenced by promotional offers. Most approval merchants allow the selections to be kept for ten days to two weeks. The unbought stamps are then returned along with payment for those kept. As soon as the selection is received back, another is mailed. This will go on, regardless of how much or how little is bought, until the company is notified to refrain from sending further selections. The reputable services will always stop when told.

Approval ads range from splashy full pagers in the stamp publications to small three line classified announcements in magazines and newspapers. Most firms catering to beginners offer loss leaders, or stamps on which they take a loss for the sake of getting new customers. If an approval dealer offers 100 pictorials for a dime, it is obvious he is losing money on that transaction, as 10¢ will not even pay the postage. It is very tempting to order these premiums. Remember that when ordering approvals. What sort of service is it? Will it offer the kind of stamps desired? Will prices be high to pay for the loss leaders? Be careful of confusing advertisements. Sometimes the premium offers seem to promise more than they actually do. A rare, early stamp may be pictured. Of course you do not receive the stamp, but merely a modern commemorative picturing it.

Auction Sales. Stamp auctions are held all over the country and account for millions of dollars in sales annually. Buying at auction is exciting and can be economical. Many sleepers turn up—stamps that can be bought at less than their actual value. To be a good auction buyer, the philatelist must know stamps and their prices pretty well, and know the ropes of auctions. An obvious drawback of auctions is that purchases are not returnable. A dealer will take back a stamp that proves not to be a collector's liking, but an auctioneer will not. Also, auctioneers require immediate payment while a dealer may extend credit.

Stamps sold at auction come from private collections and the stocks of dealers; not necessarily defunct dealers, but those who want to get shelf space. Because they were brought together from a variety of sources, the nature and condition will vary. In catalog descriptions the full book value will be given for each stamp, but of course defective stamps will sell for much less than these figures. A bidder must calculate how much less. Other lots which can be difficult for the bidder to evaluate are those containing more than one stamp. Sometimes a superb specimen will be lotted along with a defective one. Then there are bulk lots which contain odds and ends from collections and such. It is usual in auctioning a collection for the better stamps to be removed and sold separately. The remainder is then offered in a single lot, which may consist of thousands or even tens of thousands of stamps. By all means examine lots before bidding. A period of inspection is always allowed before each sale, usually for several days. There may or may not be an inspection on sale day. If the bidder is not able to make a personal examination but must bid on strength of the catalog description, he should scale his bids for bulk lots much lower than for single stamp lots. He might bid $50 on a single stamp lot with a catalog value of $100, if the condition is listed as top notch, but to bid one-half catalog value on a bulk lot would not be very wise. These lots are not scrutinized very carefully by the auctioneers and some stamps are bound to be disappointing. There may be some heavily canceled, creased, torn, etc. Also, there will very likely be duplication. A bid of one-fifth the catalog value on a bulk lot is considered high. Often a one-tenth bid is successful.

The mechanics of stamp auctions may strike the beginner as complicated. They are run no differently than other auctions. All material to be sold is lotted by the auctioneer; that is, broken down into lots or units and bidding is by lot. Everything in the lot must be bid on, even if just one of the stamps is desired. The motive of bulk lotting is to save time and give each lot a fair sales value.

Before the sale a catalog is published listing all the lots, describing the contents and sometimes picturing the better items. Catalogs are in the mail about 30 days before the sale date. If a bid is to be mailed, it must be sent early. Bids that arrive after the sale are disqualified, even if they would have been successful.

When the bid is received it is entered into a bidbook, along with the bidder's name and address. On sale day each lot opens on the floor at one level above the second highest mail bid. Say the two highest mail bids are $30 and $20. The floor bidding would begin at $25. If the two highest bids are $100 and $500, the opening bid would probably be $150. The larger the amounts involved, the bigger will be the advances. The auctioneer will not accept an advance of $5 on a $500 lot; but on low value lots even dollar advances are sometimes made. Then it becomes a contest of floor versus book. The auctioneer acts as an agent, bidding for the absentee until his limit is reached. If the floor tops him, he has lost. If the floor does not get as high as his bid, he wins the lot at one advance over the highest floor bid.

When a collector buys stamps by mail from a dealer, he should choose one who belongs to the American Stamp Dealers' Association or A.S.D.A. The emblem is carried in their ads.

SELLING YOUR STAMPS

Almost every collector becomes a stamp seller sooner or later. Duplicates are inevitably accumulated, no matter how careful one may be in avoiding them. Then there are the G and VG stamps that have been replaced with F and VF specimens, and have become duplicates by intent. In addition to duplicates, a more advanced collector is likely to have stamps that are not duplicates but for which he has no further use. These will be odds and ends, sometimes quite valuable ones, that once suited the nature of his collection but are now out of place. Collectors' tastes change. The result is a stockpile of stamps that can be converted back to cash.

The alternative to selling the stamps you no longer need or want is trading them with a collector who does want them, and taking his unwanted stamps in return. All stamp clubs hold trading sessions. Larger national stamp societies operate trade-by-mail services for their members. The APS (American Philatelic Society) keeps $8,000,000 worth of stamps constantly circulating in its trading books or "circuit" books. Trading can be an excellent way of disposing of surplus stamps. In most cases it takes a bit longer than selling. Another potential drawback, especially if you are not a club member, is finding the right person with the right stamps.

The nature and value of the material involved may help in deciding whether to sell outright or trade. Also, there are your own personal considerations. If you're not going to continue in the stamp hobby, or need cash for some purpose other than stamp buying, trading is hardly suitable. Likewise, if you have developed an interest in some very exotic group of stamps or other philatelic items it may be impossible to find someone to trade with.

Once you have decided to sell, if indeed you do make that decision, the matter revolves upon how. To a stamp shop? To another collector? Through an auction house? Possibly by running your own advertisements and issuing price lists, if you have enough stamps and spare time to make this worthwhile?

While some individuals have an absolute horror at the prospect of selling anything, stamp collectors tend to enjoy selling. It is difficult to say why. Some enjoy it so much they keep right on selling stamps, as a business, long after their original objective is achieved. Nearly all professional stamp dealers were collectors before entering the trade.

Selling your stamps outright to a dealer, especially a local dealer whom you can personally visit, is not necessarily the most financially rewarding but it is quick and very problem-free. Of course it helps if the dealer knows you and it's even better if he knows some of your stamps. Dealers have no objection to repurchasing stamps they've sold to you. You will find that the dealers encourage their customers to sell to them just as much as they encourage them to buy. The dealers are really anxious to get your stamps if you have good salable material from popular countries. In fact most dealers would prefer buying from the public rather than any other source.

The collector selling stamps to a dealer has to be reasonable in his expectations. A dealer may not be able to use all the stamps you have. It is simply not smart business for a dealer to invest money in something he may not be able to sell. So, if you have esoteric or highly specialized items for sale, it might be necessary to find a specialist who deals in those particular areas rather than selling to a neighborhood stamp shop.

The local stamp shop will almost certainly want to buy anything you can offer in the way of medium to better grade United States stamps of all kinds, including the so-called "back of the book" items. He may not want plate blocks or full sheets of commemoratives issued within the past 20 years. Most dealers are well supplied with material of this nature and have opportunities to buy more of it every day. The same is true of first day covers, with a few exceptions, issued from the 1960s to the present. The dealers either have these items abundantly or can get them from a wholesaler at rock-bottom prices. They would rather buy stamps that are a bit harder to get from the wholesalers, or for which the wholesalers charge higher prices. On the whole you will meet with a favorable reception when offering U.S. stamps to a local dealer. With foreign stamps it becomes another matter: what do you have and how flexible are you in price? Nearly all the stamp shops in this country do stock foreign stamps to one extent or another. They do not, as a rule, attempt to carry comprehensive or specialized stocks of them. In the average shop you will discover that the selection of general foreign consists of a combination of modern mint sets, topicals, souvenir sheets, packets, which come from the wholesaler, and a small sprinkling of older material, usually pre-1900. The price range of this older material will be $5 to $50. Non-specialist collectors of foreign stamps buy this type of item and that is essentially why the local shop caters to. When a local dealer buys rare foreign stamps or a large foreign collection, it is not for himself. He buys with the intent of passing them along to another dealer who has the right customers lined up. He acts only as a middleman or go-between. Therefore the price you receive for better grade foreign stamps tends to be lower than for better grade U.S., which the dealer buys for his own use.

What is a fair price to get for your stamps? This is always difficult to say, as many variable factors are involved. Consider their condition. Think in terms of what the dealer could reasonably hope to charge for them at retail and stand a good chance of selling them. Some of your stamps may have to be discounted because of no gum, poor centering, bent perfs, hinge remnants, repairs, or other problems. But even if your stamps are primarily F or VF, a dealer cannot pay book values for them. If you check his selling prices on his specimens of those same stamps, you can usually count on receiving from 40 to 50 percent of those prices. Considering the discount made from book values by the dealer in pricing his stock, your payment may work out to about 25 percent of book values. For rare United States stamps in top condition you can do better than 25 percent, but on most stamps sold to a dealer this is considered a fair offer. Keep in mind that the difference between a dealer's buying and selling prices is not just "profit margin." Most of the markup goes toward operating costs, for without this markup, there would be no stamp dealers.

IMPORTANT NOTICE: On stamps issued before 1890, prices of unused specimens are for ones without original gum. Specimens with original gum can be expected to command a premium of as much as 50 percent. Beware of regummed specimens

Scott No.		Fine Unused Each	Ave. Unused Each	Fine Used Each	Ave. Used Each
GENERAL ISSUES					
1847. FIRST ISSUE					
☐ 1	5¢ Red Brown	—	3000.00	750.00	500.00
☐ 2	10¢ Black	—	12900.00	2700.00	1600.00
1875. REPRODUCTIONS OF 1847 ISSUE					
☐ 3	5¢ Red Brown	1600.00	1100.00	—	—
☐ 4	10¢ Black	1800.00	1200.00	—	—
1851–1856. REGULAR ISSUE—IMPERFORATE					
☐ 5A	1¢ Blue (1b)	—	—	4000.00	2500.00
☐ 6	1¢ Blue (1a)	—	—	4200.00	2800.00
☐ 7	1¢ Blue (II)	500.00	300.00	160.00	95.00
☐ 8	1¢ Blue (III)	—	—	1500.00	920.00
☐ 8A	1¢ Blue (IIIa)	—	1600.00	600.00	420.00
☐ 9	1¢ Blue (IV)	320.00	210.00	120.00	72.00
☐ 10	3¢ Orange Brown (I)	—	930.00	70.00	46.00
☐ 11	3¢ Dull Red (I)	150.00	91.00	12.00	11.00
☐ 12	5¢ Red Brown (I)	—	—	1350.00	840.00
☐ 13	10¢ Green (I)	—	—	710.00	420.00
☐ 14	10¢ Green (II)	—	900.00	300.00	180.00
☐ 15	10¢ Green (III)	—	1000.00	300.00	210.00
☐ 16	10¢ Green (IV)	—	—	1410.00	920.00
☐ 17	12¢ Black	—	1100.00	280.00	191.00
1857–1861. SAME DESIGNS AS 1851–1856 ISSUE—PERF. 15					
☐ 18	1¢ Blue (I)	700.00	400.00	350.00	240.00
☐ 19	1¢ Blue (Ia)	—	2000.00	1500.00	
☐ 20	1¢ Blue (II)	550.00	300.00	160.00	92.00
☐ 21	1¢ Blue (III)	—	2100.00	1100.00	660.00
☐ 22	1¢ Blue (IIIa)	660.00	310.00	220.00	145.00
☐ 23	1¢ Blue (IV)	—	1210.00	250.00	185.00
☐ 24	1¢ Blue (V)	180.00	87.00	41.00	25.00
☐ 25	3¢ Rose (I)	—	400.00	43.00	25.00
☐ 26	3¢ Dull Red (II)	66.00	39.00	6.10	3.00
☐ 26A	3¢ Dull Red (IIa)	142.00	86.00	24.00	17.00
☐ 27	5¢ Brick Red (I)	—	4000.00	910.00	640.00
☐ 28	5¢ Red Brown (I)	—	910.00	300.00	205.00
☐ 28A	5¢ Indian Red (I)	—	1200.00	700.00	
☐ 29	5¢ Brown (I)	700.00	410.00	215.00	135.00
☐ 30	5¢ Orange Brown (II)	770.00	400.00	800.00	575.00
☐ 30A	5¢ Brown (II)	480.00	250.00	200.00	125.00
☐ 31	10¢ Green (I)	—	2500.00	600.00	315.00
☐ 32	10¢ Green (II)	1500.00	910.00	160.00	125.00

Scott No.		Fine Unused Each	Ave. Unused Each	Fine Used Each	Ave. Used Each
☐33	10¢ Green (III)	1500.00	800.00	185.00	115.00
☐34	10¢ Green (IV)	—	—	1400.00	820.00
☐35	10¢ Green (V)	190.00	121.00	91.00	62.00
☐36	12¢ Black (I)	300.00	186.00	112.00	62.00
☐36b	12¢ Black (II)	250.00	160.00	121.00	66.00
☐37	24¢ Gray Lilac	600.00	400.00	200.00	170.00
☐38	30¢ Orange	800.00	450.00	300.00	180.00
☐39	90¢ Blue	1600.00	840.00	—	—

1875. REPRINTS OF 1857–1861 ISSUE

☐40	1¢ Bright Blue	500.00	360.00	—	—
☐41	3¢ Scarlet	2100.00	1600.00	—	—
☐42	5¢ Orange Brown	850.00	610.00	—	—
☐43	10¢ Blue Green	2000.00	1460.00	—	—
☐44	12¢ Greenish Black	2000.00	1600.00	—	—
☐45	24¢ Blackish Violet	2200.00	1580.00	—	—
☐46	30¢ Yellow Orange	2200.00	1750.00	—	—
☐47	90¢ Deep Blue	3600.00	2600.00	—	—

1861. FIRST DESIGNS—PERF. 12

☐56	3¢ Brown Red	740.00	500.00	—	—
☐62B	10¢ Dark Green	—	—	520.00	335.00

1861–1862. SECOND DESIGNS

☐63	1¢ Blue	135.00	76.00	26.00	15.00
☐63b	1¢ Dark Blue	140.00	96.00	28.00	20.00
☐64	3¢ Pink	—	1900.00	300.00	176.00
☐64b	3¢ Rose Pink	280.00	181.00	50.00	30.00
☐65	3¢ Rose	61.00	38.00	3.00	2.00
☐66	3¢ Lake	—	1000.00	—	—
☐67	5¢ Buff	—	2500.00	400.00	230.00
☐68	10¢ Yellow Green	260.00	150.00	27.00	18.00
☐69	12¢ Black	420.00	300.00	57.00	35.00
☐70	24¢ Red Lilac	500.00	300.00	85.00	47.00
☐70b	24¢ Steel Blue	—	—	290.00	172.00
☐70c	24¢ Violet	—	1500.00	560.00	335.00
☐71	30¢ Orange	475.00	270.00	80.00	46.00
☐72	90¢ Blue	1100.00	620.00	250.00	160.00

1861–1866. NEW VALUES OR NEW COLORS

☐73	2¢ Black	170.00	86.00	34.00	19.00
☐74	3¢ Scarlet	3400.00	2200.00	1400.00	950.00
☐75	5¢ Red Brown	1250.00	770.00	200.00	135.00
☐76	5¢ Brown	270.00	215.00	57.00	42.00
☐77	15¢ Black	500.00	280.00	94.00	62.00
☐78	24¢ Lilac	260.00	145.00	55.00	38.00

Scott No.		Fine Unused Each	Ave. Unused Each	Fine Used Each	Ave. Used Each
1867. SAME DESIGNS AS 1861-1866 ISSUE					
GRILL WITH POINTS UP					
A. GRILL COVERING ENTIRE STAMP					
☐79	3¢ Rose	1700.00	900.00	450.00	240.00
C. GRILL ABOUT 13 x 16 MM.					
☐83	3¢ Rose	1450.00	900.00	370.00	230.00
GRILL WITH POINTS DOWN					
D. GRILL ABOUT 12 x 14 MM.					
☐84	2¢ Black	1700.00	1380.00	830.00	425.00
☐85	3¢ Rose	1150.00	670.00	340.00	195.00
Z. GRILL ABOUT 11 x 14 MM.					
☐85B	2¢ Black	990.00	575.00	320.00	185.00
☐85C	3¢ Rose	2100.00	1610.00	780.00	440.00
☐85E	12¢ Black	1400.00	880.00	510.00	300.00
E. GRILL ABOUT 11 x 13 MM.					
☐86	1¢ Blue	620.00	310.00	190.00	135.00
☐87	2¢ Black	320.00	185.00	76.00	46.00
☐88	3¢ Rose	210.00	135.00	11.00	8.00
☐89	10¢ Green	1000.00	600.00	170.00	91.00
☐90	12¢ Black	1200.00	700.00	190.00	98.00
☐91	15¢ Black	2200.00	1300.00	370.00	235.00
F. GRILL ABOUT 9 x 13 MM.					
☐92	1¢ Blue	250.00	141.00	91.00	54.00
☐93	2¢ Black	165.00	84.00	34.00	18.50
☐94	3¢ Red	92.00	55.00	400.00	3.00
☐95	5¢ Brown	700.00	440.00	200.00	118.00
☐96	10¢ Yellow Green	500.00	340.00	91.00	62.00
☐97	12¢ Black	500.00	340.00	96.00	62.00
☐98	15¢ Black	610.00	360.00	101.00	66.00
☐99	24¢ Gray Lilac	1100.00	610.00	510.00	250.00
☐100	30¢ Orange	1200.00	710.00	360.00	210.00
☐101	90¢ Blue	3150.00	1700.00	910.00	610.00
1875. RE-ISSUE OF 1861-1866 ISSUES					
☐102	1¢ Blue	—	360.00	—	465.00
☐103	2¢ Black	—	1700.00	—	2150.00
☐104	3¢ Brown Red	—	2000.00	—	2500.00
☐105	5¢ Light Brown	—	1500.00	—	1150.00
☐106	10¢ Green	—	1600.00	—	2300.00
☐107	12¢ Black	—	3400.00	—	2650.00
☐108	15¢ Black	—	2300.00	—	2700.00
☐109	24¢ Deep Violet	—	2300.00	—	3200.00
☐110	30¢ Brownish Orange	—	2800.00	—	4200.00
☐111	90¢ Blue	—	3700.00	—	6000.00

Scott No.		Fine Unused Each	Ave. Unused Each	Fine Used Each	Ave. Used Each

1869. PICTORIAL ISSUES
GRILL ABOUT 9½ x 9½ MM.

☐ 112	1¢ Buff	220.00	175.00	76.00	52.00
☐ 113	2¢ Brown	171.00	120.00	31.00	18.00
☐ 114	3¢ Ultramarine	146.00	92.00	9.50	6.50
☐ 115	6¢ Ultramarine	700.00	421.00	96.00	66.00
☐ 116	10¢ Yellow	800.00	460.00	101.00	68.00
☐ 117	12¢ Green	670.00	410.00	121.00	75.00
☐ 118	15¢ Brown & Blue (I)	1700.00	900.00	260.00	170.00
☐ 119	15¢ Brown & Blue (II)	820.00	500.00	136.00	81.00
☐ 120	24¢ Green & Violet	2400.00	1500.00	500.00	330.00
☐ 121	30¢ Blue & Carmine	2000.00	1200.00	330.00	195.00
☐ 122	90¢ Carmine & Black	7000.00	4600.00	1300.00	770.00

1875. RE-ISSUE OF 1869 ISSUE. HARD WHITE PAPER— WITHOUT GRILL

☐ 123	1¢ Buff	350.00	230.00	200.00	142.00
☐ 124	2¢ Brown	440.00	270.00	350.00	190.00
☐ 125	3¢ Blue	2400.00	1670.00	1200.00	850.00
☐ 126	6¢ Blue	—	680.00	—	350.00
☐ 127	10¢ Yellow	—	1000.00	—	725.00
☐ 128	12¢ Green	—	1100.00	—	80.00
☐ 129	15¢ Brown & Blue (III)	—	1000.00	—	420.00
☐ 130	24¢ Green & Violet	—	990.00	—	380.00
☐ 131	30¢ Blue & Carmine	—	1200.00	—	760.00
☐ 132	90¢ Carmine & Black	—	3600.00	—	5800.00

1880. SAME AS ABOVE—SOFT POROUS PAPER

☐ 133	1¢ Buff	230.00	160.00	170.00	90.00

1870–1871. PRINTED BY NATIONAL BANK NOTE CO.—GRILLED

☐ 134	1¢ Ultramarine	450.00	260.00	65.00	42.00
☐ 135	2¢ Red Brown	320.00	190.00	36.00	26.00
☐ 136	3¢ Green	200.00	150.00	12.00	8.00
☐ 137	6¢ Carmine	1300.00	600.00	260.00	160.00
☐ 138	7¢ Vermilion	1000.00	600.00	230.00	150.00
☐ 139	10¢ Brown	1200.00	700.00	380.00	270.00
☐ 140	12¢ Light Violet	—	—	2100.00	1300.00
☐ 141	15¢ Orange	1400.00	700.00	640.00	400.00
☐ 142	24¢ Purple	—	—	—	6000.00
☐ 143	30¢ Black	—	2200.00	700.00	500.00
☐ 144	90¢ Carmine	—	3000.00	600.00	420.00

1870–1871. SAME AS ABOVE—WITHOUT GRILL

☐ 145	1¢ Ultramarine	150.00	96.00	10.00	560.00
☐ 146	2¢ Red Brown	66.00	41.00	7.00	4.50
☐ 147	3¢ Green	112.00	63.00	2.00	1.00
☐ 148	6¢ Carmine	230.00	131.00	14.00	8.50
☐ 149	7¢ Vermilion	300.00	180.00	56.00	30.00
☐ 150	10¢ Brown	230.00	122.00	15.00	9.50

Scott No.		Fine Unused Each	Ave. Unused Each	Fine Used Each	Ave. Used Each
☐ 151	12¢ Dull Violet	490.00	300.00	56.00	35.00
☐ 152	15¢ Bright Orange	440.00	260.00	58.00	35.00
☐ 153	24¢ Purple	570.00	300.00	82.00	46.00
☐ 154	30¢ Black	920.00	500.00	100.00	68.00
☐ 155	90¢ Carmine	1100.00	600.00	150.00	95.00

1873. SAME DESIGNS AS 1870–1871 ISSUE—WITH SECRET MARKS
PRINTED BY THE CONTINENTAL BANK NOTE CO.
THIN HARD GRAYISH WHITE PAPER

☐ 156	1¢ Ultramarine	56.00	36.00	3.00	2.00
☐ 157	2¢ Brown	135.00	88.00	9.00	6.00
☐ 158	3¢ Green	45.00	27.00	.40	.25
☐ 159	6¢ Dull Pink	180.00	111.00	11.00	6.50
☐ 160	7¢ Orange Vermilion	370.00	216.00	58.00	39.00
☐ 161	10¢ Brown	180.00	111.00	14.00	8.10
☐ 162	12¢ Black Violet	500.00	350.00	70.00	48.00
☐ 163	15¢ Yellow Orange	460.00	270.00	50.00	38.00
☐ 165	30¢ Gray Black	420.00	250.00	50.00	36.00
☐ 166	90¢ Rose Carmine	1000.00	600.00	168.00	100.00

1875. REGULAR ISSUE

☐ 178	2¢ Vermilion	148.00	95.00	500.00	3.75
☐ 179	5¢ Blue	155.00	96.00	11.00	6.00

DESIGNS
1879. SAME AS 1870–1875 ISSUES
PRINTED BY THE AMERICAN BANK NOTE CO.
SOFT POROUS YELLOWISH WHITE PAPER

☐ 182	1¢ Dark Ultramarine	97.00	58.00	2.00	1.50
☐ 183	2¢ Vermilion	50.00	37.00	1.70	1.00
☐ 184	3¢ Green	45.00	30.00	.25	.16
☐ 185	5¢ Blue	180.00	100.00	11.00	5.90
☐ 186	6¢ Pink	420.00	280.00	13.00	7.00
☐ 187	10¢ Brown (no secret mark)	600.00	400.00	16.00	8.50
☐ 188	10¢ Brown (secret mark)	410.00	210.00	20.00	10.00
☐ 188b	10¢ Black Brown	600.00	340.00	66.00	40.00
☐ 189	15¢ Red Orange	165.00	88.00	24.00	15.00
☐ 190	30¢ Full Black	400.00	270.00	30.00	16.00
☐ 191	90¢ Carmine	950.00	630.00	150.00	100.00

1882. REGULAR ISSUE

☐ 205	5¢ Yellow Brown	90.00	55.00	6.00	3.20

1881–1882. DESIGNS OF 1873 ISSUE RE-ENGRAVED (N-H ADD 95%)

☐ 206	1¢ Gray Blue	30.00	22.00	1.00	.52
☐ 207	3¢ Blue Green	44.00	29.00	.50	.22
☐ 208	6¢ Rose	220.00	118.00	55.00	30.00
☐ 208a	6¢ Brown Red	200.00	110.00	65.00	42.00

Scott No.		Fine Unused Each	Ave. Unused Each	Fine Used Each	Ave. Used Each
☐ 209	10¢ Brown	86.00	50.00	3.00	1.65
☐ 209b	10¢ Black Brown	110.00	59.00	9.80	5.70

1883. REGULAR ISSUE

Scott No.		Fine Unused Each	Ave. Unused Each	Fine Used Each	Ave. Used Each
☐ 210	2¢ Red Brown	29.00	18.00	.22	.15
☐ 211	4¢ Blue Green	139.00	90.00	9.00	6.00

1887. REGULAR ISSUE

Scott No.		Fine Unused Each	Ave. Unused Each	Fine Used Each	Ave. Used Each
☐ 212	1¢ Ultramarine	57.00	37.00	.95	.62
☐ 213	2¢ Green	33.00	21.00	.18	.13
☐ 214	3¢ Vermilion	50.00	40.00	30.00	24.00

1888. SAME DESIGNS AS 1870–1883 ISSUES

Scott No.		Fine Unused Each	Ave. Unused Each	Fine Used Each	Ave. Used Each
☐ 215	4¢ Carmine	135.00	79.00	13.00	8.00
☐ 216	5¢ Indigo	140.00	83.00	7.00	5.00
☐ 217	30¢ Orange Brown	350.00	215.00	80.00	54.00
☐ 218	90¢ Purple	700.00	480.00	142.00	90.00

IMPORTANT NOTICE: From this point onward, values of unused stamps and blocks are for specimens with original gum. Prices given for **blocks** are for blocks of 4, **without** plate number.

Scott No.		Fine Unused Block	Ave. Unused Block	Fine Unused Each	Ave. Unused Each	Fine Used Each	Ave. Used Each
1890–1893. SMALL DESIGN (N-H ADD 95%)							
☐ 219	1¢ Dull Blue	215.00	130.00	26.00	14.00	.17	.11
☐ 219D	2¢ Lake	800.00	620.00	145.00	80.00	.60	.30
☐ 220	2¢ Carmine	140.00	100.00	17.00	13.00	.16	.11
☐ 220a	2¢ Carmine (Cap on left 2)	300.00	260.00	46.00	31.00	1.30	.82
☐ 220c	2¢ Carmine (Cap both 2's)	900.00	670.00	120.00	80.00	8.00	4.60
☐ 221	3¢ Purple	500.00	350.00	61.00	39.00	6.00	3.60
☐ 222	4¢ Dark Brown	600.00	400.00	61.00	39.00	2.50	1.40
☐ 223	5¢ Chocolate	1000.00	420.00	55.00	40.00	2.00	1.20
☐ 224	6¢ Brown Red	610.00	400.00	60.00	36.00	17.00	12.00
☐ 225	8¢ Lilac	370.00	300.00	37.00	26.00	12.00	7.00
☐ 226	10¢ Green	750.00	600.00	118.00	76.00	3.00	2.00
☐ 227	15¢ Indigo	1100.00	800.00	140.00	95.00	20.00	13.70
☐ 228	30¢ Black	1600.00	1300.00	200.00	130.00	23.00	13.60
☐ 229	90¢ Orange	3500.00	2500.00	410.00	210.00	100.00	50.00
1893. COLUMBIAN ISSUE (N-H ADD 95%)							
☐ 230	1¢ Blue	180.00	131.00	27.00	17.00	.52	.40
☐ 231	2¢ Violet	180.00	128.00	24.00	14.00	.17	.11
☐ 231c	2¢ "Broken Hat"	400.00	315.00	76.00	49.00	.60	.35
☐ 232	3¢ Green	310.00	260.00	50.00	34.00	18.00	10.50
☐ 233	4¢ Ultramarine	600.00	500.00	82.00	50.00	8.00	6.00
☐ 234	5¢ Chocolate	620.00	500.00	85.00	55.00	9.00	6.00
☐ 235	6¢ Purple	620.00	500.00	83.00	50.00	25.00	17.00
☐ 236	8¢ Magenta	580.00	450.00	50.00	32.00	10.00	6.00
☐ 237	10¢ Black Brown	900.00	600.00	120.00	80.00	7.00	6.00
☐ 238	15¢ Dark Green	1920.00	1400.00	210.00	140.00	70.00	40.00

Scott No.		Fine Unused Block	Ave. Unused Block	Fine Unused Each	Ave. Unused Each	Fine Used Each	Ave. Used Each
☐ 239	30¢ Orange Brown	2800.00	2100.00	340.00	220.00	115.00	65.00
☐ 240	50¢ Slate Blue	3100.00	2400.00	400.00	210.00	180.00	110.00
☐ 241	$1 Salmon	—	—	1000.00	700.00	500.00	380.00
☐ 242	$2 Brown Red	—	—	1200.00	800.00	500.00	315.00
☐ 243	$3 Yellow Green	—	—	2500.00	1200.00	900.00	530.00
☐ 244	$4 Crimson Lake	—	—	3500.00	1600.00	1200.00	700.00
☐ 245	$5 Black	—	—	3800.00	2400.00	1400.00	900.00

1894. UNWATERMARKED (N-H ADD 95%)

☐ 246	1¢ Ultramarine	160.00	130.00	24.00	14.00	3.70	2.00
☐ 247	1¢ Blue	350.00	200.00	60.00	33.00	2.00	1.25
☐ 248	2¢ Pink, Type I..........	115.00	70.00	20.00	13.00	2.60	1.60
☐ 249	2¢ Carmine Lake, Type I	700.00	500.00	120.00	75.00	1.40	1.00
☐ 250	2¢ Carmine, Type I	190.00	150.00	23.00	14.00	.40	.17
☐ 251	2¢ Carmine, Type II	1400.00	1200.00	165.00	115.00	3.60	2.25
☐ 252	2¢ Carmine, Type III	550.00	300.00	85.00	50.00	4.00	2.60
☐ 253	3¢ Purple	550.00	300.00	80.00	43.00	8.10	6.00
☐ 254	4¢ Dark Brown	600.00	400.00	93.00	50.00	3.50	2.00
☐ 255	5¢ Chocolate	500.00	350.00	67.00	43.00	4.60	3.00
☐ 256	6¢ Dull Brown	1000.00	700.00	140.00	73.00	18.00	11.00
☐ 257	8¢ Violet Brown	800.00	600.00	110.00	63.00	12.00	7.60
☐ 258	10¢ Dark Green	1500.00	1000.00	185.00	120.00	9.00	4.50
☐ 259	15¢ Dark Blue	2100.00	1600.00	200.00	150.00	46.00	29.00
☐ 260	50¢ Orange	2500.00	1900.00	310.00	215.00	82.00	46.00
☐ 261	$1 Black (I)	6000.00	4600.00	900.00	500.00	230.00	116.00
☐ 261A	$1 Black (II)	—	—	1820.00	1000.00	400.00	310.00
☐ 262	$2 Blue	—	—	2300.00	1300.00	500.00	340.00
☐ 263	$5 Dark Green	—	—	3500.00	1900.00	1000.00	600.00

1895. DOUBLE LINE WATERMARKED "U.S.P.S." PERF. 12 (N-H ADD 95%)

☐ 264	1¢ Blue	46.00	35.00	7.00	5.00	.17	.11
☐ 265	2¢ Carmine, Type I	240.00	170.00	27.00	14.00	.92	.70
☐ 266	2¢ Carmine, Type II	300.00	210.00	28.00	16.00	3.60	2.10
☐ 267	2¢ Carmine, Type III	46.00	33.00	6.00	4.00	.15	.11
☐ 268	3¢ Purple	280.00	190.00	36.00	19.00	1.60	.73
☐ 269	4¢ Dark Brown	300.00	215.00	35.00	20.00	1.60	.78
☐ 270	5¢ Chocolate	280.00	200.00	30.00	17.00	2.10	1.35
☐ 271	6¢ Dull Brown	415.00	320.00	70.00	46.00	4.20	2.50
☐ 272	8¢ Violet Brown	240.00	150.00	33.00	16.00	1.60	.78
☐ 273	10¢ Dark Green	360.00	200.00	58.00	30.00	1.70	.82
☐ 274	15¢ Dark Blue	800.00	600.00	170.00	100.00	10.00	6.50
☐ 275	50¢ Dull Orange	1200.00	1000.00	300.00	140.00	23.00	15.00
☐ 276	$1 Black (I)	2800.00	1900.00	600.00	300.00	76.00	49.00
☐ 276A	$1 Black (II)	—	—	1200.00	800.00	130.00	82.00
☐ 277	$2 Blue	—	—	900.00	600.00	270.00	140.00
☐ 278	$5 Dark Green	—	—	1800.00	1100.00	410.00	230.00

Scott No.		Fine Unused Block	Ave. Unused Block	Fine Unused Each	Ave. Unused Each	Fine Used Each	Ave. Used Each

1898. REGULAR ISSUE PERF. (N-H ADD 95%)

Scott No.		Fine Unused Block	Ave. Unused Block	Fine Unused Each	Ave. Unused Each	Fine Used Each	Ave. Used Each
☐279	1¢ Deep Green	70.00	44.00	12.00	7.00	.17	.11
☐279B	2¢ Red	71.00	45.00	11.00	7.00	.18	.11
☐279C	2¢ Rose Carmine	700.00	600.00	150.00	91.00	34.00	20.00
☐279D	2¢ Orange Red	68.00	4100.00	12.00	8.00	.31	.18
☐280	4¢ Rose Brown	190.00	130.00	33.00	18.00	1.60	.71
☐281	5¢ Dark Blue	200.00	150.00	38.00	20.00	1.60	.71
☐282	6¢ Lake	340.00	200.00	45.00	26.00	2.70	1.30
☐282a	6¢ Purplish Lake	470.00	300.00	56.00	30.00	3.10	1.50
☐282C	10¢ Brown (I)	850.00	600.00	160.00	90.00	3.00	1.40
☐283	10¢ Orange Brown (II)	700.00	500.00	110.00	60.00	2.50	1.20
☐284	15¢ Olive Green	800.00	550.00	130.00	77.00	7.70	4.60

1898. TRANS-MISSISSIPPI EXPOSITION ISSUE (N-H ADD 90%)

Scott No.		Fine Unused Block	Ave. Unused Block	Fine Unused Each	Ave. Unused Each	Fine Used Each	Ave. Used Each
☐285	1¢ Yellow Green	240.00	145.00	34.00	16.00	7.00	4.50
☐286	2¢ Copper Red	230.00	120.00	32.00	16.00	3.00	1.10
☐287	4¢ Orange	1000.00	700.00	150.00	100.00	280.00	18.00
☐288	5¢ Dull Blue	950.00	700.00	130.00	70.00	24.00	14.00
☐289	8¢ Violet Brown	1200.00	900.00	175.00	100.00	46.00	28.00
☐290	10¢ Gray Violet	1600.00	1200.00	200.00	120.00	25.00	16.00
☐291	50¢ Sage Green	—	—	700.00	500.00	175.00	120.00
☐292	$1 Black	—	—	1900.00	1100.00	600.00	400.00
☐293	$2 Orange Brown	—	—	3000.00	1700.00	820.00	500.00

1901. PAN-AMERICAN ISSUE (N-H ADD 75%)

Scott No.		Fine Unused Block	Ave. Unused Block	Fine Unused Each	Ave. Unused Each	Fine Used Each	Ave. Used Each
☐294	1¢ Green & Black	170.00	120.00	26.00	15.00	6.50	4.00
☐295	2¢ Carmine & Black	160.00	100.00	23.00	15.00	1.50	.78
☐296	4¢ Chocolate & Black	770.00	500.00	100.00	62.00	22.00	14.00
☐297	5¢ Ultramarine & Black	800.00	600.00	100.00	60.00	23.00	15.00
☐298	8¢ Brown Violet Black	1000.00	800.00	160.00	90.00	76.00	50.00
☐299	10¢ Yellow Brown Black	1400.00	1100.00	220.00	120.00	38.00	22.00

1902–1903. PERF. 12 (N-H ADD 80%)

Scott No.		Fine Unused Block	Ave. Unused Block	Fine Unused Each	Ave. Unused Each	Fine Used Each	Ave. Used Each
☐300	1¢ Blue Green	70.00	50.00	12.00	6.00	.16	.11
☐301	2¢ Carmine	95.00	63.00	14.00	8.00	.17	.13
☐302	3¢ Violet	450.00	300.00	55.00	35.00	4.00	2.10
☐303	4¢ Brown	500.00	300.00	60.00	36.00	1.60	.72
☐304	5¢ Blue	600.00	400.00	62.00	35.00	1.60	.72
☐305	6¢ Claret	600.00	460.00	66.00	40.00	3.00	1.60
☐306	8¢ Violet Black	300.00	260.00	41.00	25.00	3.00	1.50
☐307	10¢ Red Brown	700.00	610.00	70.00	42.00	1.80	1.00
☐308	13¢ Purple Black	300.00	180.00	42.00	26.00	10.00	7.00
☐309	15¢ Olive Green	1200.00	800.00	165.00	110.00	7.00	4.60
☐310	50¢ Orange	4000.00	2800.00	600.00	300.00	34.00	20.00
☐311	$1 Black	6000.00	4500.00	700.00	500.00	66.00	44.00
☐312	$2 Dark Blue	—	—	1200.00	700.00	200.00	121.00
☐313	$5 Dark Green	—	—	2700.00	1300.00	600.00	350.00

Scott No.		Fine Unused Block	Ave. Unused Block	Fine Unused Each	Ave. Unused Each	Fine Used Each	Ave. Used Each
1906–1908. IMPERFORATED (N-H ADD 70%)							
☐314	1¢ Blue Green	186.00	121.00	35.00	26.00	23.00	20.00
☐315	5¢ Blue	4500.00	3300.00	630.00	510.00	350.00	230.00
1903. PERF. 12 (N-H ADD 50%)							
☐319	2¢ Carmine	64.00	40.00	9.00	6.00	.16	.11
☐319a	2¢ Lake	90.00	61.00	11.00	7.00	.25	.15
1906. IMPERFORATED (N-H ADD 70%)							
☐320	2¢ Carmine	190.00	120.00	34.00	19.00	25.00	16.00
☐320a	2¢ Lake	425.00	300.00	72.00	43.00	34.00	20.00
1904. LOUISIANA PURCHASE ISSUE							
PERF. 12 (N-H ADD 75%)							
☐323	1¢ Green	215.00	140.00	31.00	18.00	7.00	4.10
☐324	2¢ Carmine	215.00	141.00	28.00	16.00	2.10	1.60
☐325	3¢ Violet	600.00	416.00	88.00	49.00	33.00	21.00
☐326	5¢ Dark Blue	700.00	610.00	120.00	73.00	23.00	15.00
☐327	10¢ Red Brown	1600.00	1100.00	215.00	130.00	35.00	24.00
1907. JAMESTOWN EXPOSITION ISSUE (N-H ADD 75%)							
☐328	1¢ Green	210.00	175.00	25.00	15.00	6.00	2.60
☐329	2¢ Carmine	250.00	165.00	31.00	17.00	5.00	2.20
☐330	5¢ Blue	1250.00	860.00	140.00	82.00	30.00	17.00
1908–1909. DOUBLE LINE WATERMARKED "U.S.P.S."							
PERF. 12 (N-H ADD 50%)							
☐331	1¢ Green	44.00	30.00	10.00	7.00	.13	.11
☐332	2¢ Carmine	43.00	30.00	10.00	6.00	.13	.11
☐333	3¢ Violet	300.00	198.00	30.00	19.00	3.80	2.15
☐334	4¢ Orange Brown	272.00	175.00	30.00	19.00	1.25	.77
☐335	5¢ Blue	361.00	250.00	40.00	26.00	2.60	1.65
☐336	6¢ Red Orange	422.00	316.00	55.00	33.00	6.00	4.60
☐337	8¢ Olive Green	285.00	171.00	32.00	19.00	3.60	1.85
☐338	10¢ Yellow	470.00	346.00	70.00	43.00	2.00	1.60
☐339	13¢ Blue Green	400.00	250.00	41.00	25.00	33.00	23.00
☐340	15¢ Pale Ultramarine	425.00	310.00	70.00	43.00	9.00	4.60
☐341	50¢ Violet	1620.00	1210.00	320.00	163.00	18.00	13.00
☐342	$1 Violet Black	2500.00	1760.00	520.00	346.00	87.00	55.00
IMPERFORATE (N-H ADD 65%)							
☐343	1¢ Green	60.00	43.00	9.00	6.00	5.00	3.00
☐344	2¢ Carmine	110.00	70.00	13.00	7.00	5.00	2.60
☐345	3¢ Deep Violet	200.00	100.00	25.00	14.00	15.00	9.00
☐346	4¢ Orange Brown	410.00	250.00	40.00	27.00	23.00	13.00
☐347	5¢ Blue	480.00	300.00	60.00	40.00	34.00	23.00

Scott No.		Fine Unused Line Pair	Ave. Unused Line Pair	Fine Unused Each	Ave. Unused Each	Fine Used Each	Ave. Used Each

1908–1910 COIL STAMPS
PERF. 12 HORIZONTALLY (N-H ADD 70%)

☐ 348	1¢ Green	180.00	125.00	25.00	14.00	16.00	9.60
☐ 349	2¢ Carmine	210.00	140.00	50.00	34.00	9.00	5.50
☐ 350	4¢ Orange Brown	7.00	400.00	121.00	81.00	78.00	44.00
☐ 351	5¢ Blue	760.00	510.00	145.00	90.00	86.00	51.00

PERF. 12 VERTICALLY (N-H ADD 70%)

☐ 352	1¢ Green	275.00	180.00	58.00	30.00	20.00	12.00
☐ 353	2¢ Carmine	250.00	150.00	49.00	29.00	8.00	7.00
☐ 354	4¢ Orange Brown	700.00	515.00	140.00	79.00	52.00	31.00
☐ 355	5¢ Blue	800.00	600.00	145.00	80.00	73.00	41.00
☐ 356	10¢ Yellow	—	—	1200.00	730.00	420.00	260.00

Scott No.		Fine Unused Block	Ave. Unused Block	Fine Unused Each	Ave. Unused Each	Fine Used Each	Ave. Used Each

1909. BLUISH GRAY PAPER
PERF. 12 (N-H ADD 70%)

☐ 357	1¢ Green	730.00	500.00	120.00	70.00	110.00	63.00
☐ 358	2¢ Carmine	710.00	480.00	115.00	60.00	85.00	54.00
☐ 359	3¢ Violet	—	—	1350.00	850.00	—	—
☐ 360	4¢ Orange Brown	—	—	9000.00	6300.00	—	—
☐ 361	5¢ Blue	—	—	3000.00	1750.00	—	—
☐ 362	6¢ Orange	—	—	950.00	625.00	—	—
☐ 363	8¢ Olive Green	—	—	1100.00	7300.00	—	—
☐ 364	10¢ Yellow	—	—	1100.00	670.00	—	—
☐ 365	13¢ Blue Green	—	—	2100.00	1240.00	—	—
☐ 366	15¢ Pale Ultramarine	—	—	970.00	620.00	—	—

1909. LINCOLN MEMORIAL ISSUE (N-H ADD 75%)

☐ 367	2¢ Carmine	60.00	40.00	9.00	6.00	4.00	2.10
☐ 368	2¢ Carmine, Impf.	310.00	220.00	50.00	29.00	33.00	20.00
☐ 369	2¢ Carmine (On B.G. Paper)	1500.00	1200.00	290.00	177.00	200.00	115.00

1909. ALASKA-YUKON ISSUE (N-H ADD 70%)

☐ 370	2¢ Carmine	120.00	87.00	14.00	9.00	3.50	1.75
☐ 371	2¢ Carmine. Impf.	300.00	200.00	56.00	38.00	42.00	28.00

1909. HUDSON-FULTON ISSUE (N-H ADD 70%)

☐ 372	2¢ Carmine	108.00	74.00	16.00	9.50	6.00	3.60
☐ 373	2¢ Carmine, Impf.	425.00	290.00	62.00	42.00	37.00	22.00

1910–1911. SINGLE LINE WATERMARKED "U.S.P.S."
PERF. 12 (N-H ADD 75%)

☐ 374	1¢ Green	72.00	48.00	9.10	7.00	.17	.12
☐ 375	2¢ Carmine	50.00	36.00	8.50	6.00	.16	.12
☐ 376	3¢ Deep Violet	120.00	102.00	18.00	13.00	2.10	1.50
☐ 377	4¢ Brown	175.00	138.00	28.00	16.00	.66	.45

Scott No.		Fine Unused Block	Ave. Unused Block	Fine Unused Each	Ave. Unused Each	Fine Used Each	Ave. Used Each
☐ 378	5¢ Blue	215.00	160.00	30.00	17.00	.65	.45
☐ 379	6¢ Red Orange	300.00	200.00	36.00	23.00	.98	.62
☐ 380	8¢ Olive Green	700.00	500.00	120.00	73.00	15.00	10.00
☐ 381	10¢ Yellow	620.00	450.00	115.00	70.00	5.50	3.50
☐ 382	15¢ Ultramarine	1500.00	1100.00	265.00	151.00	15.50	12.00

IMPERFORATE (N-H ADD 70%)

☐ 383	1¢ Green	32.00	20.00	6.00	3.00	4.00	2.20
☐ 384	2¢ Carmine	54.00	39.00	8.00	5.00	2.10	1.60

Scott No.		Fine Unused Line Pair	Ave. Unused Line Pair	Fine Unused Each	Ave. Unused Each	Fine Used Each	Ave. Used Each

1910–1913. COIL STAMPS
PERF. 12 HORIZONTALLY (N-H ADD 70%)

☐ 385	1¢ Green	185.00	110.00	26.00	15.00	16.00	10.00
☐ 386	2¢ Carmine	275.00	165.00	36.00	21.00	14.00	8.75

PERF. 12 VERTICALLY (N-H ADD 70%)

☐ 387	1¢ Green	320.00	175.00	75.00	45.00	25.00	15.00
☐ 388	2¢ Carmine	3000.00	2200.00	500.00	375.00	110.00	61.00

PERF. 8½ HORIZONTALLY (N-H ADD 70%)

☐ 390	1¢ Green	31.00	21.00	7.00	4.00	5.00	3.00
☐ 391	2¢ Carmine	215.00	140.00	37.00	21.00	9.50	7.00

PERF. 8½ VERTICALLY (N-H ADD 70%)

☐ 392	1¢ Green	105.00	68.00	22.00	13.00	16.00	13.00
☐ 393	2¢ Carmine	200.00	130.00	47.00	33.00	31.00	17.00
☐ 394	3¢ Violet	350.00	220.00	50.00	33.00	31.00	17.00
☐ 395	4¢ Brown	340.00	220.00	50.00	33.00	31.00	17.00
☐ 396	5¢ Blue	380.00	250.00	54.00	35.00	34.00	17.00

Scott No.		Fine Unused Block	Ave. Unused Block	Fine Unused Each	Ave. Unused Each	Fine Used Each	Ave. Used Each

1913–1915. PANAMA-PACIFIC ISSUE
PERF. 12 (N-H ADD 80%)

☐ 397	1¢ Green	120.00	83.00	22.00	15.00	2.10	1.50
☐ 398	2¢ Carmine	170.00	120.00	24.00	17.00	82.00	.70
☐ 399	5¢ Blue	600.00	450.00	85.00	61.00	13.00	8.00
☐ 400	10¢ Orange Yellow	950.00	700.00	150.00	98.00	30.00	18.00
☐ 400A	10¢ Orange	1600.00	1200.00	240.00	150.00	21.00	13.00

PERF. 10 (N-H ADD 80%)

☐ 401	1¢ Green	220.00	170.00	33.00	21.00	8.10	5.00
☐ 402	2¢ Carmine	550.00	380.00	93.00	54.00	2.20	1.50
☐ 403	5¢ Blue	1800.00	1300.00	220.00	133.00	22.00	13.00
☐ 404	10¢ Orange	7000.00	4600.00	1300.00	850.00	85.00	52.00

Scott No.	Fine Unused Block	Ave. Unused Block	Fine Unused Each	Ave. Unused Each	Fine Used Each	Ave. Used Each

1912–1914. REGULAR ISSUE
PERF. 12 (N-H ADD 70%)

☐405	1¢ Green	60.00	43.00	8.50	7.00	.18	.10
☐406	2¢ Carmine	85.00	61.00	8.00	5.00	.18	.11
☐407	7¢ Black	515.00	400.00	110.00	66.00	8.00	5.80

IMPERFORATE (N-H ADD 70%)

☐408	1¢ Green	15.00	12.00	2.10	1.50	.80	.57
☐409	2¢ Carmine	18.00	14.00	2.20	1.50	.86	.62

Scott No.	Fine Unused Line Pair	Ave. Unused Line Pair	Fine Unused Each	Ave. Unused Each	Fine Used Each	Ave. Used Each

1912. COIL STAMPS
PERF. 8½ HORIZONTALLY (N-H ADD 70%)

☐410	1¢ Green	70.00	45.00	8.00	6.00	4.50	2.75
☐411	2¢ Carmine	70.00	52.00	10.00	7.10	4.50	2.80

PERF. 8½ VERTICALLY (N-H ADD 80%)

☐412	1¢ Green	112.00	76.00	23.00	14.00	6.20	5.00
☐413	2¢ Carmine	175.00	130.00	35.00	21.00	1.00	.70

Scott No.	Fine Unused Block	Ave. Unused Block	Fine Unused Each	Ave. Unused Each	Fine Used Each	Ave. Used Each

1912–1914. SINGLE LINE WATERMARKED "U.S.P.S."
PERRF. 12 (N-H ADD 75%)

☐414	8¢ Olive Green	220.00	150.00	38.00	25.00	2.00	1.50
☐415	9¢ Salmon Red	270.00	200.00	50.00	33.00	15.00	9.50
☐416	10¢ Orange Yellow	270.00	200.00	39.00	25.00	42.00	.30
☐417	12¢ Claret Brown	330.00	200.00	40.00	26.00	4.00	3.50
☐418	15¢ Gray	500.00	5.00	77.00	50.00	4.00	3.50
☐419	20¢ Ultramarine	1200.00	800.00	170.00	115.00	16.00	8.20
☐420	30¢ Orange Red	900.00	700.00	120.00	73.00	17.00	8.50
☐421	50¢ Violet	2800.00	1900.00	520.00	340.00	16.00	9.00

1912. DOUBLE LINE WATERMARKED "U.S.P.S." (N-H ADD 75%)

☐422	50¢ Violet	1850.00	1500.00	270.00	160.00	17.00	10.00
☐423	$1 Violet Black	3500.00	2500.00	600.00	370.00	70.00	49.00

1914–1915. SINGLE LINE WATERMARKED "U.S.P.S." PERF. 10 (N-H ADD 55%)

☐424	1¢ Green	40.00	30.00	4.50	2.50	.17	.12
☐425	2¢ Carmine	26.00	17.00	4.50	2.10	.18	.13
☐426	3¢ Deep Violet	2.00	66.00	13.00	10.00	2.00	1.40
☐427	4¢ Brown	218.00	146.00	30.00	20.00	.67	.42
☐428	5¢ Blue	215.00	130.00	31.00	17.00	.65	.45
☐429	6¢ Orange	280.00	175.00	42.00	25.00	1.60	.98

Scott No.		Fine Unused Block	Ave. Unused Block	Fine Unused Each	Ave. Unused Each	Fine Used Each	Ave. Used Each
☐ 430	7¢ Black	470.00	340.00	93.00	58.00	6.00	4.50
☐ 431	8¢ Olive Green	260.00	180.00	38.00	22.00	2.10	1.25
☐ 432	9¢ Salmon Red	450.00	320.00	48.00	26.00	12.00	6.60
☐ 433	12¢ Orange Yellow	350.00	200.00	46.00	26.00	.46	.26
☐ 434	11¢ Dark Green	170.00	100.00	23.00	13.00	6.60	4.50
☐ 435	12¢ Claret Brown	200.00	140.00	26.00	14.00	5.00	2.40
☐ 435a	12¢ Copper Red	225.00	160.00	30.00	16.00	5.10	3.50
☐ 437	15¢ Gray	850.00	600.00	120.00	63.00	7.10	4.50
☐ 438	20¢ Ultramarine	1210.00	900.00	200.00	120.00	5.00	2.60
☐ 439	30¢ Orange Red	1350.00	1020.00	200.00	150.00	15.00	8.60
☐ 440	50¢ Violet	3900.00	2900.00	700.00	450.00	20.00	12.00

Scott No.		Fine Unused Line Pair	Ave. Unused Line Pair	Fine Unused Each	Ave. Unused Each	Fine Used Each	Ave. Used Each

1914. COIL STAMPS
PERF. 10 HORIZONTALLY (N-H ADD 75%)

☐ 441	1¢ Green	9.00	6.10	1.25	.80	1.25	.68
☐ 442	2¢ Carmine	49.00	35.00	12.50	8.50	9.10	6.50

PERF. 10 VERTICALLY (N-H ADD 70%)

☐ 443	1¢ Green	100.00	65.00	26.00	15.00	6.50	4.00
☐ 444	2¢ Carmine	155.00	115.00	38.00	20.00	2.00	1.50
☐ 445	3¢ Violet	1300.00	1000.00	246.00	120.00	130.00	81.00
☐ 446	4¢ Brown	600.00	400.00	160.00	95.00	41.00	27.00
☐ 447	5¢ Blue	200.00	130.00	45.00	30.00	27.00	17.00

1914–1916. ROTARY PRESS COIL STAMPS
PERF. 10 HORIZONTALLY (N-H ADD 70%)

☐ 448	1¢ Green	48.00	32.00	8.50	6.00	3.75	2.50
☐ 449	2¢ Red (I)	—	—	1400.00	1000.00	140.00	95.00
☐ 450	2¢ Carmine (III)	83.00	55.00	15.00	9.10	3.50	2.50

PERF. 10 VERTICALLY (N-H ADD 70%)

☐ 452	1¢ Green	82.00	54.00	10.00	7.00	2.10	2.00
☐ 453	2¢ Red (I)	710.00	500.00	130.00	85.00	5.00	4.00
☐ 454	2¢ Carmine (II)	750.00	500.00	140.00	80.00	16.00	9.10
☐ 455	2¢ Carmine (III)	95.00	63.00	15.00	9.00	2.00	.90
☐ 456	3¢ Violet	1200.00	800.00	250.00	130.00	110.00	70.00
☐ 457	4¢ Brown	130.00	90.00	36.00	20.00	19.00	13.00
☐ 458	5¢ Blue	140.00	96.00	38.00	20.00	19.00	14.00

IMPERFORATE (N-H ADD 60%)

☐ 459	2¢ Carmine	2100.00	1400.00	450.00	350.00	—	—

Scott No.		Fine Unused Block	Ave. Unused Block	Fine Unused Each	Ave. Unused Each	Fine Used Each	Ave. Used Each

1915. DOUBLE LINE WATERMARKED "U.S.P.S." PERF. 10 (N-H ADD 60%)

| ☐ 460 | $1 Violet Black | 4100.00 | 3900.00 | 880.00 | 610.00 | 95.00 | 61.00 |

1915. SINGLE LINE WATERMARKED "U.S. P.S." PERF. 11 (N.H. ADD 60%)

| ☐ 461 | 2¢ Pale Carmine Rose | 340.00 | 100.00 | 65.00 | 85.00 | 55.00 | — |

1916–1917. UNWATERMARKED PERF. 10 (N-H ADD 70%)

☐ 462	1¢ Green	90.00	56.00	7.80	6.00	.42	.26
☐ 463	2¢ Carmine	40.00	28.00	6.00	3.50	.21	.16
☐ 464	3¢ Violet	400.00	310.00	87.00	60.00	18.00	11.50
☐ 465	4¢ Orange Brown	390.00	270.00	55.00	30.00	3.00	1.40
☐ 466	5¢ Blue	430.00	310.00	82.00	51.00	2.50	1.40
☐ 467	5¢ Carmine (error)	—	800.00	540.00	570.00	—	—
☐ 468	6¢ Red Orange	510.00	370.00	91.00	61.00	7.70	6.00
☐ 469	7¢ Black	620.00	500.00	120.00	70.00	16.00	9.10
☐ 470	.58¢ Olive Green	400.00	300.00	50.00	35.00	6.00	3.75
☐ 471	9¢ Salmon Red	360.00	200.00	58.00	36.00	15.00	9.90
☐ 472	12¢ Orange Yellow	630.00	460.00	115.00	75.00	1.50	.70
☐ 473	11¢ Dark Green	210.00	150.00	33.00	21.00	16.50	12.00
☐ 474	12¢ Claret Brown	370.00	220.00	50.00	32.00	7.00	5.00
☐ 475	15¢ Gray	1120.00	850.00	180.00	120.00	13.00	8.50
☐ 476	20¢ Ultramarine	2500.00	1800.00	320.00	170.00	13.00	9.00
☐ 477	50¢ Light Violet	6400.00	4600.00	1300.00	970.00	83.00	50.00
☐ 478	$1 Violet Black	4400.00	2800.00	850.00	650.00	19.50	13.00

1916–1917. DESIGN OF 1902–03 PERF. 10 (N-H ADD 70%)

| ☐ 479 | $2 Dark Blue | 2600.00 | 1800.00 | 600.00 | 350.00 | 46.00 | 29.00 |
| ☐ 480 | $5 Light Green | 2300.00 | 1700.00 | 450.00 | 260.00 | 55.00 | 33.00 |

IMPERFORATE (N-H ADD 70%)

☐ 481	1¢ Green	12.00	8.00	1.50	.95	1.60	.85
☐ 482	2¢ Carmine	22.00	17.00	2.10	1.20	2.00	1.20
☐ 483	3¢ Violet (I)	125.00	125.00	22.00	15.00	10.00	6.50
☐ 484	3¢ Violet (II)	80.00	55.00	16.00	16.00	5.00	3.50

Scott No.		Fine Unused Line Pair	Ave. Unused Line Pair	Fine Unused Each	Ave. Unused Each	Fine Used Each	Ave. Used Each

1916–1922. ROTARY PRESS COIL STAMPS PERF. 10 HORIZONTALLY (N-H ADD 60%)

☐ 486	1¢ Green	6.00	5.00	1.20	.67	.25	.17
☐ 487	2¢ Carmine (II)	155.00	120.00	23.00	14.00	4.00	2.70
☐ 488	2¢ Carmine (III)	28.00	20.00	5.00	3.00	2.00	1.20
☐ 489	3¢ Violet	35.00	20.00	6.00	4.00	140.00	.90

Scott No.	Fine Unused Line Pair	Ave. Unused Line Pair	Fine Unused Each	Ave. Unused Each	Fine Used Each	Ave. Used Each

PERF. 10 VERTICALLY (N-H ADD 60%)

☐ 490	1¢ Green	6.70	5.00	.80	.60	.25	.16
☐ 491	2¢ Carmine (II)	—	—	1100.00	800.00	190.00	125.00
☐ 492	2¢ Carmine (III)	64.00	43.00	13.00	7.50	.26	.18
☐ 493	3¢ Violet (I)	130.00	81.00	26.00	18.00	3.10	1.70
☐ 494	3¢ Violet (II)	95.00	61.00	16.00	9.10	.95	.60
☐ 495	4¢ Orange Brown	100.00	65.00	14.00	8.50	4.00	2.30
☐ 496	5¢ Blue	36.00	24.00	6.00	3.00	1.15	.60
☐ 497	10¢ Orange Yellow	165.00	112.00	25.00	18.00	14.00	7.70

Scott No.	Fine Unused Block	Ave. Unused Block	Fine Unused Each	Ave. Unused Each	Fine Used Each	Ave. Used Each

1917–1919. FLAT PLATE PRINTING
PERF. 11 (N-H ADD 60%)

☐ 498	1¢ Green	8.00	7.00	.60	.41	.16	.12
☐ 499	2¢ Rose (I)	9.00	7.00	.65	.42	.15	.12
☐ 500	2¢ Deep Rose (Ia)	1600.00	1210.00	290.00	160.00	122.00	75.00
☐ 501	3¢ Violet (I)	130.00	85.00	16.00	11.00	.18	.17
☐ 502	3¢ Violet (II)	140.00	100.00	21.00	14.00	.41	.26
☐ 503	4¢ Brown	115.00	74.00	16.00	10.00	.28	.21
☐ 504	5¢ Blue	80.00	59.00	12.00	7.50	.22	.16
☐ 505	5¢ Rose (error)	—	—	500.00	300.00	—	—
☐ 506	6¢ Red Orange	120.00	90.00	17.00	10.00	.50	.22
☐ 507	7¢ Black	210.00	140.00	36.00	21.00	1.60	.96
☐ 508	8¢ Olive Bistre	125.00	87.00	15.00	9.00	1.00	.65
☐ 509	9¢ Salmon Red	160.00	95.00	18.00	12.00	3.00	1.50
☐ 510	10¢ Orange Yellow	175.00	110.00	21.00	12.00	.20	.15
☐ 511	11¢ Light Green	90.00	62.00	13.00	8.00	4.00	2.30
☐ 512	12¢ Claret Brown	80.00	54.00	10.00	9.00	.68	.42
☐ 513	13¢ Apple Green	88.00	60.00	11.00	7.50	8.00	5.20
☐ 514	15¢ Gray	350.00	250.00	51.00	31.00	1.00	.80
☐ 515	20¢ Ultramarine	500.00	390.00	60.00	37.00	.40	.23
☐ 516	30¢ Orange Red	400.00	315.00	60.00	34.00	1.30	.80
☐ 517	50¢ Red Violet	600.00	400.00	115.00	60.00	1.00	.65
☐ 518	$1 Violet Brown	800.00	600.00	89.00	60.00	2.00	1.10
☐ 518b	$1 Deep Brown	2900.00	2300.00	600.00	420.00	190.00	125.00

1917. DOUBLE LINE WATERMARKED ''U.S.P.S.''
DESIGN OF 1908–1909
PERF. 11 (N-H ADD 60%)

☐ 519	2¢ Carmine	1300.00	1100.00	250.00	160.00	240.00	150.00

1918. UNWATERMARKED
PERF. 11 (N-H ADD 55%)

☐ 523	$2 Orange Red & Black ..	7900.00	5900.00	1170.00	1100.00	200.00	115.00
☐ 524	$5 Deep Green & Black ..	3000.00	2200.00	440.00	360.00	29.00	18.00

Scott No.		Fine Unused Block	Ave. Unused Block	Fine Unused Each	Ave. Unused Each	Fine Used Each	Ave. Used Each
1918–1920. OFFSET PRINTING							
PERF. 11 (N-H ADD 60%)							
☐ 525	1¢ Gray Green	23.00	13.00	2.80	2.00	.85	.60
☐ 526	2¢ Carmine (IV)	210.00	150.00	33.00	23.00	4.70	2.75
☐ 527	2¢ Carmine (V)	140.00	110.00	20.00	13.00	1.15	.65
☐ 528	2¢ Carmine (Va)	60.00	40.00	11.00	6.00	.26	.18
☐ 528A	2¢ Carmine (VI)	285.00	211.00	52.00	29.00	1.20	.75
☐ 528B	2¢ Carmine (VII)	160.00	112.00	23.00	14.00	.18	.14
☐ 529	3¢ Violet (III)	30.00	24.00	3.00	2.00	.25	.18
☐ 530	3¢ Purple (IV)	13.00	7.00	1.50	.75	.16	.12
IMPERFORATE (N-H ADD 60%)							
☐ 531	1¢ Gray Green	78.00	60.00	14.00	9.00	12.00	9.00
☐ 532	2¢ Carmine (IV)	280.00	200.00	53.00	35.00	34.00	22.00
☐ 533	2¢ Carmine (V)	1500.00	1000.00	250.00	160.00	77.00	50.00
☐ 534	2¢ Carmine (Va)	115.00	72.00	20.00	14.00	13.00	9.00
☐ 534A	2¢ Carmine (VI)	240.00	175.00	45.00	29.00	33.00	19.50
☐ 534B	2¢ Carmine (VII)	—	—	1700.00	1000.00	415.00	275.00
☐ 535	3¢ Violet	70.00	51.00	14.00	10.00	9.00	6.10
PERF. 12½ (N-H ADD 65%)							
☐ 536	1¢ Gray Green	125.00	90.00	18.00	12.00	16.00	9.00

IMPORTANT NOTICE: Beginning here, prices of **blocks** are for blocks of 4 with **plate number attached.** Ordinary blocks of 4 bring lower prices. Plate blocks consisting of more than 4 stamps would sell higher than these sums. Always check the **headings** of price columns to accurately value your stamps.

Scott No.		Fine Unused Plate Blk	Ave. Unused Plate Blk	Fine Unused Each	Ave. Unused Each	Fine Used Each	Ave. Used Each
1919. VICTORY ISSUE (N-H ADD 45%)							
☐ 537	3¢ Violet	220.00	145.00	13.00	9.00	5.60	3.00
1919–1921. REGULAR ISSUE							
ROTARY PRESS PRINTING							
PERF. 11 x 10 (N-H ADD 70%)							
☐ 538	1¢ Green	110.00	77.00	12.00	7.50	10.00	7.00
☐ 538a	Same Impf. Horiz. Pair	—	—	62.00	38.00	—	—
☐ 539	2¢ Carmine Rose (II) ...	—	—	2200.00	1275.00	680.00	400.00
☐ 540	2¢ Carmine Rose (III)	110.00	73.00	13.00	8.00	10.00	7.00
☐ 540a	Same Impf. Horiz. Pair	—	—	65.00	41.00	—	—
☐ 541	3¢ Violet	390.00	270.00	46.00	30.00	41.00	26.00
PERF. 10 x 11 (N-H ADD 70%)							
☐ 542	1¢ Green	117.00	79.00	7.10	6.50	1.25	.90
PERF. 10 x 10 (N-H ADD 70%)							
☐ 543	1¢ Green	18.00	13.00	.90	.70	.18	.13

Scott No.		Fine Unused Plate Blk	Ave. Unused Plate Blk	Fine Unused Each	Ave. Unused Each	Fine Used Each	Ave. Used Each
PERF. 11 x 11 (N-H ADD 70%)							
☐ 544	1¢ Green	—	—	—	—	1600.00	1100.00
☐ 545	1¢ Green	800.00	700.00	165.00	120.00	98.00	63.00
☐ 546	2¢ Carmine Rose	550.00	450.00	95.00	76.00	68.00	45.00
FLAT PLATE PRINTING							
PERF. 11 (N-H ADD 60%)							
☐ 547	$2 Carmine & Black	—	—	410.00	240.00	37.00	26.00
1920. PILGRIM ISSUE (N-H ADD 55%)							
☐ 548	1¢ Green	62.00	50.00	7.50	5.00	3.60	2.00
☐ 549	2¢ Carmine Rose	90.00	68.00	12.00	7.10	2.70	1.70
☐ 550	5¢ Deep Blue	700.00	550.00	60.00	37.00	23.00	13.00
1922–1925 PERF. FLAT PLATE PRINTING							
PERF. 11 (N-H ADD 55%)							
☐ 551	½¢ Olive Brown	13.00	9.00	18.00	12.00	16.00	.11
☐ 552	1¢ Deep Green	35.00	22.00	3.10	1.70	.16	.11
☐ 553	1½¢ Yellow Brown	50.00	35.00	5.00	3.20	.40	.21
☐ 554	2¢ Carmine	46.00	33.00	2.00	1.15	.13	.09
☐ 555	3¢ Violet	26.00	185.00	25.00	14.00	1.40	.90
☐ 556	4¢ Yellow Brown	270.00	200.00	26.00	14.00	.21	.17
☐ 557	5¢ Dark Blue	290.00	215.00	24.00	15.00	.20	.14
☐ 558	6¢ Red Orange	570.00	400.00	42.00	26.00	1.00	.65
☐ 559	7¢ Black	115.00	82.00	12.00	6.60	1.00	.60
☐ 560	8¢ Olive Green	9.00	710.00	48.00	32.00	1.10	.65
☐ 561	9¢ Rose	220.00	160.00	19.00	13.00	1.60	.83
☐ 562	10¢ Orange	400.00	270.00	25.00	16.00	.21	.15
☐ 563	11¢ Blue	48.00	31.00	2.60	1.50	.50	.26
☐ 564	12¢ Brown Violet	120.00	80.00	9.10	6.50	.20	.16
☐ 565	14¢ Dark Blue	90.00	71.00	8.00	5.00	1.10	.62
☐ 566	15¢ Gray	320.00	220.00	26.00	15.00	.16	.15
☐ 567	20¢ Carmine Rose	315.00	220.00	31.00	18.00	.15	.10
☐ 568	25¢ Green	300.00	220.00	31.00	17.00	.60	.42
☐ 569	30¢ Olive Brown	500.00	300.00	43.00	25.00	.51	.34
☐ 570	50¢ Lilac	11.00	700.00	70.00	50.00	.26	.18
☐ 571	$1 Violet Black	610.00	400.00	58.00	38.00	.48	.31
☐ 572	$2 Deep Blue	1600.00	1200.00	160.00	96.00	12.00	8.00
☐ 573	$5 Carmine & Blue	9200.00	5900.00	350.00	225.00	20.00	13.00
IMPERFORATE (N-H ADD 45%)							
☐ 575	1¢ Green	155.00	122.00	13.00	8.00	5.50	3.50
☐ 576	1½¢ Yellow Brown	34.00	23.00	3.00	1.60	2.10	1.50
☐ 577	2¢ Carmine	37.00	25.00	3.00	1.70	2.10	1.60
1923–1926. ROTARY PRESS PRINTING							
PERF. 11 x 10 (N-H ADD 55%)							
☐ 578	1¢ Green	700.00	600.00	79.00	55.00	75.00	46.00
☐ 579	2¢ Carmine	450.00	300.00	55.00	37.00	46.00	30.00

Scott No.		Fine Unused Plate Blk	Ave. Unused Plate Blk	Fine Unused Each	Ave. Unused Each	Fine Used Each	Ave. Used Each
PERF. 10 (N-H ADD 55%)							
☐ 581	1¢ Green	123.00	85.00	8.50	5.00	1.25	.72
☐ 582	1½¢ Brown	50.00	34.00	5.00	3.10	1.00	.65
☐ 583	2¢ Carmine	33.00	21.00	3.00	1.70	.17	.08
☐ 584	3¢ Violet	300.00	200.00	31.00	19.00	2.50	1.10
☐ 585	4¢ Yellow Brown	200.00	145.00	17.00	10.00	.70	.35
☐ 586	5¢ Blue	188.00	123.00	15.00	9.00	.40	.25
☐ 587	6¢ Red Orange	85.00	63.00	10.00	6.50	.70	.45
☐ 588	7¢ Black	110.00	74.00	13.00	8.00	6.20	4.50
☐ 589	8¢ Olive Green	310.00	210.00	33.00	19.00	4.00	2.30
☐ 590	9¢ Rose	62.00	40.00	7.00	4.20	3.00	1.50
☐ 591	10¢ Orange	700.00	500.00	65.00	40.00	.18	.12
PERF. 11							
☐ 595	2¢ Carmine	1600.00	1100.00	190.00	125.00	170.00	115.00

Scott No.		Fine Unused Line Pair	Ave. Unused Line Pair	Fine Unused Each	Ave. Unused Each	Fine Used Each	Ave. Used Each
1923–1929. ROTARY PRESS COIL STAMPS							
PERF. 10 VERTICALLY (N-H ADD 55%)							
☐ 597	1¢ Green	3.80	3.00	.55	.27	.14	.12
☐ 598	1½¢ Deep Brown	7.70	6.00	.75	.46	.21	.16
☐ 599	2¢ Carmine (I)	2.70	2.00	.42	.25	.14	.10
☐ 599A	2¢ Carmine (II)	700.00	510.00	140.00	90.00	14.00	7.70
☐ 600	3¢ Deep Violet	57.00	38.00	9.00	6.00	.16	.14
☐ 601	4¢ Yellow Brown	60.00	40.00	6.10	4.00	.62	.43
☐ 602	5¢ Dark Blue	16.00	12.00	2.00	1.00	.24	.16
☐ 603	10¢ Orange	30.00	20.00	5.00	3.00	.18	.13
PERF. 10 HORIZONTALLY (N-H ADD 55%)							
☐ 604	1¢ Green	5.00	3.60	.30	.18	.15	.11
☐ 605	1½¢ Yellow Brown	4.00	2.00	.30	.18	.21	.15
☐ 606	2¢ Carmine	3.00	2.00	.32	.21	.16	.12

Scott No.		Fine Unused Plate Blk	Ave. Unused Plate Blk	Fine Unused Each	Ave. Unused Each	Fine Used Each	Ave. Used Each
1923. HARDING MEMORIAL ISSUE (N-H ADD 45%)							
☐ 610	2¢ Black, pf. 11	38.00	26.00	1.25	.66	.17	.11
☐ 611	2¢ Black, imperf.	180.00	130.00	14.00	9.10	6.50	4.50
☐ 612	2¢ Black, pf. 10 rotary ...	490.00	370.00	24.00	15.00	2.80	1.50
1924. HUGUENOT-WALLOON ISSUE (N-H ADD 45%)							
☐ 614	1¢ Green	85.00	63.00	6.50	3.40	4.70	3.00
☐ 615	2¢ Carmine Rose	115.00	80.00	8.10	6.50	3.80	2.00
☐ 616	5¢ Dark Blue	500.00	375.00	48.00	29.00	23.00	14.00

Scott No.		Fine Unused Plate Blk	Ave. Unused Plate Blk	Fine Unused Each	Ave. Unused Each	Fine Used Each	Ave. Used Each

1925. LEXINGTON-CONCORD SESQUICENTENNIAL (N-H ADD 45%)

☐ 617	1¢ Green	85.00	56.00	6.00	3.60	5.00	3.30
☐ 618	2¢ Carmine Rose	140.00	100.00	9.00	7.00	6.20	4.20
☐ 619	5¢ Dark Blue	500.00	370.00	46.00	31.00	23.00	14.00

1925. NORSE-AMERICAN ISSUE (N-H ADD 40%)

☐ 620	2¢ Carmine & Black	180.00	120.00	8.00	5.00	6.00	4.00
☐ 621	5¢ Dark Blue & Black	800.00	600.00	24.00	15.00	23.00	13.00

1925–1926

☐ 622	13¢ Green	210.00	130.00	20.00	13.00	.85	.60
☐ 623	17¢ Black	230.00	165.00	23.00	15.00	.45	.30

1926–1927. COMMEMORATIVES

1926. SESQUICENTENNIAL EXPOSITION (N-H ADD 50%)

☐ 627	2¢ Carmine Rose	65.00	43.00	5.00	3.00	.76	.53

1926. ERICSSON MEMORIAL ISSUE (N-H ADD 50%)

☐ 628	5¢ Gray Lilac	135.00	110.00	13.00	8.00	6.00	3.00

1926. BATTLE OF WHITE PLAINS (N-H ADD 45%)

☐ 629	2¢ Carmine Rose	—	63.00	4.00	3.00	4.00	1.50
☐ 630	2¢ Souv. Sheet of 25	—	—	450.00	350.00	—	—

1926–1928. DESIGNS OF 1922–1925
ROTARY PRESS PRINTING IMPERFORATE (N-H ADD 40%)

☐ 631	1½¢ Brown	90.00	65.00	3.00	2.10	2.50	1.60

PERF. 11 x 10½ (N-H ADD 50%)

☐ 632	1¢ Green	3.50	2.50	.19	.14	.15	.10
☐ 633	1½¢ Yellow Brown	121.00	84.00	3.50	2.00	.17	.11
☐ 634	2¢ Carmine (I)	2.40	1.70	.19	.12	.13	.09
☐ 634A	2¢ Carmine (II)	—	—	360.00	250.00	18.00	12.00
☐ 635	3¢ Violet	7.50	6.00	.60	.42	.13	.10
☐ 636	4¢ Yellow Brown	125.00	80.00	4.10	2.10	.19	.14
☐ 637	5¢ Dark Blue	30.00	19.00	3.50	2.10	.13	.10
☐ 638	6¢ Red Orange	33.00	21.00	4.60	2.10	.13	.10
☐ 639	7¢ Black	28.00	19.00	4.00	2.10	.15	.10
☐ 640	8¢ Olive Green	29.00	20.00	4.10	2.10	.12	.10
☐ 641	9¢ Orange Red	33.00	20.00	4.00	2.10	.13	.10
☐ 642	10¢ Orange	50.00	34.00	7.10	3.60	.13	.10

1927. VERMONT SESQUICENTENNIAL (N.H ADD 45%)

☐ 643	2¢ Carmine Rose	65.00	50.00	2.20	1.60	1.50	1.00

1927. BURGOYNE CAMPAIGN ISSUE (N.H ADD 45%)

☐ 644	2¢ Carmine	70.00	50.00	5.10	3.10	3.90	2.50

1928. VALLEY FORGE ISSUE (N.H ADD 45%)

☐ 645	2¢ Carmine	60.00	45.00	1.35	1.00	.70	.50

1928. BATTLE OF MONMOUTH (N.H ADD 45%)

☐ 646	2¢ Carmine	70.00	50.00	1.70	1.20	1.50	1.00

Scott No.		Fine Unused Plate Blk	Ave. Unused Plate Blk	Fine Unused Each	Ave. Unused Each	Fine Used Each	Ave. Used Each
1928. DISCOVERY OF HAWAII (N.H ADD 45%)							
☐647	2¢ Carmine Rose	240.00	146.00	6.00	5.00	5.50	3.50
☐648	5¢ Blue	500.00	350.00	21.00	13.00	21.00	14.50
1928. AERONAUTICS CONFERENCE (N.H ADD 40%)							
☐649	2¢ Carmine	26.00	17.00	1.75	1.00	1.50	1.10
☐650	5¢ Blue	100.00	70.00	7.50	5.10	5.00	3.50
1929. GEORGE ROGERS CLARK (N.H ADD 40%)							
☐651	2¢ Carmine & Black	18.00	13.00	.85	.60	.86	.65
1929. DESIGNS OF 1922–1925							
ROTARY PRESS PRINTING—PERF. 11 x 10½ (N.H ADD 40%)							
☐653	½¢ Olive Brown	2.40	1.50	.12	.11	.14	.11
1929. EDISON COMMEMORATIVE							
FLAT PLATE PRINTING—PERF. 11 (N.H ADD 40%)							
☐654	2¢ Carmine Rose	50.00	33.00	.99	.66	1.30	1.00
ROTARY PRESS PRINTING—PERF. 11 x 10½ (N.H ADD 40%)							
☐655	2¢ Carmine Rose	91.00	55.00	.95	.72	.42	.28

Scott No.		Fine Unused Line Pair	Ave. Unused Line Pair	Fine Unused Each	Ave. Unused Each	Fine Used Each	Ave. Used Each
ROTARY PRESS COIL STAMPS—PERF. 10 VERTICALLY (N-H ADD 40%)							
☐656	2¢ Carmine Rose	93.00	61.00	15.00	11.00	2.70	1.80

Scott No.		Fine Unused Plate Blk	Ave. Unused Plate Blk	Fine Unused Each	Ave. Unused Each	Fine Used Each	Ave. Used Each
1929. SULLIVAN EXPEDITION (N-H ADD 40%)							
☐657	2¢ Carmine Rose	30.00	20.00	1.20	.75	.95	.75
1929. 632–42 OVERPRINTED (KANS.) (N.H ADD 45%)							
☐658	1¢ Green	42.00	24.00	2.60	1.75	2.50	1.50
☐659	1½¢ Brown	50.00	31.00	4.10	2.70	4.50	3.20
☐660	2¢ Carmine	60.00	41.00	3.80	2.50	1.00	.70
☐661	3¢ Violet	200.00	130.00	22.00	14.00	15.00	8.80
☐662	4¢ Yellow Brown	200.00	150.00	25.00	18.00	9.00	6.20
☐663	5¢ Deep Blue	170.00	120.00	16.00	12.00	11.00	7.70
☐664	6¢ Red Orange	460.00	320.00	29.00	18.00	17.00	12.10
☐665	7¢ Black	460.00	300.00	32.00	20.00	26.00	16.50
☐666	8¢ Olive Green	800.00	600.00	91.00	62.00	69.00	46.00
☐667	9¢ Light Rose	225.00	170.00	16.00	13.00	11.00	10.00
☐668	10¢ Orange Yellow	360.00	260.00	25.00	18.00	12.00	7.50
1929. 632–42 OVERPRINTED (NEBR.) (N.H ADD 45%)							
☐669	1¢ Green	38.00	25.00	2.60	1.75	2.40	1.60
☐670	1½¢ Brown	61.00	36.00	3.40	2.30	2.90	1.90

Scott No.		Fine Unused Plate Blk	Ave. Unused Plate Blk	Fine Unused Each	Ave. Unused Each	Fine Used Each	Ave. Used Each
☐ 671	2¢ Carmine	44.00	30.00	2.50	1.70	1.00	.75
☐ 672	3¢ Violet	210.00	130.00	14.00	9.00	10.00	6.75
☐ 673	4¢ Brown	230.00	170.00	21.00	13.00	12.00	8.00
☐ 674	5¢ Blue	250.00	175.00	19.00	12.00	13.00	8.00
☐ 675	6¢ Orange	510.00	400.00	39.00	25.00	27.00	16.00
☐ 676	7¢ Black	275.00	180.00	22.00	13.00	17.00	12.00
☐ 677	8¢ Olive Green	310.00	200.00	28.00	17.00	24.00	16.00
☐ 678	9¢ Rose	425.00	230.00	39.00	24.00	33.00	22.00
☐ 679	10¢ Orange Yellow	860.00	650.00	100.00	71.00	21.00	13.00

1929. BATTLE OF FALLEN TIMBERS (N-H ADD 35%)

☐ 680	2¢ Carmine Rose	45.00	33.00	1.25	.73	1.10	.66

1929. OHIO RIVER CANALIZATION (N-H ADD 30%)

☐ 681	2¢ Carmine Rose	31.00	23.00	.90	.60	.85	.53

1930–1931. COMMEMORATIVES

1930. MASSACHUSETTS BAY COLONY (N-H ADD 35%)

☐ 682	2¢ Carmine Rose	46.00	30.00	.75	.53	.67	.45

1930. CAROLINA-CHARLESTON ISSUE (N-H ADD 35%)

☐ 683	2¢ Carmine Rose	76.00	50.00	1.60	1.20	1.75	1.20

1930. REGULAR ISSUE
ROTARY PRESS PRINTING—PERF. 11 x 10½ (N-H ADD 35%)

☐ 684	1½¢ Brown	4.50	3.50	.50	.34	.14	.12
☐ 685	4¢ Brown	11.00	9.10	1.00	.65	.15	.13

Scott No.		Fine Unused Line Pair	Ave. Unused Line Pair	Fine Unused Each	Ave. Unused Each	Fine Used Each	Ave. Used Each

ROTARY PRESS COIL STAMPS
PERF. 10 VERTICALLY (N-H ADD 40%)

☐ 686	1½¢ Brown	13.00	10.00	2.10	1.50	.14	.10
☐ 687	4¢ Brown	18.00	13.00	3.60	2.50	.62	.13

Scott No.		Fine Unused Plate Blk	Ave. Unused Plate Blk	Fine Unused Each	Ave. Unused Each	Fine Used Each	Ave. Used Each

1930. BATTLE OF BRADDOCK'S FIELD (N-H ADD 40%)

☐ 688	2¢ Carmine Rose	64.00	42.00	1.30	.90	1.70	1.50

1930. VON STEUBEN ISSUE (N-H ADD 40%)

☐ 689	2¢ Carmine Rose	37.00	23.00	.70	.46	.76	.55

1931. PULASKI ISSUE (N-H ADD 40%)

☐ 690	2¢ Carmine Rose	27.00	20.00	.33	.22	.25	.16

1931. DESIGNS OF 1922–1926
ROTARY PRESS PRINTING—PERF. 11 x 10½ (N-H ADD 40%)

☐ 692	11¢ Light Blue	34.00	22.00	3.80	2.60	.19	.13
☐ 693	12¢ Brown Violet	49.00	35.00	6.50	5.20	.13	.11

Scott No.		Fine Unused Plate Blk	Ave. Unused Plate Blk	Fine Unused Each	Ave. Unused Each	Fine Used Each	Ave. Used Each
☐ 694	13¢ Yellow Green	29.00	21.00	3.00	2.00	.27	.19
☐ 695	14¢ Dark Blue	40.00	30.00	6.00	3.50	.65	.45
☐ 696	15¢ Gray	80.00	53.00	13.00	9.10	.14	.12

PERF. 10½ x 11 (N-H ADD 40%)

☐ 697	17¢ Black	48.00	33.00	7.00	5.50	.41	.25
☐ 698	20¢ Carmine Rose	110.00	70.00	14.00	8.60	.14	.10
☐ 699	25¢ Blue Green	92.00	66.00	12.00	8.00	.16	.13
☐ 700	30¢ Brown..............	130.00	110.00	19.00	12.00	.15	.10
☐ 701	50¢ Lilac	360.00	240.00	61.00	38.00	.15	.12

1931. RED CROSS ISSUE (N-H ADD 40%)

☐ 702	2¢ Black & Red	3.70	2.25	.20	.15	.23	.18

1931. SURRENDER OF YORKTOWN (N-H ADD 40%)

☐ 703	2¢ Carmine Rose & Black	4.60	3.70	.60	.45	.50	.43

1932. WASHINGTON BICENTENNIAL (N-H ADD 40%)

☐ 704	½¢ Olive Brown	6.00	5.00	.14	.10	.15	.11
☐ 705	1¢ Green	7.00	6.00	.20	.16	.14	.11
☐ 706	1½¢ Brown	33.00	22.00	.58	.40	.19	.13
☐ 707	2¢ Carmine	3.50	3.00	.14	.11	.16	.13
☐ 708	3¢ Purple	30.00	17.00	.87	.60	.14	.13
☐ 709	4¢ Light Brown	10.00	7.00	.40	.25	.15	.13
☐ 710	5¢ Blue	26.00	14.00	2.40	1.30	.18	.16
☐ 711	6¢ Orange	95.00	60.00	6.50	4.00	.18	.13
☐ 712	7¢ Black	12.00	8.50	.62	.46	.22	.18
☐ 713	8¢ Olive Bistre	110.00	70.00	6.70	5.20	1.00	.67
☐ 714	9¢ Pale Red	75.00	48.00	4.50	2.60	.32	.22
☐ 715	10¢ Orange Yellow	210.00	140.00	19.00	11.00	.18	.14

1932. COMMEMORATIVES

1932. OLYMPIC WINTER GAMES (N-H ADD 30%)

☐ 716	2¢ Carmine Rose	18.00	14.00	.65	.47	.34	.20

1932. ARBOR DAY ISSUE (N-H ADD 30%)

☐ 717	2¢ Carmine Rose	13.00	9.00	.21	.16	.16	.15

1932. OLYMPIC SUMMER GAMES (N-H ADD 30%)

☐ 718	3¢ Purple	27.00	19.00	2.50	2.70	.18	.14
☐ 719	5¢ Blue	42.00	27.00	4.10	3.50	.36	.25

Scott No.		Fine Unused Line Pair	Ave. Unused Line Pair	Fine Unused Each	Ave. Unused Each	Fine Used Each	Ave. Used Each

1932. ROTARY PRESS COIL STAMPS

☐ 720	3¢ Deep Violet	2.60	1.85	.26	.18	.12	.08

PERF. 10 VERTICALLY (N-H ADD 30%)

☐ 721	3¢ Deep Violet	11.10	6.60	3.50	2.70	.14	.10

Scott No.		Fine Unused Line Pair	Ave. Unused Line Pair	Fine Unused Each	Ave. Unused Each	Fine Used Each	Ave. Used Each
PERF. 10 HORIZONTALLY (N-H ADD 30%)							
☐ 722	3¢ Deep Violet	6.00	4.20	2.10	1.25	1.00	.62
DESIGN OF 1922–1925—PERF. 10 VERTICALLY (N-H ADD 30%)							
☐ 723	6¢ Deep Orange	73.00	49.10	16.80	10.00	.31	.22

Scott No.		Fine Unused Plate Blk	Ave. Unused Plate Blk	Fine Unused Each	Ave. Unused Each	Fine Used Each	Ave. Used Each
1932. WILLIAM PENN ISSUE (N-H ADD 30%)							
☐ 724	3¢ Violet	21.00	13.00	.52	.33	.28	.22
1932. DANIEL WEBSTER ISSUE (N-H ADD 30%)							
☐ 725	3¢ Violet	39.00	25.00	.69	.51	.43	.31
1933. COMMEMORATIVES							
1933. GEORGIA BICENTENNIAL (N-H ADD 30%)							
☐ 726	3¢ Violet	25.00	17.00	.43	.31	.27	.20
1933. PEACE SESQUICENTENNIAL (N-H ADD 30%)							
☐ 727	3¢ Violet	8.10	5.10	.17	.15	.14	.11
1933. CENTURY OF PROGRESS EXPOSITION (N-H ADD 30%)							
☐ 728	1¢ Yellow Green	4.00	2.60	.17	.11	.12	.09
☐ 729	3¢ Purple	7.00	3.70	.21	.12	.10	.09
1933. A.P.S. CONVENTION AND EXHIBITION AT CHICAGO IMPERFORATE—UNGUMMED (N-H ADD 30%)							
☐ 730	1¢ Yellow Green, Sheet of 25	—	—	49.00	35.00	—	—
☐ 730a	1¢ Yellow Green, sgl.	—	—	.95	.70	.79	.62
☐ 731	3¢ Violet Sheet of 25	—	—	42.00	—	39.00	—
☐ 731a	3¢ Violet, single	—	—	.88	.67	.61	.42
1933. N.R.A. ISSUE (N-H ADD 25%)							
☐ 732	3¢ Violet	3.90	2.50	.17	.14	.11	.09
1933. BYRD ANTARCTIC EXPEDITION (N-H ADD 30%)							
☐ 733	3¢ Dark Blue	33.00	22.00	.95	.67	1.10	.77
1933. KOSCIUSZKO ISSUE (N-H ADD 30%)							
☐ 734	5¢ Blue	71.00	47.00	.86	.65	.42	.27
1934. NATIONAL PHILATELIC EXHIBITION IMPERFORATE—UNGUMMED (N-H ADD 30%)							
☐ 735	3¢ Dark Blue Sheet of 6	—	—	27.00	—	23.00	16.00
☐ 735a	3¢ Dark Blue, sgl.	—	—	4.10	2.50	3.00	2.00
1934. COMMEMORATIVES							
1934. MARYLAND TERCENTENARY (N-H ADD 30%)							
☐ 736	3¢ Rose	19.00	12.50	.22	.15	.20	.13

Scott No.	Fine Unused Plate Blk	Ave. Unused Plate Blk	Fine Unused Each	Ave. Unused Each	Fine Used Each	Ave. Used Each

1934. MOTHER'S DAY ISSUE
ROTARY PRESS PRINTING—PERF. 11 x 10½ (N-H ADD 30%)

| ☐737 | 3¢ Deep Violet . . . . | 2.50 | 1.90 | .20 | .15 | .13 | .09 |

FLAT PRESS PRINTING-PERF. 11 (N-H ADD 30%)

| ☐738 | 3¢ Deep Violet . . . . | 8.00 | 7.00 | .29 | .19 | .36 | .23 |

1934. WISCONSIN TERCENTENARY (N-H ADD 30%)

| ☐739 | 3¢ Deep Violet . . . . | 8.00 | 5.00 | .26 | .18 | .18 | .14 |

1934. NATIONAL PARKS ISSUE (N-H ADD 25%)

☐740	1¢ Green	2.50	1.75	.17	.11	.16	.10
☐741	2¢ Red	2.40	1.60	.20	.15	.16	.13
☐742	3¢ Purple	4.70	3.50	.26	.18	.17	.13
☐743	4¢ Brown	18.10	12.00	.62	.42	.63	.45
☐744	5¢ Blue	20.10	14.00	1.21	.86	.90	.66
☐745	6¢ Indigo	36.10	21.00	1.50	.95	1.30	.96
☐746	7¢ Black	21.00	12.00	1.30	.86	1.20	.78
☐747	8¢ Green	35.00	21.00	3.70	2.41	2.70	1.75
☐748	9¢ Salmon	34.00	21.00	3.50	2.21	.81	.56
☐749	10¢ Gray Black	58.00	40.00	5.10	3.60	1.60	.97

1934. A.P.S. CONVENTION AND EXHIBITION AT ATLANTIC CITY
IMPERFORATE SOUVENIR SHEET (N-H ADD 25%)

| ☐750 | 3¢ Purple, sheet of 6 . . . . | — | — | 42.00 | — | 46.00 | 39.00 |
| ☐750a | 3¢ Purple, single . . . . . . | — | — | 6.10 | 4.10 | 5.10 | 3.00 |

1934. TRANS-MISSISSIPPI PHILATELIC EXPOSITION AND
CONVENTION AT OMAHA
IMPERFORATE SOUVENIR SHEET (N-H ADD 25%)

| ☐751 | 1¢ Green, sheet of 6 . . . . | — | — | 21.00 | — | 21.00 | 14.00 |
| ☐751a | 1¢ Green, single . . . . | — | — | 3.00 | 2.10 | 1.60 | 1.20 |

Scott No.	Plate Block	Block Plain	Mint Each	Used Each

1935. "FARLEY SPECIAL PRINTINGS"
DESIGNS OF 1933–1934
PERF. 10½ x 11—UNGUMMED (N-H ADD 25%)

| ☐752 | 3¢ Violet . . . . | 17.00 | 1.50 | .18 | .16 |

PERF. 11—GUMMED (N-H ADD 25%)

| ☐753 | 3¢ Dark Blue . . . . | 26.00 | 5.10 | .60 | .65 |

IMPERFORATE—UNGUMMED (N-H ADD 25%)

| ☐754 | 3¢ Deep Violet . . . . | 27.00 | 5.20 | .85 | .88 |
| ☐755 | 3¢ Deep Violet . . . . | 27.00 | 6.10 | .90 | .99 |

NATIONAL PARKS
IMPERFORATE—UNGUMMED (N-H ADD 25%)

| ☐756 | 1¢ Green . . . . | 11.00 | 1.25 | .23 | .35 |
| ☐757 | 2¢ Red . . . . | 12.00 | 1.80 | .38 | .35 |

Scott No.		Plate Block	Block Plain	Mint Each	Used Each
☐ 758	3¢ Deep Violet	24.00	3.15	.75	.75
☐ 759	4¢ Brown	33.00	9.10	1.20	1.10
☐ 760	5¢ Blue	36.00	15.00	2.10	2.00
☐ 761	6¢ Dark Blue	62.00	17.00	4.00	3.00
☐ 762	7¢ Black	55.00	14.00	2.00	2.00
☐ 763	8¢ Sage Green	67.00	13.00	2.50	2.00
☐ 764	9¢ Red Orange	71.00	15.00	2.50	2.00
☐ 765	10¢ Gray Black	81.00	28.00	4.00	4.00

IMPERFORATE—UNGUMMED (N-H ADD 25%)

☐ 766a	1¢ Yellow Green	—	14.50	1.00	.70
☐ 767a	3¢ Violet	—	14.50	1.10	.70
☐ 768a	3¢ Dark Blue	—	21.00	4.00	3.10
☐ 769a	1¢ Green	—	13.00	1.50	1.50
☐ 770a	3¢ Deep Violet	—	20.00	3.30	3.50

DESIGN OF CE 1 (N-H ADD 30%)

☐ 771	16¢ Dark Blue	121.00	22.00	4.00	3.60

1935–1936. COMMEMORATIVES

Scott No.		Fine Unused Plate Blk	Ave. Unused Plate Blk	Mint Each	Used Each
1935. CONNECTICUT TERCENTENARY (N-H ADD 25%)					
☐ 772	3¢ Red Violet	2.50	2.00	.18	.12
1935. CALIFORNIA PACIFIC EXPOSITION (N-H ADD 25%)					
☐ 773	3¢ Purple	2.50	1.60	.17	.15
1935. BOULDER DAM ISSUE (N-H ADD 25%)					
☐ 774	3¢ Purple	2.00	1.50	.17	.14
1935. MICHIGAN CENTENARY (N-H ADD 25%)					
☐ 775	3¢ Purple	2.50	1.30	.16	.13
1936. TEXAS CENTENNIAL (N-H ADD 25%)					
☐ 776	3¢ Purple	2.10	1.50	.20	.15
1936. RHODE ISLAND TERCENTENARY (N-H ADD 25%)					
☐ 777	3¢ Purple	2.60	1.60	.24	.16
1936. THIRD INTL. PHILATELIC EXHIBITION "TIPEX" IMPERFORATE SOUVENIR SHEET DESIGNS OF 772, 773, 775, 776 (N-H ADD 25%)					
☐ 778	3¢ Red Violet, sheet of 4	—	—	4.00	3.20
☐ 778a	3¢ Red Violet, single	—	—	1.00	1.10
☐ 778b	3¢ Red Violet, single	—	—	1.00	1.10
☐ 778c	3¢ Red Violet, single	—	—	1.00	1.10
☐ 778d	3¢ Red Violet, single	—	—	1.00	1.10
1936. ARKANSAS CENTENNIAL (N-H ADD 25%)					
☐ 782	3¢ Purple	2.15	1.50	.15	.13

Scott No.		Fine Unused Plate Blk	Ave. Unused Plate Blk	Fine Unused Each	Ave. Unused Each	Fine Used Each	Ave. Used Each

1936. OREGON TERRITORY CENTENNIAL (N-H ADD 25%)

| ☐783 | 3¢ Purple | 1.50 | 1.20 | .16 | .13 | .11 | .10 |

1936. SUFFRAGE FOR WOMEN ISSUE (N-H ADD 25%)

| ☐784 | 3¢ Dark Violet .... | 1.10 | .95 | .14 | .11 | .12 | .09 |

1936–1937. ARMY AND NAVY ISSUE
ARMY COMMEMORATIVES (N-H ADD 20%)

☐785	1¢ Green	1.70	1.00	.13	.10	.11	.07
☐786	2¢ Carmine	1.35	1.20	.18	.13	.11	.08
☐787	3¢ Purple	2.00	1.60	.26	.21	.15	.12
☐788	4¢ Gray	18.00	16.00	.85	.61	.26	.19
☐789	5¢ Ultramarine	21.00	16.00	.94	.69	.25	.20

NAVY COMMEMORATIVES (N-H ADD 25%)

☐790	1¢ Green	—	1.15	.17	.16	.11	.09
☐791	2¢ Carmine	1.60	1.21	.22	.16	.11	.08
☐792	3¢ Purple	1.80	1.26	.25	.19	.15	.12
☐793	4¢ Gray	22.00	17.00	.75	.54	.24	.17
☐794	5¢ Ultramarine	24.00	17.00	.95	.70	.24	.18

1937. COMMEMORATIVES

1937. NORTHWEST ORDINANCE ISSUE (N-H ADD 25%)

| ☐795 | 3¢ Violet .... | 2.12 | 1.70 | .21 | .13 | .11 | .09 |

1937. VIRGINIA DARE ISSUE (N-H ADD 20%)

| ☐796 | 5¢ Gray Blue .... | 11.00 | 9.00 | .51 | .26 | .26 | .19 |

1937. S.P.A. CONVENTION ISSUE (N-H ADD 25%)
DESIGN OF 749 IMPERFORATE SOUVENIR SHEET

| ☐797 | 10¢ Blue Green .... | — | — | 1.45 | — | .87 | .66 |

1937. CONSTITUTIONAL SESQUICENTENNIAL (N-H ADD 25%)

| ☐798 | 3¢ Red Violet .... | 1.40 | 1.20 | .20 | .15 | .12 | .10 |

1937. TERRITORIAL PUBLICITY ISSUE (N-H ADD 25%)

☐799	3¢ Violet	3.00	2.00	.19	.14	.10	.09
☐800	3¢ Violet	3.00	2.00	.19	.14	.10	.09
☐801	3¢ Bright Violet	3.00	2.00	.19	.14	.10	.09
☐802	3¢ Light Violet	3.00	2.00	.19	.14	.10	.09

1938. PRESIDENTIAL SERIES
ROTARY PRESS PRINTING—PERF. 11 x 10½ (N-H ADD 25%)

☐803	½¢ Red Orange	.82	.62	.12	.08	.11	.08
☐804	1¢ Green	.50	.37	.14	.09	.10	.07
☐805	1½¢ Bistre Brown	.52	.39	.14	.11	.10	.07
☐806	2¢ Rose Carmine	.74	.54	.18	.14	.11	.08
☐807	3¢ Deep Violet	.64	.48	.16	.11	.11	.08
☐808	4¢ Red Violet	2.70	1.93	.45	.29	.11	.08
☐809	4½¢ Dark Gray	2.41	1.85	.25	.18	.12	.11

Scott No.		Fine Unused Plate Blk	Ave. Unused Plate Blk	Fine Unused Each	Ave. Unused Each	Fine Used Each	Ave. Used Each
☐810	5¢ Bright Blue	2.30	1.80	.31	.22	.14	.11
☐811	6¢ Red Orange	2.65	1.82	.48	.31	.13	.10
☐812	7¢ Sepia	2.70	1.87	.43	.27	.13	.09
☐813	8¢ Olive Green	3.50	2.70	.66	.41	.13	.09
☐814	9¢ Rose Pink	3.70	2.80	.78	.47	.13	.10
☐815	10¢ Brown Red	2.75	2.00	.61	.30	.11	.10
☐816	11¢ Ultramarine	6.20	4.50	.92	.52	.16	.12
☐817	12¢ Bright Violet	13.00	8.20	1.28	.75	.15	.12
☐818	13¢ Blue Green	13.00	8.70	1.50	.80	.17	.13
☐819	14¢ Blue	8.70	6.90	1.30	.75	.17	.14
☐820	15¢ Blue Gray	4.30	3.30	.95	.56	.13	.09
☐821	16¢ Black	12.00	8.20	1.20	.62	.65	.42
☐822	17¢ Rose Red	11.00	7.80	1.30	.73	.16	.13
☐823	18¢ Brown Carmine	16.75	14.00	3.00	1.82	.14	.12
☐824	19¢ Bright Violet	14.00	9.00	1.60	.93	.84	.63
☐825	20¢ Bright Blue Green	8.75	6.50	1.21	.63	.11	.09
☐826	21¢ Dull Blue	16.00	11.50	2.80	2.20	.27	.22
☐827	22¢ Vermilion	18.50	14.00	1.32	.77	.78	.56
☐828	24¢ Gray Black	38.00	29.00	5.40	4.20	.30	.20
☐829	25¢ Deep Red Lilac	9.50	7.10	1.25	.67	.13	.09
☐830	30¢ Deep Ultramarine	45.00	34.00	7.70	5.30	.12	.09
☐831	50¢ Light Red Violet	60.00	42.00	12.50	7.70	.12	.10

FLAT PLATE PRINTING—PERF. 11 (N-H ADD 20%)

☐832	$1 Purple & Black	60.00	43.00	13.00	9.00	.15	.12
☐832b	$1 Watermarked	—	—	251.00	187.00	76.00	56.00
☐832c	$1 Dry Printing, Thick Paper (1954)	51.00	41.00	11.00	8.00	.19	.14
☐833	$2 Green & Black	212.00	172.00	36.00	23.00	7.70	6.10
☐834	$5 Carmine & Black	785.00	600.00	142.00	100.00	7.30	6.00

1938–1939. COMMEMORATIVES

1938. CONSTITUTION RATIFICATION (N-H ADD 25%)

☐835	3¢ Deep Violet	6.10	4.75	.24	.18	.16	.12

1938. SWEDISH-FINNISH TERCENTENARY (N-H ADD 25%)

☐836	3¢ Red Violet	6.10	4.50	.23	.16	.18	.13

1938. NORTHWEST COLONIZATION (N-H ADD 25%)

☐837	3¢ Bright Violet	16.00	12.00	.30	.22	.16	.11

1938. IOWA TERRITORY CENTENNIAL (N-H ADD 25%)

☐838	3¢ Violet	12.00	9.00	.30	.21	.17	.13

Scott No.	Fine Unused Line Pair	Ave. Unused Line Pair	Fine Unused Each	Ave. Unused Each	Fine Used Each	Ave. Used Each

1939. ROTARY PRESS COIL STAMPS
PERF. 10 VERTICALLY (N-H ADD 25%)

Scott No.		Fine Unused Line Pair	Ave. Unused Line Pair	Fine Unused Each	Ave. Unused Each	Fine Used Each	Ave. Used Each
☐839	1¢ Green	1.70	1.50	.47	.32	.13	.10
☐840	1½¢ Bistre Brown	2.30	1.80	.53	.44	.13	.10
☐841	2¢ Rose Carmine	2.70	1.90	.67	.53	.11	.10
☐842	3¢ Deep Violet	2.80	2.00	.62	.41	.12	.09
☐843	4¢ Red Violet	36.00	29.00	11.00	9.00	.57	.39
☐844	4½¢ Dark Gray	8.50	6.00	.96	.67	.70	.55
☐845	5¢ Bright Blue	30.00	25.00	8.00	6.00	.42	.27
☐846	6¢ Red Orange	13.00	10.00	1.75	.86	.21	.13
☐847	10¢ Brown Red	63.00	48.00	19.00	14.20	.09	.46

PERF. 10 HORIZONTALLY (N-H ADD 25%)

Scott No.		Fine Unused Line Pair	Ave. Unused Line Pair	Fine Unused Each	Ave. Unused Each	Fine Used Each	Ave. Used Each
☐848	1¢ Green	3.70	2.50	.92	.72	.17	.15
☐849	1½¢ Bistre Brown	4.40	3.60	1.65	1.15	.56	.41
☐850	2¢ Rose Carmine	7.60	6.10	2.80	2.10	.72	.44
☐851	3¢ Deep Violet	8.20	6.10	2.80	2.20	.66	.44

Scott No.		Fine Unused Plate Blk	Ave. Unused Plate Blk	Fine Unused Each	Ave. Unused Each	Fine Used Each	Ave. Used Each
1939. GOLDEN GATE INTERNATIONAL EXPOSITION (N-H ADD 25%)							
☐852	3¢ Bright Purple	2.30	1.60	.23	.18	.13	.11
1939. NEW YORK WORLD'S FAIR (N-H ADD 20%)							
☐853	3¢ Deep Purple	2.60	1.80	.24	.17	.13	.12
1939. WASHINGTON INAUGURATION SESQUICENTENNIAL (N-H ADD 20%)							
☐854	3¢ Bright Red Violet	4.90	3.40	.34	.23	.17	.13
1939. BASEBALL CENTENNIAL (N-H ADD 20%)							
☐855	3¢ Violet	4.20	2.90	.57	.43	.13	.11
1939. 25TH ANNIVERSARY PANAMA CANAL (N-H ADD 20%)							
☐856	3¢ Deep Red Violet	5.50	3.60	.31	.21	.14	.13
1939. COLONIAL PRINTING TERCENTENARY (N-H ADD 20%)							
☐857	3¢ Rose Violet	1.91	1.70	.19	.15	.12	.13
1939. 50TH ANNIVERSARY OF STATEHOOD (N-H ADD 20%)							
☐858	3¢ Rose Violet	2.65	1.85	.20	.16	.14	.11

1940. FAMOUS AMERICANS SERIES
AMERICAN AUTHORS (N-H ADD 20%)

		Fine Unused Plate Blk	Ave. Unused Plate Blk	Fine Unused Each	Ave. Unused Each	Fine Used Each	Ave. Used Each
☐859	1¢ Bright Blue Green	1.90	1.35	.14	.10	.14	.09
☐860	2¢ Rose Carmine	2.15	1.45	.20	.15	.16	.12
☐861	3¢ Bright Red Violet	2.65	1.80	.21	.16	.13	.10
☐862	5¢ Ultramarine	21.00	17.00	.43	.31	.41	.29
☐863	10¢ Dark Brown	74.00	57.00	2.40	2.20	2.00	1.70

Scott No.		Fine Unused Plate Blk	Ave. Unused Plate Blk	Fine Unused Each	Ave. Unused Each	Fine Used Each	Ave. Used Each
AMERICAN POETS (N-H ADD 20%)							
☐864	1¢ Bright Blue Green	3.30	2.50	.17	.14	.18	.14
☐865	2¢ Rose Carmine	3.50	2.70	.17	.13	.13	.10
☐866	3¢ Bright Red Violet	5.00	3.30	.23	.17	.12	.10
☐867	5¢ Ultramarine	18.00	15.00	.81	.60	.37	.23
☐868	10¢ Dark Brown	66.00	50.00	2.70	1.87	2.60	1.80
AMERICAN EDUCATORS (N-H ADD 20%)							
☐869	1¢ Bright Blue Green	300.00	2.20	.16	.10	.15	.10
☐870	2¢ Rose Carmine	300.00	2.70	.16	.11	.15	.10
☐871	3¢ Bright Red Violet	5.50	4.20	.33	.20	.13	.10
☐872	5¢ Ultramarine	20.00	14.00	.70	.55	.45	.34
☐873	10¢ Dark Brown	53.00	38.00	2.50	1.30	2.30	1.60
AMERICAN SCIENTISTS (N-H ADD 20%)							
☐874	1¢ Bright Blue Green	2.40	1.90	.14	.10	.13	.09
☐875	2¢ Rose Carmine	2.20	2.00	.16	.13	.14	.09
☐876	3¢ Bright Red Violet	2.30	1.80	.21	.14	.14	.08
☐877	5¢ Ultramarine	18.00	15.00	.39	.31	.36	.25
☐878	10¢ Dark Brown	52.00	38.00	2.30	1.50	2.00	1.40
AMERICAN COMPOSERS (N-H ADD 20%)							
☐879	1¢ Bright Blue Green	1.71	1.36	.13	.10	.13	.09
☐880	2¢ Rose Carmine	1.70	1.30	.22	.13	.13	.10
☐881	3¢ Bright Red Violet	2.35	1.60	.21	.14	.16	.13
☐882	5¢ Ultramarine	22.00	16.00	.80	.63	.41	.28
☐883	10¢ Dark Brown	61.00	46.00	6.00	4.50	2.30	1.65
AMERICAN ARTISTS (N-H ADD 20%)							
☐884	1¢ Bright Blue Green	1.75	1.25	.13	.10	.13	.10
☐885	2¢ Rose Carmine	1.75	1.25	.16	.13	.14	.10
☐886	3¢ Bright Red Violet	1.75	1.60	.28	.22	.13	.10
☐887	5¢ Ultramarine	23.00	15.00	.73	.50	.45	.33
☐888	10¢ Dark Brown	53.00	44.00	2.50	1.71	2.45	1.72
AMERICAN INVENTORS (N-H ADD 20%)							
☐889	1¢ Bright Blue Green	4.00	2.90	.17	.13	.15	.11
☐890	2¢ Rose Carmine	1.90	1.21	.17	.14	.13	.10
☐891	3¢ Bright Red Violet	3.40	2.30	.31	.24	.11	.10
☐892	5¢ Ultramarine	33.00	24.00	1.31	.94	.62	.43
☐893	10¢ Dark Brown	160.00	132.00	19.00	12.50	3.70	2.65

1940. COMMEMORATIVES

1940. 80TH ANNIVERSARY OF PONY EXPRESS (N-H ADD 20%)

☐894	3¢ Henna Brown	6.20	4.90	.60	.41	.26	.21

1940. 50TH ANNIVERSARY OF PAN-AMERICAN UNION (N-H ADD 20%)

☐895	3¢ Light Violet	6.20	4.60	.57	.41	.20	.17

Scott No.		Fine Unused Plate Blk	Ave. Unused Plate Blk	Fine Unused Each	Ave. Unused Each	Fine Used Each	Ave. Used Each
1940. 50TH ANNIVERSARY OF IDAHO (N-H ADD 20%)							
☐ 896	3¢ Bright Violet	4.15	3.20	.26	.17	.17	.11
1940. 50TH ANNIVERSARY OF WYOMING (N-H ADD 20%)							
☐ 897	3¢ Brown Violet	3.40	2.60	.23	.19	.16	.12
1940. 400TH ANNIVERSARY OF COLORADO EXPEDITION (N-H ADD 20%)							
☐ 898	3¢ Violet	3.30	2.80	.26	.21	.17	.14
1940. NATIONAL DEFENSE ISSUE (N-H ADD 20%)							
☐ 899	1¢ Bright Blue Green	1.15	.82	.18	.14	.11	.09
☐ 900	2¢ Rose Carmine	1.15	.82	.21	.14	.10	.09
☐ 901	3¢ Bright Violet	1.15	.82	.21	.14	.10	.09
1940. 75TH ANNIVERSARY EMANCIPATION AMENDMENT (N-H ADD 20%)							
☐ 902	3¢ Deep Violet	6.90	6.20	.34	.25	.21	.16

IMPORTANT NOTICE: Values for mint sheets are provided for the following listings. To command the stated prices, sheets must be complete as issued with the plate number (or numbers) intact.

Scott No.		Mint Sheet	Plate Block	Fine Unused Each	Fine Used Each
1941–1943. COMMEMORATIVES					
1941. VERMONT STATEHOOD					
☐ 903	3¢ Light Violet	13.00	4.10	.25	.17
1942. KENTUCKY SESQUICENTENNIAL ISSUE					
☐ 904	3¢ Violet	12.00	2.50	.31	.17
1942. WIN THE WAR ISSUE					
☐ 905	3¢ Violet	12.50	.86	.18	.10
1942. CHINA ISSUE					
☐ 906	5¢ Bright Blue	36.00	25.00	.61	.34
1943. ALLIED NATIONS ISSUE					
☐ 907	2¢ Rose Carmine	7.20	.77	.18	.12
1943. FOUR FREEDOMS ISSUE					
☐ 908	1¢ Green	6.20	1.15	.15	.10
1943–1944. OVERRUN COUNTRIES SERIES					
☐ 909	5¢ (Poland)	25.00	16.00	.31	.26
☐ 910	5¢ (Czechoslovakia)	20.00	6.10	.32	.23
☐ 911	5¢ (Norway)	9.50	2.90	.24	.19
☐ 912	5¢ (Luxembourg)	9.50	2.90	.24	.19
☐ 913	5¢ (Netherlands)	9.50	2.90	.24	.19
☐ 914	5¢ (Belgium)	9.50	2.90	.24	.19
☐ 915	5¢ (France)	9.50	2.90	.24	.19
☐ 916	5¢ (Greece)	47.00	27.00	.77	.70

*No hinge pricing from 1941 to date is figured at (N-H ADD 15%)

Scott No.		Mint Sheet	Plate Block	Fine Unused Each	Fine Used Each
☐917	5¢ (Yugoslavia)	35.00	12.00	.52	.42
☐918	5¢ (Albania)	30.00	13.00	.47	.46
☐919	5¢ (Austria)	23.00	11.00	.31	.33
☐920	5¢ (Denmark)	30.00	12.00	.39	.42
☐921	5¢ (Korea)	20.00	11.00	.28	.25

1944. COMMEMORATIVES

1944. RAILROAD ISSUE
☐922	3¢ Violet	17.50	2.70	.28	.17

1944. STEAMSHIP ISSUE
☐923	3¢ Violet	9.80	2.50	.22	.14

1944. TELEGRAPH ISSUE
☐924	3¢ Bright Red Violet	7.80	1.80	.20	.14

1944. CORREGIDOR ISSUE
☐925	3¢ Deep Violet	9.00	2.50	.21	.16

1944. MOTION PICTURE ISSUE
☐926	3¢ Deep Violet	8.00	1.70	.16	.16

1945. COMMEMORATIVES

1945. FLORIDA ISSUE
☐927	3¢ Bright Red Violet	6.50	1.35	.16	.12

1945. PEACE CONFERENCE ISSUE
☐928	5¢ Ultramarine	8.00	.92	.21	.13

1945. IWO JIMA ISSUE
☐929	3¢ Yellow Green	7.10	.63	.15	.12

1945–1946. ROOSEVELT MEMORIAL ISSUE
☐930	1¢ Blue Green	3.10	.27	.11	.08
☐931	2¢ Carmine Rose	4.60	.47	.13	.10
☐932	3¢ Purple	6.20	.65	.17	.13
☐933	5¢ Bright Blue	8.60	.95	.21	.12

1945. ARMY ISSUE
☐934	3¢ Olive Gray	6.60	.60	.15	.09

1945. NAVY ISSUE
☐935	3¢ Blue	5.60	.63	.14	.10

1945. COAST GUARD ISSUE
☐936	3¢ Bright Blue Green	5.60	.63	.14	.10

1945. ALFRED SMITH ISSUE
☐937	3¢ Purple	10.00	.56	.15	.11

1945. TEXAS CENTENNIAL ISSUE
☐938	3¢ Blue	5.60	.56	.15	.10

*No hinge pricing from 1941 to date is figured at (N-H ADD 15%)

Scott No.		Mint Sheet	Plate Block	Fine Unused Each	Fine Used Each
1946–1947. COMMEMORATIVES					
1946. MERCHANT MARINE ISSUE					
☐ 939	3¢ Blue Green	5.40	.55	.14	.09
1946. HONORABLE DISCHARGE EMBLEM ISSUE					
☐ 940	3¢ Dark Violet	9.70	.55	.14	.09
1946. TENNESSEE ISSUE					
☐ 941	3¢ Dark Violet	5.60	.56	.14	.09
1946. IOWA STATEHOOD ISSUE					
☐ 942	3¢ Deep Blue	5.30	.52	.14	.09
1946. SMITHSONIAN INSTITUTION ISSUE					
☐ 943	3¢ Violet Brown	5.30	.55	.14	.09
1946. NEW MEXICO ISSUE					
☐ 944	3¢ Brown Violet	5.30	.54	.14	.09
1947. EDISON ISSUE					
☐ 945	3¢ Bright Red Violet	7.00	.55	.14	.09
1947. PULITZER PRIZE					
☐ 946	3¢ Purple	6.00	.54	.14	.09
1947. U.S. POSTAGE STAMP CENTENARY					
☐ 947	3¢ Deep Blue	5.50	.54	.14	.09
1947. "CIPEX" SOUVENIR SHEET					
☐ 948	5¢ & 10 Sheet of 2	—	—	1.42	1.40
☐ 948a	5¢ Blue, sgl. stp.	—	—	.54	.41
☐ 948b	10¢ Brown Orange, sgl. stp.	—	—	.84	.50
1947. DOCTORS ISSUE					
☐ 949	3¢ Brown Violet	5.30	.54	.13	.10
1947. UTAH ISSUE					
☐ 950	3¢ Dark Violet	5.30	.52	.32	.10
1947. U.S.F. CONSTITUTION ISSUE					
☐ 951	3¢ Blue Green	5.50	.55	.13	.09
1947. EVERGLADES ISSUE					
☐ 952	3¢ Bright Green	5.30	.54	.14	.09
1948. COMMEMORATIVES					
1948. CARVER ISSUE					
☐ 953	3¢ Red Violet	7.00	.54	.14	.09
1948. GOLD RUSH ISSUE					
☐ 954	3¢ Dark Violet	5.30	.54	.14	.09
1948. MISSISSIPPI TERRITORY ISSUE					
☐ 955	3¢ Brown Violet	5.40	.54	.14	.09

*No hinge pricing from 1941 to date is figured at (N-H ADD 15%)

Scott No.		Mint Sheet	Plate Block	Fine Unused Each	Fine Used Each
1948. FOUR CHAPLAINS ISSUE					
☐ 956	3¢ Gray Black	5.00	.54	.12	.09
1948. WISCONSIN CENTENNIAL ISSUE					
☐ 957	3¢ Dark Violet	5.70	.54	.12	.09
1948. SWEDISH PIONEER ISSUE					
☐ 958	5¢ Deep Blue	7.50	1.10	.15	.14
1948. 100 YEARS PROGRESS OF WOMEN					
☐ 959	3¢ Dark Violet	5.70	.60	.14	.09
1948. WILLIAM ALLEN WHITE ISSUE					
☐ 960	3¢ Red Violet	6.20	.90	.14	.09
1948. U.S.-CANADA FRIENDSHIP					
☐ 961	3¢ Blue	5.30	.50	.14	.09
1948. FRANCIS SCOTT KEY ISSUE					
☐ 962	3¢ Rose Pink	5.30	.50	.14	.09
1948. SALUTE TO YOUTH ISSUE					
☐ 963	3¢ Deep Blue	5.40	.50	.14	.09
1948. OREGON TERRITORY ISSUE					
☐ 964	3¢ Brown Red	5.70	.76	.17	.13
1948. HARLAN FISKE STONE					
☐ 965	3¢ Bright Red Violet	8.50	2.00	.23	.14
1948. MT. PALOMAR OBSERVATORY					
☐ 966	3¢ Blue	12.00	2.60	.25	.14
1948. CLARA BARTON ISSUE					
☐ 967	3¢ Rose Pink	5.30	.51	.14	.09
1948. POULTRY ISSUE					
☐ 968	3¢ Sepia	5.60	.55	.14	.09
1948. GOLD STAR MOTHERS					
☐ 969	3¢ Orange Yellow	5.70	.54	.14	.09
1948. FORT KEARNY ISSUE					
☐ 970	3¢ Violet	5.70	.55	.14	.11
1948. VOLUNTEER FIREMEN					
☐ 971	3¢ Bright Rose Carmine	5.60	.57	.14	.11
1948. INDIAN CENTENNIAL					
☐ 972	3¢ Dark Brown	5.75	.55	.14	.11
1948. ROUGH RIDERS					
☐ 973	3¢ Violet Brown	6.20	.64	.13	.11
1948. JULIETTE LOW					
☐ 974	3¢ Blue Green	6.00	.64	.14	.11

*No hinge pricing from 1941 to date is figured at (N-H ADD 15%)

Scott No.		Mint Sheet	Plate Block	Fine Unused Each	Fine Used Each
1948. WILL ROGERS					
☐ 975	3¢ Bright Red Violet	6.20	.66	.17	.11
1948. FORT BLISS					
☐ 976	3¢ Henna Brown	10.00	3.00	.20	.16
1948. MOINA MICHAEL					
☐ 977	3¢ Rose Pink	6.00	.56	.15	.13
1948. GETTYSBURG ADDRESS					
☐ 978	3¢ Bright Blue	5.75	.55	.15	.13
1948. AMERICAN TURNERS					
☐ 979	3¢ Carmine	5.70	.55	.15	.13
1948. JOEL CHANDLER HARRIS					
☐ 980	3¢ Bright Red Violet	7.70	.92	.15	.13
1949-1950. COMMEMORATIVES					
1949. MINNESOTA CENTENNIAL					
☐ 981	3¢ Blue Green	5.80	.57	.15	.11
1949. WASHINGTON & LEE UNIVERSITY					
☐ 982	3¢ Ultramarine	5.50	.56	.14	.11
1949. PUERTO RICO ISSUE					
☐ 983	3¢ Green	5.50	.55	.13	.12
1949. ANNAPOLIS TERCENTENARY					
☐ 984	3¢ Aquamarine	5.20	.55	.12	.11
1949. G.A.R. ISSUE					
☐ 985	3¢ Bright Rose Carmine	5.75	.55	.13	.12
1950. EDGAR ALLAN POE					
☐ 986	3¢ Bright Red Violet	7.00	.55	.15	.11
1950. BANKERS ASSOCIATION					
☐ 987	3¢ Yellow Green	5.50	.55	.15	.12
1950. SAMUEL GOMPERS					
☐ 988	3¢ Bright Red Violet	7.00	.62	.14	.12
1950. WASHINGTON SESQUICENTENNIAL					
☐ 989	3¢ Bright Blue	5.70	.62	.16	.12
☐ 990	3¢ Deep Green	6.00	.63	.16	.12
☐ 991	3¢ Light Violet	6.00	.56	.16	.12
☐ 992	3¢ Rose Violet	6.00	.56	.16	.12
1950. RAILROAD ENGINEERS					
☐ 993	3¢ Violet Brown	5.30	.57	.15	.11
1950. KANSAS CITY CENTENARY					
☐ 994	3¢ Violet	5.30	.57	.15	.11

*No hinge pricing from 1941 to date is figured at (N-H ADD 15%)

Scott No.	Mint Sheet	Plate Block	Fine Unused Each	Fine Used Each

1950. BOY SCOUTS ISSUE
☐ 995	3¢ Sepia	5.70	.60	.16	.11

1950. INDIANA SESQUICENTENNIAL
☐ 996	3¢ Bright Blue	5.50	.56	.15	.11

1950. CALIFORNIA STATEHOOD
☐ 997	3¢ Yellow Orange	5.50	.56	.15	.11

1951-1952 COMMEMORATIVES

1951. UNITED CONFEDERATE VETERANS
☐ 998	3¢ Gray	5.70	.61	.16	.12

1951. NEVADA SETTLEMENT
☐ 999	3¢ Light Olive Green	5.50	.56	.15	.12

1951. LANDING OF CADILLAC
☐ 1000	3¢ Bright Blue	5.50	.56	.16	.12

1951. COLORADO STATEHOOD
☐ 1001	3¢ Violet Blue	5.30	.55	.15	.12

1951. AMERICAN CHEMICAL SOCIETY
☐ 1002	3¢ Violet Brown	5.70	.58	.16	.11

1951. BATTLE OF BROOKLYN ISSUE
☐ 1003	3¢ Violet	5.30	.56	.16	.11

1952. BETSY ROSS ISSUE
☐ 1004	3¢ Carmine Rose	5.90	.58	.16	.12

1952. 4-H CLUB ISSUE
☐ 1005	3¢ Blue Green	5.70	.56	.15	.12

1952. BALTIMORE & OHIO RAILROAD
☐ 1006	3¢ Bright Blue	8.00	.61	.17	.11

1952. AMERICAN AUTOMOBILE ASSOCIATION (AAA)
☐ 1007	3¢ Deep Blue	5.70	.56	.16	.11

1952. NORTH ATLANTIC TREATY ORGANIZATION
☐ 1008	3¢ Deep Violet	10.00	.56	.15	.11

1952. GRAND COULEE DAM ISSUE
☐ 1009	3¢ Blue Green	5.50	.56	.15	.11

1952. ARRIVAL OF LAFAYETTE
☐ 1010	3¢ Ultramarine	5.60	.56	.16	.11

1952. MOUNT RUSHMORE
☐ 1011	3¢ Blue Green	5.20	.57	.15	.11

1952. SOCIETY OF CIVIL ENGINEERS
☐ 1012	3¢ Violet Blue	5.20	.57	.15	.11

*No hinge pricing from 1941 to date is figured at (N-H ADD 15%)

Scott No.	Mint Sheet	Plate Block	Fine Unused Each	Fine Used Each
1952. WOMEN IN ARMED FORCES				
☐ 1013 3¢ Deep Blue	5.20	.56	.16	.11
1952. GUTENBERG PRINTING				
☐ 1014 3¢ Violet	5.30	.57	.17	.10
1952. NEWSPAPERBOYS				
☐ 1015 3¢ Violet	5.15	.57	.16	.10
1952. INTERNATIONAL RED CROSS				
☐ 1016 3¢ Deep Blue & Carmine	5.30	.56	.15	.10
1953-1954. COMMEMORATIVES				
1953. NATIONAL GUARD				
☐ 1017 3¢ Bright Blue	5.20	.50	.16	.10
1953. OHIO STATEHOOD				
☐ 1018 3¢ Chocolate	8.20	.67	.16	.10
1953. WASHINGTON TERRITORY				
☐ 1019 3¢ Green	5.30	.55	.16	.10
1953. LOUISIANA PURCHASE				
☐ 1020 3¢ Violet Brown	5.30	.55	.15	.10
1953. OPENING OF JAPAN				
☐ 1021 3¢ Green	9.60	1.70	.20	.10
1953. AMERICAN BAR ASSOCIATION				
☐ 1022 3¢ Rose Violet	5.20	.56	.16	.10
1953. SAGAMORE HILL				
☐ 1023 3¢ Yellow Green	5.20	.56	.15	.10
1953. FUTURE FARMERS				
☐ 1024 3¢ Deep Blue	5.20	.55	.16	.10
1953. TRUCKING INDUSTRY				
☐ 1025 3¢ Violet	5.30	.55	.15	.10
1953. GENERAL PATTON				
☐ 1026 3¢ Blue Violet	8.60	.93	.16	.11
1953. NEW YORK CITY				
☐ 1027 3¢ Bright Red Violet	6.10	.56	.16	.10
1953. GADSDEN PURCHASE				
☐ 1028 3¢ Copper Brown	5.20	.56	.15	.09
1954. COLUMBIA UNIVERSITY				
☐ 1029 3¢ Blue	5.20	.55	.15	.09
1954-1961. LIBERTY SERIES				
☐ 1030 ½¢ Red Orange	4.60	.57	.15	.09
☐ 1031 1¢ Dark Green	5.20	.33	.10	.09
☐ 1031A 1¼¢ Turquoise	5.20	1.10	.12	.09

*No hinge pricing from 1941 to date is figured at (N-H ADD 15%)

Scott No.		Mint Sheet	Plate Block	Fine Unused Each	Fine Used Each
☐ 1032	1½¢ Brown	11.00	4.60	.13	.10
☐ 1033	2¢ Rose Carmine	7.20	.51	.12	.09
☐ 1034	2½¢ Dark Blue	9.00	.96	.11	.10
☐ 1035	3¢ Deep Violet	9.00	.46	.11	.09
☐ 1036	4¢ Red Violet	11.00	.56	.15	.09
☐ 1037	4½¢ Green	13.50	1.24	.30	.11
☐ 1038	5¢ Deep Blue	17.00	.93	.25	.10
☐ 1039	6¢ Orange Red	63.00	2.60	.53	.09
☐ 1040	7¢ Deep Carmine	27.00	2.50	.41	.09
☐ 1041	8¢ Dark Violet Blue, Carmine	27.00	3.40	.20	.09
☐ 1042	8¢ Violet Blue, Carmine (Re-engraved)	31.00	1.60	.50	.11
☐ 1042A	8¢ Brown	31.00	2.20	.39	.10
☐ 1043	9¢ Rose Lilac	29.00	2.70	.39	.09
☐ 1044	10¢ Rose Lake	37.00	1.70	.50	.09
☐ 1044A	11¢ Carmine, Violet Blue	29.00	2.10	.39	.11
☐ 1045	12¢ Red	44.00	2.30	.54	.11
☐ 1046	15¢ Maroon	70.00	3.60	.78	.11
☐ 1047	20¢ Ultramarine	91.00	3.70	.83	.12
☐ 1048	25¢ Green	252.00	11.00	2.30	.12
☐ 1049	30¢ Black	164.00	9.00	1.75	.12
☐ 1050	40¢ Brown Carmine	340.00	15.00	3.30	.12
☐ 1051	50¢ Bright Violet	322.00	14.00	3.00	.12
☐ 1052	$1 Deep Violet	1480.00	55.00	13.00	.12
☐ 1053	$5 Black	13800.00	490.00	100.00	9.00

1954-1965. ROTARY PRESS COIL STAMPS
PERF. 10 VERTICALLY OR HORIZONTALLY

Scott No.		Fine Unused Line Pair	Ave. Unused Line Pair	Fine Unused Each	Ave. Unused Each	Fine Used Each	Ave. Used Each
☐ 1054	1¢ Deep Green	1.50	1.10	.33	.26	.12	.10
☐ 1055	2¢ Rose Carmine	.78	.37	.12	.10	.12	.10
☐ 1056	2½¢ Gray Blue	7.50	5.50	.43	.31	.33	.23
☐ 1057	3¢ Deep Violet	1.00	.77	.16	.12	.11	.09
☐ 1058	4¢ Red Violet	1.50	.82	.22	.16	.12	.09
☐ 1059	4½¢ Green	21.00	19.00	2.15	1.70	2.00	1.20
☐ 1059A	25¢ Green	2.70	2.30	.58	.44	.33	.21

Scott No.		Mint Sheet	Plate Block	Fine Unused Each	Fine Used Each

1954. NEBRASKA TERRITORY
| ☐ 1060 | 3¢ Violet | 5.15 | .59 | .16 | .11 |

1954. KANSAS TERRITORY
| ☐ 1061 | 3¢ Brown Orange | 5.15 | .59 | .16 | .11 |

1954. GEORGE EASTMAN ISSUE
| ☐ 1062 | 3¢ Violet Brown | 7.10 | .60 | .16 | .11 |

*No hinge pricing from 1941 to date is figured at (N H ADD 15%)

Scott No.		Mint Sheet	Plate Block	Fine Unused Each	Fine Used Each
1954. LEWIS & CLARK EXPEDITION					
☐ 1063	3¢ Dark Brown	5.40	.62	.16	.10
1955. COMMEMORATIVES					
1955. PENNSYLVANIA ACADEMY OF FINE ARTS					
☐ 1064	3¢ Rose Brown	5.70	.58	.16	.11
1955. LAND GRANT COLLEGES					
☐ 1065	3¢ Green	5.16	.57	.15	.10
1955. ROTARY INTERNATIONAL ISSUE					
☐ 1066	8¢ Deep Blue	14.00	.16	.28	.13
1955. ARMED FORCES RESERVE					
☐ 1067	3¢ Red Violet	5.70	.59	.17	.11
1955. OLD MAN OF THE MOUNTAINS					
☐ 1068	3¢ Blue Green	5.80	.59	.16	.10
1955. SOO LOCKS CENTENNIAL					
☐ 1069	3¢ Blue	5.70	.59	.16	.10
1955. ATOMS FOR PEACE					
☐ 1070	3¢ Blue	5.50	.63	.17	.10
1955. FORT TICONDEROGA BICENTENNIAL					
☐ 1071	3¢ Sepia	6.00	.58	.17	.10
1955. ANDREW MELLON ISSUE					
☐ 1072	3¢ Deep Carmine	7.00	.57	.17	.10
1956. COMMEMORATIVES					
1956. 250TH ANNIVERSARY FRANKLIN'S BIRTH					
☐ 1073	3¢ Rose Carmine	5.20	.58	.17	.10
1956. BOCKER T. WASHINGTON ISSUE					
☐ 1074	3¢ Deep Blue	5.00	.59	.17	.10
1956. FIFTH INTL. PHILATELIC EXHIBITION DESIGNS OF 1035 & 1041 IN IMPERF. SOUVENIR SHEET					
☐ 1075	3¢ & 8¢ Sheet of 2	—	—	5.20	5.10
1956. FIFTH INTL. PHILATELIC EXHIBITION					
☐ 1076	3¢ Deep Violet	5.50	.66	.18	—
1956. WILDLIFE CONSERVATION ISSUE					
☐ 1077	3¢ Rose Lake	6.00	.74	.17	.12
☐ 1078	3¢ Brown	6.00	.74	.17	.12
☐ 1079	3¢ Green	6.00	.74	.17	.12
1956. PURE FOOD & DRUG ACT					
☐ 1080	3¢ Dark Blue Green	5.30	.58	.16	.09
1956. HOME OF PRESIDENT BUCHANAN					
☐ 1081	3¢ Black Brown	5.30	.58	.16	.09

*No hinge pricing from 1941 to date is figured at (N-H ADD 15%)

Scott No.	Mint Sheet	Plate Block	Fine Unused Each	Fine Used Each
1956. LABOR DAY ISSUE				
☐ 1082 3¢ Deep Blue	5.40	.58	.16	.09
1956. NASSAU HALL—PRINCETON				
☐ 1083 3¢ Black on Orange	5.15	.58	.16	.09
1956. DEVIL'S TOWER				
☐ 1084 3¢ Purple	5.40	.60	.16	.09
1956. CHILDREN'S ISSUE				
☐ 1085 3¢ Dark Blue	5.40	.60	.16	.09
1957. COMMEMORATIVES				
1957. ALEXANDER HAMILTON ISSUE				
☐ 1086 3¢ Rose Red	5.70	.56	.16	.09
1957. POLIO ISSUE				
☐ 1087 3¢ Light Purple	5.20	.56	.16	.09
1957. COAST & GEODETIC SURVEY				
☐ 1088 3¢ Dark Blue	5.20	.56	.16	.09
1957. ARCHITECTS ISSUE				
☐ 1089 3¢ Red Lilac	5.20	.56	.16	.09
1957. STEEL INDUSTRY CENTENNIAL				
☐ 1090 3¢ Bright Ultra	5.20	.56	.16	.09
1957. INTERNATIONAL NAVAL REVIEW				
☐ 1091 3¢ Blue Green	5.20	.56	.16	.09
1957. OKLAHOMA STATEHOOD				
☐ 1092 3¢ Dark Blue	5.30	.62	.16	.09
1957. SCHOOL TEACHERS				
☐ 1093 3¢ Rose Lake	5.20	.58	.14	.09
1957. U.S. FLAG ISSUE				
☐ 1094 4¢ Blue & Red	5.50	.67	.16	.09
1957. 350TH SHIPBUILDING ANNIVERSARY				
☐ 1095 3¢ Purple	6.00	.56	.16	.09
1957. PHILIPPINES—CHAMPION OF LIBERTY				
☐ 1096 8¢ Red, Blue, & Gold	11.00	1.21	.21	.15
1957. BIRTH OF LAFAYETTE				
☐ 1097 3¢ Maroon	6.00	.56	.15	.10
1957. WILDLIFE CONSERVATION ISSUE				
☐ 1098 3¢ Blue, Green & Yellow	5.00	.56	.15	.09
1957. RELIGIOUS FREEDOM				
☐ 1099 3¢ Black	5.00	.56	.15	.09

*No hinge pricing from 1941 to date is figured at (N-H ADD 15%)

Scott No.	Mint Sheet	Plate Block	Fine Unused Each	Fine Used Each
1958. COMMEMORATIVES				
1958. GARDENING & HORTICULTURE				
☐ 1100 3¢ Deep Green	5.40	.58	.15	.09
1958. BRUSSELS EXHIBITION				
☐ 1104 3¢ Deep Claret	5.40	.58	.15	.09
1958. JAMES MONROE BICENTENNIAL				
☐ 1105 3¢ Purple	7.00	.58	.16	.11
1958. MINNESOTA STATEHOOD				
☐ 1106 3¢ Green	5.25	.58	.15	.10
1958. INTERNATIONAL GEOPHYSICAL YEAR				
☐ 1107 3¢ Black & Orange	5.40	.70	.15	.11
1958. GUNSTON HALL BICENTENARY				
☐ 1108 3¢ Light Green	5.40	.59	.15	.10
1958. MACKINAC BRIDGE ISSUE				
☐ 1109 3¢ Bluish Green	5.25	.58	.14	.10
1958. SOUTH AMERICA—CHAMPION OF LIBERTY				
☐ 1110 4¢ Olive Bistre	7.60	.66	.17	.11
☐ 1111 8¢ Red, Blue & Gold	19.10	3.70	.28	.20
1958. ATLANTIC CABLE CENTENNIAL				
☐ 1112 4¢ Reddish Purple	5.50	.66	.14	.10
1958–1959. LINCOLN COMMEMORATIVE ISSUE				
☐ 1113 1¢ Green	2.30	.29	.13	.10
☐ 1114 3¢ Rust Brown	5.10	.66	.15	.10
☐ 1115 4¢ Sepia	6.60	.72	.15	.09
☐ 1116 4¢ Blue	6.00	.72	.15	.09
1958. HUNGARY—CHAMPION OF LIBERTY				
☐ 1117 4¢ Bluish Green	7.80	.67	.16	.10
☐ 1118 8¢ Red, Blue & Gold	21.00	3.00	.26	.16
1958. FREEDOM OF THE PRESS				
☐ 1119 4¢ Black	6.70	.66	.16	.10
1958. OVERLAND MAIL CENTENNIAL				
☐ 1120 4¢ Crimson Rose	6.20	.61	.16	.10
1958. NOAH WEBSTER				
☐ 1121 4¢ Dark Carmine Rose	7.60	.61	.16	.11
1958. FOREST CONSERVATION				
☐ 1122 4¢ Yellow, Brown & Green	6.10	.61	.16	.10
1958. FORT DUQUESNE BICENTENNIAL				
☐ 1123 4¢ Blue	5.70	.61	.16	.12

*No hinge pricing from 1941 to date is figured at (N-H ADD 15%)

Scott No.		Mint Sheet	Plate Block	Fine Unused Each	Fine Used Each
1959. COMMEMORATIVES					
1959. OREGON STATEHOOD					
☐ 1124	4¢ Blue Green	5.70	.62	.16	.10
1959. ARGENTINA & CHILE—CHAMPION OF LIBERTY					
☐ 1125	4¢ Blue	7.60	.63	.16	.10
☐ 1126	8¢ Red, Blue & Gold	16.50	1.70	.28	.17
1959. 10TH ANNIVERSARY N.A.T.O.					
☐ 1127	4¢ Blue	7.50	.55	.16	.10
1959. ARCTIC EXPLORATIONS					
☐ 1128	4¢ Blue	5.50	.87	.16	.10
1959. WORLD PEACE & TRUST					
☐ 1129	8¢ Maroon	12.00	1.95	.26	.17
1959. SILVER DISCOVERY CENTENNIAL					
☐ 1130	4¢ Black	5.60	.58	.16	.17
1959. ST. LAWRENCE SEAWAY ISSUE					
☐ 1131	4¢ Red & Blue	5.60	.58	.16	.17
1959. 49-STAR FLAG ISSUE					
☐ 1132	4¢ Blue, Red & Yellow	5.60	.58	.16	.17
1959. SOIL CONSERVATION					
☐ 1133	4¢ Yellow, Green & Blue	5.70	.64	.16	.17
1959. PETROLEUM INDUSTRY CENTENNIAL					
☐ 1134	4¢ Brown	5.20	.58	.16	.17
1959. DENTAL HEALTH ISSUE					
☐ 1135	4¢ Green	5.20	.58	.16	.10
1959. GERMANY—CHAMPION OF LIBERTY					
☐ 1136	4¢ Gray	7.50	.72	.17	.10
☐ 1137	8¢ Red, Blue & Gold	18.00	2.70	.27	.15
1959. DR. EPHRAIM MCDOWELL					
☐ 1138	4¢ Maroon	7.20	.62	.17	.12
1960–1961. CREDO OF AMERICA SERIES					
☐ 1139	4¢ Dark Violet, Blue & Carmine	6.40	.67	.17	.12
☐ 1140	4¢ Olive Bistre & Green	6.40	.67	.17	.12
☐ 1141	4¢ Gray & Red	6.40	.81	.17	.12
☐ 1142	4¢ Red & Blue	6.40	.81	.17	.12
☐ 1143	4¢ Violet & Green	8.70	1.05	.26	.12
☐ 1144	4¢ Green & Brown	8.00	1.05	.26	.12
1960. COMMEMORATIVES					
1960. BOY SCOUTS GOLDEN JUBILEE					
☐ 1145	4¢ Red, Khaki & Blue	5.70	.75	.15	.12

*No hinge pricing from 1941 to date is figured at (N-H ADD 15%)

Scott No.		Mint Sheet	Plate Block	Fine Unused Each	Fine Used Each
1960. WINTER OLYMPIC GAMES					
☐ 1146	4¢ Blue	7.50	.87	.19	.12
1960. CZECHOSLOVAKIA—CHAMPION OF LIBERTY					
☐ 1147	4¢ Blue	7.80	.60	.17	.11
☐ 1148	8¢ Yellow, Blue & Red	17.00	1.85	.29	.19
1960. WORLD REFUGEE YEAR					
☐ 1149	4¢ Gray Black	5.70	.58	.17	.11
1960. WATER CONSERVATION					
☐ 1150	4¢ Blue, Green & Orange Brown	5.70	.58	.17	.11
1960. SOUTHEAST ASIA TREATY ORGANIZATION					
☐ 1151	4¢ Blue	7.60	.67	.17	.11
1960. HONORING AMERICAN WOMAN					
☐ 1152	4¢ Violet	5.70	.71	.16	.11
1960. 50-STAR FLAG ISSUE					
☐ 1153	4¢ Red & Blue	5.70	.67	.16	.11
1960. PONY EXPRESS CENTENNIAL					
☐ 1154	4¢ Sepia	6.20	.73	.20	.12
1960. EMPLOY THE HANDICAPPED					
☐ 1155	4¢ Blue	5.70	.65	.20	.11
1960. WORLD FORESTRY CONGRESS					
☐ 1156	4¢ Green	6.10	.73	.17	.11
1960. MEXICAN INDEPENDENCE SESQUICENTENNIAL					
☐ 1157	4¢ Red & Green	5.70	.62	.17	.11
1960. UNITED STATES—JAPAN TREATY CENTENNIAL					
☐ 1158	4¢ Blue & Pink	5.70	.62	.18	.12
1960. POLAND—CHAMPION OF LIBERTY					
☐ 1159	4¢ Blue	8.10	.62	.18	.12
☐ 1160	8¢ Red, Blue & Gold	15.00	2.00	.31	.15
1960. ROBERT A. TAFT MEMORIAL ISSUE					
☐ 1161	4¢ Dull Violet	7.60	.62	.18	.10
1960. WHEELS OF FREEDOM					
☐ 1162	4¢ Dark Blue	5.70	.62	.17	.09
1960. BOYS' CLUBS OF AMERICA					
☐ 1163	4¢ Indigo, Slate & Red	5.70	.62	.17	.09
1960. FIRST AUTOMATED POST OFFICE					
☐ 1164	4¢ Dark Blue & Carmine	5.70	.60	.17	.09
1960. FINLAND—CHAMPION OF LIBERTY					
☐ 1165	4¢ Blue	7.70	.62	.17	.10
☐ 1166	8¢ Red, Blue & Gold	16.50	2.10	.30	.17

*No hinge pricing from 1941 to date is figured at (N-H ADD 15%)

Scott No.		Mint Sheet	Plate Block	Fine Unused Each	Fine Used Each
1960. CAMP FIRE GIRLS					
☐ 1167	4¢ Dark Blue & Red	5.60	.61	.17	.12
1960. ITALY—CHAMPION OF LIBERTY					
☐ 1168	4¢ Green	7.50	.62	.17	.10
☐ 1169	8¢ Red, Blue & Gold	15.00	1.70	.35	.17
1960. WALTER F. GEORGE MEMORIAL ISSUE					
☐ 1170	4¢ Dull Violet	7.30	.62	.18	.11
1960. ANDREW CARNEGIE					
☐ 1171	4¢ Deep Claret	8.10	.67	.19	.12
1960. JOHN FOSTER DULLES MEMORIAL ISSUE					
☐ 1172	4¢ Dull Violet	7.00	.63	.19	.10
1960. "ECHO I" SATELLITE					
☐ 1173	4¢ Deep Violet	18.00	2.20	.52	.12
1961. COMMEMORATIVES					
1961. INDIA—CHAMPION OF LIBERTY					
☐ 1174	4¢ Red Orange	7.70	.62	.19	.10
☐ 1175	8¢ Red, Blue & Gold	15.00	2.10	.29	.18
1961. RANGE CONSERVATION					
☐ 1176	4¢ Blue, Slate & Brown Orange	5.60	.66	.18	.11
1961. HORACE GREELEY					
☐ 1177	4¢ Dull Violet	7.50	.66	.18	.11
1961-1965. CIVIL WAR CENTENNIAL SERIES					
1961. FORT SUMTER					
☐ 1178	4¢ Light Green	8.50	.95	.22	.12
1962. BATTLE OF SHILOH					
☐ 1179	4¢ Black on Peach	6.50	.72	.28	.11
1963. BATTLE OF GETTYSBURG					
☐ 1180	5¢ Blue & Gray	8.00	.72	.21	.11
1964. BATTLE OF THE WILDERNESS					
☐ 1181	5¢ Dark Red & Black	8.00	.82	.21	.11
1965. APPOMATTOX					
☐ 1182	5¢ Black & Blue	8.00	1.20	.21	.11
1961. KANSAS STATEHOOD					
☐ 1183	4¢ Brown, Dark Red & Green on Yellow Paper	5.70	.72	.18	.11
1961. GEORGE W. NORRIS BIRTH CENTENARY					
☐ 1184	4¢ Blue Green	5.60	.65	.18	.11
1961. NAVAL AVIATION GOLDEN JUBILEE					
☐ 1185	4¢ Blue	5.60	.65	.18	.11

*No hinge pricing from 1941 to date is figured at (N-H ADD 15%)

Scott No.		Mint Sheet	Plate Block	Fine Unused Each	Fine Used Each
1961. WORKMEN'S COMPENSATION LAW					
☐ 1186	4¢ Ultramarine	5.70	.63	.18	.13
1961. F. REMINGTON BIRTH CENTENNIAL					
☐ 1187	4¢ Blue, Red & Yellow	6.20	.82	.18	.11
1961. REPUBLIC OF CHINA ISSUE					
☐ 1188	4¢ Blue	5.60	.65	.18	.11
1961. DR. J. NAISMITH—BASKETBALL FOUNDER					
☐ 1189	4¢ Brown	6.10	.82	.18	.11
1961. NURSING PROFESSION					
☐ 1190	4¢ Blue, Red, Black & Green	5.60	.72	.18	.10
1962. COMMEMORATIVES					
1962. NEW MEXICO STATEHOOD					
☐ 1191	4¢ Blue, Maroon, Bistre	5.70	.66	.19	.13
1962. ARIZONA STATEHOOD					
☐ 1192	4¢ Red, Deep Blue, Green	5.70	.73	.19	.13
1962. PROJECT MERCURY					
☐ 1193	4¢ Dark Blue & Yellow	6.50	.93	.19	.13
1962. MALARIA ERADICATION					
☐ 1194	4¢ Blue & Bistre	5.60	.68	.16	.11
1962. CHARLES EVANS HUGHES BIRTH CENTENNIAL					
☐ 1195	4¢ Black on Buff	5.60	.72	.16	.11
1962. SEATTLE WORLD'S FAIR					
☐ 1196	4¢ Red & Dark Blue	5.60	.72	.16	.11
1962. LOUISIANA STATEHOOD					
☐ 1197	4¢ Blue, Green, Red	5.60	.72	.17	.11
1962. THE HOMESTEAD ACT					
☐ 1198	4¢ Slate	6.00	.72	.14	.11
1962. GIRL SCOUTS 50TH ANNIVERSARY					
☐ 1199	4¢ Red	5.60	.68	.14	.11
1962. BRIEN MCMAHON MEMORIAL ISSUE					
☐ 1200	4¢ Purple	6.00	.72	.14	.11
1962. NATIONAL APPRENTICESHIP ACT					
☐ 1201	4¢ Black on Buff	5.60	.67	.14	.11
1962. SAM RAYBURN MEMORIAL ISSUE					
☐ 1202	4¢ Brown & Blue	5.60	.67	.14	.11
1962. DAG HAMMARSKJOLD MEMORIAL					
☐ 1203	4¢ Yellow, Brown & Black	5.60	.67	.14	.11
☐ 1204	4¢ Yellow Color Inverted	12.50	3.70	.21	.20

*No hinge pricing from 1941 to date is figured at (N-H ADD 15%)

Scott No.		Mint Sheet	Plate Block	Fine Unused Each	Fine Used Each
1962. CHRISTMAS TREE					
☐ 1205	4¢ Green & Red	13.00	.72	.16	.09
1962. HIGHER EDUCATION					
☐ 1206	4¢ Green & Black	6.60	.72	.16	.11
1962. WINSLOW HOMER					
☐ 1207	4¢ Brown & Blue	7.50	.76	.21	.11
1963. 50-STAR FLAG					
☐ 1208	5¢ Red & Blue	13.00	.71	.16	.11
1962-1963. REGULAR ISSUE					
☐ 1209	1¢ Green	4.00	.35	.12	.11
☐ 1213	5¢ Dark Blue Gray	13.70	.82	.24	.11

1962-1963. ROTARY PRESS COIL STAMPS PERF. 10 VERTICALLY

Scott No.		Fine Unused Plate Blk	Ave. Unused Plate Blk	Fine Unused Each	Ave. Unused Each	Fine Used Each	Ave. Used Each
☐ 1225	1¢ Green	1.20	.83	.19	.14	.14	.19
☐ 1229	5¢ Dark Blue Gray	4.10	3.50	1.50	1.15	.13	.19

Scott No.		Mint Sheet	Plate Block	Fine Unused Each	Fine Used Each
1963. COMMEMORATIVES—CAROLINA CHARTER TERCENTENARY					
☐ 1230	5¢ Dark Carmine & Brown	6.90	.90	.21	.11
1963. FOOD FOR PEACE—FREEDOM FROM HUNGER					
☐ 1231	5¢ Green, Buff & Red	6.70	.76	.18	.11
1963. WEST VIRGINIA STATEHOOD					
☐ 1232	5¢ Green, Red & Black	6.70	.76	.18	.10
1963. EMANCIPATION PROCLAMATION					
☐ 1233	5¢ Black, Blue & Red	6.70	.76	.18	.10
1963. ALLIANCE FOR PROGRESS					
☐ 1234	5¢ Bright Blue & Green	6.70	.76	.18	.10
1963. CORDELL HULL					
☐ 1235	5¢ Blue Green	6.70	.76	.18	.10
1963. ELEANOR ROOSEVELT					
☐ 1236	5¢ Light Purple	6.70	.76	.18	.10
1963. THE SCIENCES					
☐ 1237	5¢ Blue & Black	6.70	.84	.21	.10
1963. CITY MAIL DELIVERY					
☐ 1238	5¢ Red, Blue & Gray	6.70	.76	.16	.10

*No hinge pricing from 1941 to date is figured at (N-H ADD 15%)

Scott No.		Mint Sheet	Plate Block	Fine Unused Each	Fine Used Each
1963. INTERNATIONAL RED CROSS CENTENARY					
☐ 1239	5¢ Slate & Carmine	6.70	.75	.18	.10
1963. CHRISTMAS ISSUE					
☐ 1240	5¢ Dark Blue, Blue Black & Red	13.50	.83	.18	.10
1963. JOHN JAMES AUDUBON					
☐ 1241	5¢ Blue, Brown, Bistre	7.00	.85	.20	.10
1964. COMMEMORATIVES					
1964. SAM HOUSTON					
☐ 1242	5¢ Black	6.70	.77	.19	.10
1964. CHARLES M. RUSSELL					
☐ 1243	5¢ Indigo, Red Brown & Olive	8.50	.90	.20	.12
1964. NEW YORK WORLD'S FAIR					
☐ 1244	5¢ Green	7.00	.80	.20	.11
1964. JOHN MUIR—CONSERVATIONIST					
☐ 1245	5¢ Brown, Green & Olive	6.70	.80	.18	.11
1964. JOHN F. KENNEDY MEMORIAL					
☐ 1246	5¢ Blue Gray	6.70	.79	.18	.11
1964. NEW JERSEY TERCENTENARY					
☐ 1247	5¢ Ultramarine	8.50	.93	.22	.10
1964. NEVADA STATEHOOD					
☐ 1248	5¢ Red, Yellow & Blue	7.00	.76	.18	.11
1964. REGISTER AND VOTE					
☐ 1249	5¢ Dark Blue & Red	7.00	.76	.18	.11
1964. WILLIAM SHAKESPEARE					
☐ 1250	5¢ Brown on Tan	7.00	.76	.18	.11
1964. DOCTORS MAYO					
☐ 1251	5¢ Green	7.00	.76	.18	.11
1964. AMERICAN MUSIC					
☐ 1252	5¢ Red, Black & Blue	7.00	.76	.18	.11
1964. AMERICAN HOMEMAKERS					
☐ 1253	5¢ Multicolored	7.00	.76	.18	.11
1964. CHRISTMAS ISSUE					
☐ 1254	5¢ Red & Green	—	—	.65	.11
☐ 1255	5¢ Red & Green	—	—	.65	.11
☐ 1256	5¢ Red & Green	—	—	.65	.11
☐ 1257	5¢ Red & Green	—	—	.65	.11
1964. VERRAZANO—NARROWS BRIDGE					
☐ 1258	5¢ Green	6.70	.76	.19	.11

*No hinge pricing from 1941 to date is figured at (N-H ADD 15%)

Scott No.		Mint Sheet	Plate Block	Fine Unused Each	Fine Used Each
1964. STUART DAVIS—MODERN ART					
☐ 1259	5¢ Ultramarine, Black & Red	6.70	.76	.19	.11
1964. RADIO AMATEURS					
☐ 1260	5¢ Red Lilac	6.70	.76	.19	.11
1965. COMMEMORATIVES					
1965. BATTLE OF NEW ORLEANS					
☐ 1261	5¢ Carmine, Blue & Gray	6.50	.76	.19	.11
1965. PHYSICAL FITNESS—SOKOL CENTENNIAL					
☐ 1262	5¢ Maroon & Black	6.50	.76	.19	.11
1965. CRUSADE AGAINST CANCER					
☐ 1263	5¢ Black, Purple, Orange	6.50	.76	.19	.11
1965. SIR WINSTON CHURCHILL MEMORIAL					
☐ 1264	5¢ Black	6.60	.82	.19	.11
1965. MAGNA CARTA 750TH ANNIVERSARY					
☐ 1265	5¢ Black, Ochre, Red Lilac	6.60	.76	.19	.11
1965. INTERNATIONAL COOPERATION YEAR					
☐ 1266	5¢ Dull Blue & Black	6.60	.76	.19	.11
1965. SALVATION ARMY					
☐ 1267	5¢ Red, Black & Blue	6.60	.76	.19	.11
1965. DANTE ALIGHIERI					
☐ 1268	5¢ Maroon on Tan	6.60	.76	.19	.10
1965. HERBERT HOOVER					
☐ 1269	5¢ Red Rose	6.60	.76	.19	.10
1965. ROBERT FULTON BIRTH BICENTENNIAL					
☐ 1270	5¢ Black & Blue	6.60	.76	.19	.10
1965. FLORIDA SETTLEMENT QUADRICENTENNIAL					
☐ 1271	5¢ Red, Yellow & Black	6.60	.82	.19	.10
1965. TRAFFIC SAFETY					
☐ 1272	5¢ Green, Black, Red	6.60	.85	.19	.10
1965. JOHN SINGLETON COPLEY—ARTIST					
☐ 1273	5¢ Black, Brown, Olive	7.70	.90	.19	.12
1965. INTERNATIONAL TELECOMMUNICATION UNION					
☐ 1274	11¢ Black, Carmine, Bistre	36.00	12.50	.63	.30
1965. ADLAI E. STEVENSON MEMORIAL					
☐ 1275	5¢ Light & Dark Blue, Black & Red	6.50	.75	.19	.11
1965. CHRISTMAS ISSUE					
☐ 1276	5¢ Red, Green & Yellow	14.50	.75	.19	.11

*No hinge pricing from 1941 to date is figured at (N-H ADD 15%)

Scott No.		Mint Sheet	Plate Block	Fine Unused Each	Fine Used Each

1965-1968. PROMINENT AMERICANS SERIES

Scott No.			Mint Sheet	Plate Block	Fine Unused Each	Fine Used Each
☐ 1278	1¢	Green	4.10	.35	.11	.08
☐ 1279	1¼¢	Green	41.00	.34	.13	.13
☐ 1280	2¢	Slate Blue	6.50	.41	.11	.09
☐ 1281	3¢	Purple	8.60	.60	.13	.09
☐ 1282	4¢	Black	12.00	.84	.12	.09
☐ 1283	5¢	Blue	14.00	1.15	.21	.11
☐ 1283B	5¢	Blue	14.00	.87	.21	.11
☐ 1284	6¢	Gray Brown	21.00	1.20	.21	.11
☐ 1285	8¢	Violet	21.00	1.50	.30	.11
☐ 1286	10¢	Lilac	26.00	1.70	.30	.11
☐ 1286A	12¢	Black	30.00	2.30	.34	.11
☐ 1287	13¢	Brown	34.00	2.60	.34	.13
☐ 1288	15¢	Rose Claret	45.00	3.10	.35	.14
☐ 1289	20¢	Olive Green	45.00	3.00	.55	.09
☐ 1290	25¢	Rose Lake	54.00	3.40	.56	.09
☐ 1291	30¢	Light Purple	80.00	4.00	.75	.13
☐ 1292	40¢	Dark Blue	87.00	5.00	1.10	.13
☐ 1293	50¢	Maroon	120.00	6.00	1.60	.10
☐ 1294	$1	Purple	260.00	15.00	2.60	.17
☐ 1295	$5	Gray	1310.00	53.00	13.00	4.10

Scott No.		Fine Unused Line Pair	Ave. Unused Line Pair	Fine Unused Each	Ave. Unused Each	Fine Used Each	Ave. Used Each

PERF. 10 HORIZONTALLY

Scott No.			Fine Unused Line Pair	Ave. Unused Line Pair	Fine Unused Each	Ave. Unused Each	Fine Used Each	Ave. Used Each
☐ 1297	3¢	Purple	.76	.62	.14	.10	.13	.11
☐ 1298	6¢	Gray Brown	2.00	1.50	.33	.24	.13	.11

PERF. 10 VERTICALLY

Scott No.			Fine Unused Line Pair	Ave. Unused Line Pair	Fine Unused Each	Ave. Unused Each	Fine Used Each	Ave. Used Each
☐ 1299	1¢	Green	.33	.24	.11	.08	.12	.11
☐ 1303	4¢	Black	1.10	.82	.20	.14	.12	.12
☐ 1304	5¢	Blue	.72	.52	.20	.15	.11	.12
☐ 1305	6¢	Gray Brown	1.00	.72	.31	.22	.11	.12
☐ 1305C	$1	Purple	6.50	4.80	2.20	1.75	.92	.65

Scott No.		Mint Sheet	Plate Block	Fine Unused Each	Fine Used Each

1966. COMMEMORATIVES
1966. MIGRATORY BIRD TREATY

			Mint Sheet	Plate Block	Fine Unused Each	Fine Used Each
☐ 1306	5¢	Red, Blue, Black	7.40	.85	.18	.10

1966. HUMANE TREATMENT OF ANIMALS

☐ 1307	5¢	Orange Brown & Black	7.00	.75	.18	.10

1966. INDIANA STATEHOOD

☐ 1308	5¢	Ochre, Brown & Violet Blue	7.00	.75	.18	.10

*No hinge pricing from 1941 to date is figured at (N-H ADD 15%)

Scott No.	Mint Sheet	Plate Block	Fine Unused Each	Fine Used Each
1966. AMERICAN CIRCUS				
☐ 1309 5¢ Red, Blue, Pink, Black	7.50	.75	.19	.11
1966. SIXTH INTL. PHILATELIC EXHIBITION "SIPEX"				
☐ 1310 5¢ Multicolored	7.00	.69	.18	.11
IMPERFORATE SOUVENIR SHEET				
☐ 1311 5¢ Multicolored	—	—	.36	.31
1966. BILL OF RIGHTS				
☐ 1312 5¢ Red, Dark & Light Blue	6.90	.68	.19	.10
1966. POLISH MILLENNIUM				
☐ 1313 5¢ Red	7.20	.68	.19	.10
1966. NATIONAL PARK SERVICE				
☐ 1314 5¢ Yellow, Black & Green	6.70	.67	.19	.10
1966. MARINE CORPS RESERVE				
☐ 1315 5¢ Black, Red, Blue, Olive	6.70	.67	.19	.10
1966. GENERAL FEDERATION OF WOMEN'S CLUBS				
☐ 1316 5¢ Blue, Pink, Black	6.70	.67	.19	.10
1966. AMERICAN FOLKLORE—JOHNNY APPLESEED				
☐ 1317 5¢ Red, Black, Green	6.70	.67	.19	.10
1966. BEAUTIFICATION OF AMERICA				
☐ 1318 5¢ Emerald, Pink, Black	7.30	.93	.19	.10
1966. GREAT RIVER ROAD				
☐ 1319 5¢ Yellow, Red, Blue, Green	7.00	.78	.21	.11
1966. SERVICEMEN & SAVINGS BONDS				
☐ 1320 5¢ Red, Light Blue, Dark Blue	7.00	.78	.20	.11
1966. CHRISTMAS ISSUE				
☐ 1321 5¢ Multicolored	13.50	.85	.20	.11
1966. MARY CASSATT—ARTIST				
☐ 1322 5¢ Multicolored	9.70	1.60	.25	.11
1967. COMMEMORATIVES				
1967. NATIONAL GRANGE CENTENARY				
☐ 1323 5¢ Orange, Yellow, Black, Brown & Green . . .	7.30	.71	.18	.11
1967. CANADA CENTENNIAL				
☐ 1324 5¢ Green, Light & Dark Blue, Black	7.50	.78	.18	.11
1967. ERIE CANAL SESQUICENTENNIAL				
☐ 1325 5¢ Light & Dark Blue, Red & Black	7.30	.78	.18	.11
1967. SEARCH FOR PEACE—LIONS INTL.				
☐ 1326 5¢ Red, Blue & Black	7.40	.71	.18	.11
1967. HENRY DAVID THOREAU				
☐ 1327 5¢ Black, Red & Green	8.00	.78	.20	.11

*No hinge pricing from 1941 to date is figured at (N-H ADD 15%)

Scott No.		Mint Sheet	Plate Block	Fine Unused Each	Fine Used Each
1967. NEBRASKA STATEHOOD CENTENNIAL					
☐ 1328	5¢ Yellow Green & Brown	7.40	.72	.18	.11
1967. VOICE OF AMERICA					
☐ 1329	5¢ Red, Blue & Black	7.40	.72	.18	.11
1967. AMERICAN FOLKLORE—DAVY CROCKETT					
☐ 1330	5¢ Green & Black	7.40	.76	.18	.11
1967. SPACE ACCOMPLISHMENTS					
☐ 1331	5¢ Light & Dark Blue, Red, Black	—	—	.90	.31
☐ 1332	5¢ Light & Dark Blue, Red, Black	—	—	.90	.31
1967. URBAN PLANNING					
☐ 1333	5¢ Blue & Black	8.60	1.45	.19	.11
1967. FINNISH INDEPENDENCE					
☐ 1334	5¢ Blue	8.60	1.45	.19	.11
1967. THOMAS EAKINS—ARTIST					
☐ 1335	5¢ Gold & Multicolored	9.00	1.50	.19	.11
1967. CHRISTMAS ISSUE					
☐ 1336	5¢ Multicolored	7.50	.85	.19	.11
1967. MISSISSIPPI STATEHOOD					
☐ 1337	5¢ Multicolored	8.70	1.40	.21	.11
1968–1971. REGULAR ISSUES					
1968. FLAG ISSUE					
☐ 1338	6¢ Red, Blue, Green	18.00	.85	.21	.11
1968. COMMEMORATIVES					
1968. ILLINOIS STATEHOOD					
☐ 1339	6¢ Black, Gold, Pink	9.00	.92	.24	.12
1968. HEMISFAIR '68					
☐ 1340	6¢ Indigo, Carmine, White	9.00	.92	.24	.12
1968. AIRLIFT TO SERVICEMEN					
☐ 1341	$1 Multicolored	280.00	33.00	6.70	4.10
1968. SUPPORT OUR YOUTH (ELKS)					
☐ 1342	6¢ Red & Blue	9.00	.92	.25	.12
1968. LAW AND ORDER					
☐ 1343	6¢ Blue & Black	9.00	.92	.25	.12
1968. REGISTER & VOTE					
☐ 1344	6¢ Black & Gold	9.00	.89	.25	.12
1968. HISTORIC AMERICAN FLAGS					
☐ 1345	6¢ Dark Blue	—	—	1.50	.72
☐ 1346	6¢ Red & Dark Blue	—	—	1.30	.72

*No hinge pricing from 1941 to date is figured at (N-H ADD 15%)

Scott No.		Mint Sheet	Plate Block	Fine Unused Each	Fine Used Each
☐ 1347	6¢ Dark, Blue, Olive Green	—	—	.61	.48
☐ 1348	6¢ Dark Blue & Red	—	—	.61	.51
☐ 1349	6¢ Black, Yellow, Red	—	—	.61	.50
☐ 1350	6¢ Dark Blue & Red	—	—	.61	.50
☐ 1351	6¢ Blue, Olive Green, Red	—	—	.61	.50
☐ 1352	6¢ Dark Blue & Red	—	—	.61	.50
☐ 1353	6¢ Blue, Yellow, Red	—	—	.61	.50
☐ 1354	6¢ Blue Red, Yellow	—	—	.81	.50

1968. WALT DISNEY

☐ 1355	6¢ Multicolored	11.75	2.30	.29	.10

1968. FATHER MARQUETTE—EXPLORATIONS

☐ 1356	6¢ Black, Brown, Green	9.00	.96	.21	.10

1968. AMERICAN FOLKLORE—DANIEL BOONE

☐ 1357	6¢ Brown, Yellow, Black, Red	9.00	.95	.21	.10

1968. ARKANSAS RIVER NAVIGATION

☐ 1358	6¢ Black & Blue	9.00	.95	.22	.10

1968. LEIF ERIKSON

☐ 1359	6¢ Dark Brown on Brown	9.00	.95	.22	.10

1968. CHEROKEE STRIP LAND RUSH

☐ 1360	6¢ Brown	11.00	1.20	.25	.11

1968. JOHN TRUMBULL PAINTING

☐ 1361	6¢ Yellow Red, Black	13.00	1.26	.28	.11

1968. WILDLIFE CONSERVATION—DUCKS

☐ 1362	6¢ Multicolored	13.00	1.65	.35	.11

1968. CHRISTMAS ISSUE

☐ 1363	6¢ Multicolored	9.00	1.35	.26	.11

1968. AMERICAN INDIAN

☐ 1364	6¢ Multicolored	17.00	3.20	.38	.14

1969. COMMEMORATIVES

1969. BEAUTIFICATION OF AMERICA

☐ 1365	6¢ Multicolored	—	—	.91	.17
☐ 1366	6¢ Multicolored	—	—	.91	.17
☐ 1367	6¢ Multicolored	—	—	.91	.17
☐ 1368	6¢ Multicolored	—	—	.91	.17

1969. AMERICAN LEGION

☐ 1369	6¢ Red, Blue, Black	9.00	.86	.24	.11

1969. GRANDMA MOSES PAINTING

☐ 1370	6¢ Multicolored	9.00	.91	.24	.10

1969. APOLLO 8 MOON ORBIT

☐ 1371	6¢ Black, Blue, Ochre	14.00	1.96	.30	.12

*No hinge pricing from 1941 to date is figured at (N-H ADD 15%)

Scott No.		Mint Sheet	Plate Block	Fine Unused Each	Fine Used Each
1969. W. C. HANDY—MUSICIAN					
☐ 1372	6¢ Multicolored	8.40	.82	.23	.10
1969. SETTLEMENT OF CALIFORNIA					
☐ 1373	6¢ Multicolored	8.40	.82	.23	.10
1969. MAJOR JOHN WESLEY POWELL—GEOLOGIST					
☐ 1374	6¢ Multicolored	8.40	.82	.23	.10
1969. ALABAMA STATEHOOD					
☐ 1375	6¢ Red, Yellow, Brown	8.40	.82	.23	.10
1969. XI INTL. BOTANICAL CONGRESS					
☐ 1376	6¢ Multicolored	—	—	1.50	.20
☐ 1377	6¢ Multicolored	—	—	1.50	.20
☐ 1378	6¢ Multicolored	—	—	1.50	.20
☐ 1379	6¢ Multicolored	—	—	1.50	.20
1969. DARTMOUTH COLLEGE CASE					
☐ 1380	6¢ Green	8.60	.81	.22	.11
1969. PROFESSIONAL BASEBALL CENTENARY					
☐ 1381	6¢ Multicolored	22.00	2.40	.57	.13
1969. INTERCOLLEGIATE FOOTBALL CENTENARY					
☐ 1382	6¢ Red & Green	13.00	1.50	.35	.11
1969. DWIGHT D. EISENHOWER MEMORIAL					
☐ 1383	6¢ Blue, Black & Red	6.50	.82	.24	.11
1969. CHRISTMAS ISSUE					
☐ 1384	6¢ Multicolored	8.10	2.15	.24	.11
1969. HOPE FOR THE CRIPPLED					
☐ 1385	6¢ Multicolored	8.30	.82	.23	.11
1969. WILLIAM M. HARNETT PAINTING					
☐ 1386	6¢ Multicolored	5.50	.82	.23	.11
1970. COMMEMORATIVES					
1970. NATURAL HISTORY					
☐ 1387	6¢ Multicolored	—	—	.24	.15
☐ 1388	6¢ Multicolored	—	—	.24	.15
☐ 1389	6¢ Multicolored	—	—	.24	.15
☐ 1390	6¢ Multicolored	—	—	.24	.15
1970. MAINE STATEHOOD SESQUICENTENNIAL					
☐ 1391	6¢ Multicolored	8.00	.86	.24	.13
1970. WILDLIFE CONSERVATION—BUFFALO					
☐ 1392	6¢ Black on Tan	8.00	.86	.24	.12
1970–1974. REGULAR ISSUE					
☐ 1393	6¢ Blue Gray	17.00	1.10	.22	.11
☐ 1393D	7¢ Light Blue	17.70	.97	.22	.11

*No hinge pricing from 1941 to date is figured at (N-H ADD 15%)

Scott No.		Mint Sheet	Plate Block	Fine Unused Each	Fine Used Each
☐ 1394	8¢ Black, Blue, Red	19.00	1.10	.24	.11
☐ 1395	8¢ Rose Violet	—	—	.36	.11
☐ 1396	8¢ Multicolored	21.00	6.70	.24	.11
☐ 1397	14¢ Brown	31.00	1.90	.42	.15
☐ 1398	16¢ Orange Brown	36.00	2.00	.44	.17
☐ 1399	18¢ Purple	41.00	2.00	.48	.17
☐ 1400	21¢ Green	48.00	2.40	.56	.27

Scott No.		Fine Unused Line Pair	Ave. Unused Line Pair	Fine Unused Each	Ave. Unused Each	Fine Used Each	Ave. Used Each
1970–1971. ROTARY PRESS COIL STAMPS—PERF. 10 VERTICALLY							
☐ 1401	6¢ Blue Gray	.73	.62	.23	.18	.14	.12
☐ 1402	8¢ Rose Violet	.73	.62	.23	.18	.14	.12

Scott No.		Mint Sheet	Plate Block	Fine Unused Each	Fine Used Each
1970. EDGAR LEE MASTERS—POET					
☐ 1405	6¢ Black & Olive Bistre	8.10	.95	.22	.12
1970. 50th ANNIVERSARY WOMEN'S SUFFRAGE					
☐ 1406	6¢ Blue	8.00	.95	.22	.12
1970. SOUTH CAROLINA TERCENTENARY					
☐ 1407	6¢ Multicolored	8.00	.95	.22	.12
1970. STONE MOUNTAIN MEMORIAL					
☐ 1408	6¢ Gray Black	8.00	.95	.22	.12
1970. FORT SNELLING					
☐ 1409	6¢ Multicolored	8.00	.95	.22	.12
1970. ANTI-POLLUTION					
☐ 1410	6¢ Multicolored	—	—	.35	.18
☐ 1411	6¢ Multicolored	—	—	.35	.18
☐ 1412	6¢ Multicolored	—	—	.35	.18
☐ 1413	6¢ Multicolored	—	—	.35	.18
1970. CHRISTMAS ISSUE					
☐ 1414	6¢ Multicolored	9.40	2.20	.24	.08
☐ 1415	6¢ Multicolored	—	—	.71	.15
☐ 1416	6¢ Multicolored	—	—	.71	.15
☐ 1417	6¢ Multicolored	—	—	.71	.15
☐ 1418	6¢ Multicolored	—	—	.71	.15
1970. PRECANCELLED CHRISTMAS ISSUE					
☐ 1414a	6¢ Multicolored	11.00	4.50	.26	.14
☐ 1415a	6¢ Multicolored	—	—	1.50	.18
☐ 1416a	6¢ Multicolored	—	—	1.50	.18
☐ 1417a	6¢ Multicolored	—	—	1.50	.18
☐ 1418a	6¢ Multicolored	—	—	1.50	.18

*No hinge pricing from 1941 to date is figured at (N-H ADD 15%)

Scott No.		Mint Sheet	Plate Block	Fine Unused Each	Fine Used Each
1970. UNITED NATIONS 25th ANNIVERSARY					
☐ 1419	6¢ Black, Red, Blue	8.00	.88	.22	.12
1970. PILGRIM LANDING 350th ANNIVERSARY					
☐ 1420	6¢ Multicolored	8.00	.88	.22	.12
1970. DISABLED AMERICAN VETERANS AND SERVICEMEN ISSUE					
☐ 1421	6¢ Blue, Black, Red	—	—	.21	.15
☐ 1422	6¢ Blue, Black, Red	—	—	.21	.15
1971. COMMEMORATIVES					
1971. ADVENT OF SHEEP TO AMERICA					
☐ 1423	6¢ Multicolored	8.00	.84	.20	.11
1971. GENERAL DOUGLAS MacARTHUR					
☐ 1424	6¢ Red, Blue, Black	8.00	.84	.20	.12
1971. BLOOD DONORS PROGRAM					
☐ 1425	6¢ Light Blue, Scarlet, Indigo	7.90	.84	.20	.12
1971. MISSOURI STATEHOOD					
☐ 1426	8¢ Multicolored	11.00	3.50	.26	.13
1971. WILDLIFE CONSERVATION					
☐ 1427	8¢ Multicolored	—	—	.56	.16
☐ 1428	8¢ Multicolored	—	—	.25	.16
☐ 1429	8¢ Multicolored	—	—	.25	.16
☐ 1430	8¢ Multicolored	—	—	.25	.16
1971. ANTARCTIC TREATY					
☐ 1431	8¢ Red & Blue	10.90	1.25	.30	.11
1971. AMERICAN REVOLUTION BICENTENNIAL					
☐ 1432	8¢ Red, Blue, Black	20.00	2.30	1.15	.11
1971. JOHN SLOAN PAINTING					
☐ 1433	8¢ Multicolored	11.00	1.20	.27	.11
1971. DECADE OF SPACE ACHIEVEMENTS					
☐ 1434	8¢ Multicolored	—	—	.25	.12
☐ 1435	8¢ Multicolored	—	—	.25	.12
1971. EMILY DICKINSON—POET					
☐ 1436	8¢ Multicolored	9.45	1.12	.22	.11
1971. SAN JUAN 450th ANNIVERSARY					
☐ 1437	8¢ Brown, Carmine, Blk.	9.45	1.12	.24	.11
1971. DRUG ADDICTION					
☐ 1438	8¢ Blue & Black	9.45	1.12	.24	.11
1971. CARE ANNIVERSARY					
☐ 1439	8¢ Multicolored	9.45	1.12	.26	.11
☐ 1440	8¢ Dark Brown & Ochre	—	—	.28	.12

*No hinge pricing from 1941 to date is figured at (N-H ADD 15%)

Scott No.		Mint Sheet	Plate Block	Fine Unused Each	Fine Used Each
☐ 1441	8¢ Dark Brown & Ochre	—	—	.28	.14
☐ 1442	8¢ Dark Brown & Ochre	—	—	.28	.14
☐ 1443	8¢ Dark Brown & Ochre	—	—	.28	.14

1971. CHRISTMAS

| ☐ 1444 | 8¢ Multicolored .... | 9.50 | 2.80 | .27 | .12 |
| ☐ 1445 | 8¢ Multicolored .... | 9.50 | 2.80 | .27 | .12 |

1972. COMMEMORATIVES

1972. SIDNEY LANIER—POET

| ☐ 1446 | 8¢ Multicolored .... | 9.75 | 1.10 | .25 | .11 |

1972. PEACE CORPS

| ☐ 1447 | 8¢ Red & Blue .... | 9.75 | 1.60 | .26 | .11 |

1972. NATIONAL PARKS CENTENNIAL

☐ 1448	2¢ Multicolored	—	—	.12	.11
☐ 1449	2¢ Multicolored	—	—	.14	.13
☐ 1450	2¢ Multicolored	—	—	.14	.13
☐ 1451	2¢ Multicolored	—	—	.14	.13
☐ 1452	6¢ Multicolored	8.10	1.10	.24	.16
☐ 1453	8¢ Multicolored	6.60	1.20	.28	.11
☐ 1454	15¢ Multicolored	19.10	2.00	.42	.45

1972. FAMILY PLANNING

| ☐ 1455 | 8¢ Multicolored .... | 10.00 | 1.15 | .26 | .12 |

1972. AMERICAN REVOLUTION BICENTENNIAL—COLONIAL CRAFTMEN

☐ 1456	8¢ Deep Brown, Yellow	—	—	.25	.15
☐ 1457	8¢ Deep Brown, Yellow	—	—	.25	.15
☐ 1458	8¢ Deep Brown, Yellow	—	—	.25	.15
☐ 1459	8¢ Deep Brown, Yellow	—	—	.25	.15

1972. OLYMPIC GAMES

☐ 1460	6¢ Multicolored	11.75	3.00	.31	.15
☐ 1461	8¢ Multicolored	14.00	3.00	.31	.10
☐ 1462	15¢ Multicolored	23.00	4.00	.50	.55

1972. PARENT TEACHER ASSOCIATION

| ☐ 1463 | 8¢ Black & Yellow .... | 9.50 | 1.20 | .26 | .11 |
| ☐ 1463a | 8¢ Black & Yellow, Reversed Pl. No. .... | — | 1.20 | — | — |

1972. WILDLIFE CONSERVATION

☐ 1464	8¢ Multicolored	—	—	.25	.13
☐ 1465	8¢ Multicolored	—	—	.25	.13
☐ 1466	8¢ Multicolored	—	—	.25	.13
☐ 1467	8¢ Multicolored	—	—	.25	.13

1972. MAIL ORDER BUSINESS

| ☐ 1468 | 8¢ Multicolored .... | 9.60 | 2.90 | .26 | .11 |

*No hinge pricing from 1941 to date is figured at (N-H ADD 15%)

Scott No.		Mint Sheet	Plate Block	Fine Unused Each	Fine Used Each
1972. OSTEOPATHIC MEDICINE					
☐ 1469	8¢ Yellow Orange, Brown	9.60	1.60	.27	.10
1972. TOM SAWYER—AMERICAN FOLKLORE					
☐ 1470	8¢ Multicolored	9.60	1.25	.27	.09
1972. CHRISTMAS					
☐ 1471	8¢ Multicolored	9.60	3.00	.27	.10
☐ 1472	8¢ Multicolored	9.60	3.00	.27	.10
1972. PHARMACY					
☐ 1473	8¢ Multicolored	9.60	1.25	.27	.09
1972. STAMP COLLECTING					
☐ 1474	8¢ Multicolored	8.70	1.20	.27	.11
1973. COMMEMORATIVES					
1973. LOVE—"FOR SOMEONE SPECIAL"					
☐ 1475	8¢ Red, Green, Blue	9.60	1.50	.23	.09
1973. COLONIAL COMMUNICATIONS					
☐ 1476	8¢ Black, Red, Blue	9.60	1.21	.25	.11
☐ 1477	8¢ Blue, Red, Brown	9.60	1.21	.24	.12
☐ 1478	8¢ Multicolored	9.60	1.21	.24	.11
☐ 1479	8¢ Multicolored	9.60	1.21	.24	.12
1973. BOSTON TEA PARTY					
☐ 1480	8¢ Multicolored	—	—	.25	.15
☐ 1481	8¢ Multicolored	—	—	.25	.15
☐ 1482	8¢ Multicolored	—	—	.25	.15
☐ 1483	8¢ Multicolored	—	—	.25	.15
1973. GEORGE GERSHWIN—COMPOSER					
☐ 1484	8¢ Multicolored	8.40	3.00	.23	.11
1973. ROBINSON JEFFERS—POET					
☐ 1485	8¢ Multicolored	8.30	3.00	.23	.11
1973. HENRY OSSAWA TANNER—ARTIST					
☐ 1486	6¢ Multicolored	8.40	3.00	.23	.11
1973. WILLA CATHER—NOVELIST					
☐ 1487	8¢ Multicolored	8.40	3.00	.23	.11
1973. NICOLAUS COPERNICUS					
☐ 1488	8¢ Black & Orange	10.50	1.25	.23	.12
1973. POSTAL PEOPLE					
☐ 1489	8¢ Multicolored	—	—	.22	.13
☐ 1490	8¢ Multicolored	—	—	.22	.14
☐ 1491	8¢ Multicolored	—	—	.22	.13
☐ 1492	8¢ Multicolored	—	—	.22	.13
☐ 1493	8¢ Multicolored	—	—	.22	.14
☐ 1494	8¢ Multicolored	—	—	.22	.14

*No hinge pricing from 1941 to date is figured at (N-H ADD 15%)

Scott No.		Mint Sheet	Plate Block	Fine Unused Each	Fine Used Each
☐ 1495	8¢ Multicolored	—	—	.22	.14
☐ 1496	8¢ Multicolored	—	—	.22	.14
☐ 1497	8¢ Multicolored	—	—	.22	.14
☐ 1498	8¢ Multicolored	—	—	.22	.14

1973. HARRY S. TRUMAN MEMORIAL
☐ 1499	8¢ Black, Red, Blue	7.25	1.15	.26	.13

1973. PROGRESS IN ELECTRONICS
☐ 1500	6¢ Multicolored	9.00	1.25	.22	.22
☐ 1501	8¢ Multicolored	9.85	1.20	.26	.11
☐ 1502	15¢ Multicolored	19.00	2.60	.45	.50

1973. LYNDON B. JOHNSON MEMORIAL
☐ 1503	8¢ Multicolored	7.25	3.00	.25	.13

1973. ANGUS CATTLE—RURAL AMERICA
☐ 1504	8¢ Multicolored	10.50	.96	.26	.12

1974. CHAUTAUQUA—RURAL AMERICA
☐ 1505	10¢ Multicolored	12.50	1.30	.27	.12

1974. WINTER WHEAT—RURAL AMERICA
☐ 1506	10¢ Multicolored	12.00	1.22	.29	.12

1973. CHRISTMAS
☐ 1507	8¢ Multicolored	10.50	3.90	.28	.10
☐ 1508	8¢ Multicolored	10.50	3.90	.26	.10

1973–1974. REGULAR ISSUES
☐ 1509	10¢ Red & Blue	23.00	5.50	.29	.10
☐ 1510	10¢ Blue	23.00	1.22	.29	.10
☐ 1511	10¢ Multicolored	23.00	2.20	.29	.10

Scott No.		Fine Unused Line Pair	Ave. Unused Line Pair	Fine Unused Each	Ave. Unused Each	Fine Used Each	Ave. Used Each
1973–1974. COIL STAMPS—PERF. 10 VERTICALLY							
☐ 1518	63¢ Orange	.92	.76	.21	.16	.19	.15
☐ 1519	10¢ Red & Blue	—	—	.32	.24	.16	.12
☐ 1520	10¢ Blue	.92	.71	.34	.24	.16	.12

Scott No.		Mint Sheet	Plate Block	Fine Unused Each	Fine Used Each
1974. COMMEMORATIVES					
1974. VETERANS OF FOREIGN WARS					
☐ 1525	10¢ Carmine & Blue	11.75	1.30	.28	.12

1974. ROBERT FROST—POET
☐ 1526	10¢ Black	11.75	1.30	.28	.12

1974. EXPO '74—PRESERVE THE ENVIRONMENT
☐ 1527	10¢ Multicolored	9.20	3.60	.28	.12

*No hinge pricing from 1941 to date is figured at (N-H ADD 15%)

Scott No.		Mint Sheet	Plate Block	Fine Unused Each	Fine Used Each
1974. HORSE RACING					
☐ 1528	10¢ Multicolored	11.90	3.50	.27	.12
1974. SKYLAB PROJECT					
☐ 1529	10¢ Multicolored	11.90	1.30	.27	.11
1974. UNIVERSAL POSTAL UNION CENTENARY					
☐ 1530	10¢ Multicolored	—	—	.27	.25
☐ 1531	10¢ Multicolored	—	—	.27	.25
☐ 1532	10¢ Multicolored	—	—	.27	.25
☐ 1533	10¢ Multicolored	—	—	.27	.25
☐ 1534	10¢ Multicolored	—	—	.27	.25
☐ 1535	10¢ Multicolored	—	—	.27	.25
☐ 1536	10¢ Multicolored	—	—	.27	.25
☐ 1537	10¢ Multicolored	—	—	.27	.25
1974. MINERALS HERITAGE ISSUE					
☐ 1538	10¢ Multicolored	—	—	.24	.15
☐ 1539	10¢ Multicolored	—	—	.24	.15
☐ 1540	10¢ Multicolored	—	—	.27	.14
☐ 1541	10¢ Multicolored	—	—	.27	.14
1974. FORT HARROD BICENTENNIAL					
☐ 1542	10¢ Multicolored	1.50	1.25	.30	.11
1974. CONTINENTAL CONGRESS					
☐ 1543	10¢ Red, Blue, Gray	—	—	.28	.13
☐ 1544	10¢ Red, Blue, Gray	—	—	.28	.13
☐ 1545	10¢ Red, Blue, Gray	—	—	.28	.13
☐ 1546	10¢ Red, Blue, Gray	—	—	.28	.13
1974. ENERGY CONSERVATION					
☐ 1547	10¢ Multicolored	11.75	1.20	.28	.12
1974. LEGEND OF SLEEPY HOLLOW					
☐ 1548	10¢ Multicolored	11.75	1.20	.28	.12
1974. RETARDED CHILDREN					
☐ 1549	10¢ Light & Dark Brown	11.75	1.20	.28	.12
1974. CHRISTMAS					
☐ 1550	10¢ Multicolored	11.70	2.70	.33	.11
☐ 1551	10¢ Multicolored	11.70	3.70	.33	.11
☐ 1552	10¢ Multicolored	11.70	5.30	.35	.12
☐ 1552	10¢ Multicolored, Plate Block of 12	—	3.70	—	—
1975. COMMEMORATIVES—AMERICAN ARTS					
1975. BENJAMIN WEST—ARTIST					
☐ 1553	10¢ Multicolored	11.75	3.10	.30	.12
1975. PAUL LAURENCE DUNBAR—POET					
☐ 1554	10¢ Multicolored	11.75	3.00	.30	.13

*No hinge pricing from 1941 to date is figured at (N-H ADD 15%)

Scott No.		Mint Sheet	Plate Block	Fine Unused Each	Fine Used Each
1975. D. W. GRIFFITH—MOTION PICTURES					
☐ 1555	10¢ Multicolored	11.50	1.25	.30	.12
1975. PIONEER 10 SPACE MISSION					
☐ 1556	10¢ Multicolored	11.50	1.25	.30	.12
1975. MARINER 10 SPACE MISSION					
☐ 1557	10¢ Multicolored	11.50	1.25	.30	.12
1975. COLLECTIVE BARGAINING					
☐ 1558	10¢ Blue, Red, Purple	11.50	2.50	.30	.12
1975. CONTRIBUTORS TO THE CAUSE					
☐ 1559	8¢ Multicolored	9.80	2.75	.25	.22
☐ 1560	10¢ Multicolored	11.50	3.10	.30	.12
☐ 1561	10¢ Multicolored	11.50	3.10	.31	.12
☐ 1562	18¢ Multicolored	25.00	5.80	.62	.51
1975. LEXINGTON AND CONCORD BATTLES BICENTENNIAL					
☐ 1563	10¢ Multicolored	11.50	4.10	.38	.12
1975. BATTLE OF BUNKER HILL					
☐ 1564	10¢ Multicolored	11.00	3.80	.38	.12
1975. CONTINENTAL MILITARY SERVICE UNIFORMS					
☐ 1565	10¢ Multicolored	—	—	.28	.13
☐ 1566	10¢ Multicolored	—	—	.28	.13
☐ 1567	10¢ Multicolored	—	—	.28	.13
☐ 1568	10¢ Multicolored	—	—	.28	.13
1975. U.S.—SOVIET JOINT SPACE MISSION					
☐ 1569	10¢ Multicolored	—	—	.27	.17
☐ 1570	10¢ Multicolored	—	—	.27	.17
1975. INTERNATIONAL WOMEN'S YEAR					
☐ 1571	10¢ Multicolored	11.90	1.90	.24	.09
1975. U.S. POSTAL SERVICE BICENTENNIAL					
☐ 1572	10¢ Multicolored	—	—	.28	.15
☐ 1573	10¢ Multicolored	—	—	.28	.15
☐ 1574	10¢ Multicolored	—	—	.28	.15
☐ 1575	10¢ Multicolored	—	—	.28	.15
1975. WORLD PEACE THROUGH LAW					
☐ 1576	10¢ Blue, Green, Brown	11.50	1.40	.27	.11
1975. BANKING AND COMMERCE					
☐ 1577	10¢ Multicolored	—	—	.27	.10
☐ 1578	10¢ Multicolored	—	—	.27	.10
1975. CHRISTMAS					
☐ 1579	10¢ Multicolored	11.50	3.40	.28	.13
☐ 1580	10¢ Multicolored	11.50	3.40	.28	.13

*No hinge pricing from 1941 to date is figured at (N-H ADD 15%)

Scott No.		Mint Sheet	Plate Block	Fine Unused Each	Fine Used Each
1975–1980. AMERICANA SERIES					
☐ 1581	1¢ Blue on Green	4.40	.41	.11	.11
☐ 1582	2¢ Brown on Green	5.40	.45	.11	.11
☐ 1584	3¢ Olive on Green	7.60	.50	.12	.11
☐ 1585	4¢ Maroon on Green	9.00	.59	.12	.11
☐ 1590	9¢ Slate on Green	—	—	.20	.11
☐ 1591	9¢ Green on Gray	17.00	.98	.24	.11
☐ 1592	10¢ Purple	23.00	1.12	.24	.11
☐ 1593	11¢ Orange on Gray	27.00	1.30	.27	.11
☐ 1594	12¢ Maroon	19.50	1.95	.37	.11
☐ 1595	13¢ Brown	—	—	.37	.11
☐ 1596	13¢ Multicolored	27.00	4.80	.37	.11
☐ 1597	15¢ Multicolored	34.00	2.90	.37	.11
☐ 1598	15¢ Multicolored	—	—	.68	.11
☐ 1599	16¢ Blue & Black	36.00	2.40	.53	.11
☐ 1603	24¢ Red on Blue	59.00	3.40	.72	.13
☐ 1604	28¢ Brown & Blue	66.00	3.90	.71	.15
☐ 1605	29¢ Blue & Blue	66.00	4.30	.71	.24
☐ 1606	30¢ Green on Blue	48.00	3.50	.65	.16
☐ 1608	50¢ Black & Orange	76.00	5.60	1.10	.18
☐ 1610	$1 Multicolored	132.00	11.00	2.00	.18
☐ 1611	$2 Multicolored	285.00	21.00	3.80	.66
☐ 1612	$5 Multicolored	800.00	44.00	9.20	3.60

Scott No.		Fine Unused Line Pair	Ave. Unused Line Pair	Fine Unused Each	Ave. Unused Each	Fine Used Each	Ave. Used Each
1975–1978. COIL STAMPS							
☐ 1613	3.1¢ Brown on Yellow	1.10	.86	.15	.12	.14	.11
☐ 1614	7.7¢ Gold on Yellow	1.60	1.25	.31	.24	.18	.14
☐ 1615	7.9¢ Red on Yellow	1.70	1.40	.35	.26	.14	.11
☐ 1615C	8.4¢ Blue on White	2.00	1.45	.30	.22	.19	.16
☐ 1616	9¢ Green on Gray	1.30	.95	.24	.20	.15	.12
☐ 1617	10¢ Purple on Gray	1.10	.85	.24	.20	.15	.12
☐ 1618	13¢ Brown	1.20	.90	.24	.27	.19	.14

Scott No.		Mint Sheet	Plate Block	Fine Unused Each	Fine Used Each
1975–1977. REGULAR ISSUES					
☐ 1622	13¢ Red, Brown, Blue	30.00	8.50	.32	.11
☐ 1623	13¢ Blue, Red	30.00	8.50	.32	.11
☐ 1623c	13¢ Blue, Red, pf 10	—	—	.35	.11

Scott No.		Fine Unused Each	Ave. Unused Each	Fine Used Each	Ave. Used Each
1975. COIL STAMPS					
☐ 1625	13¢ Red, Brown, Blue	.43	.33	.12	.09

*No hinge pricing from 1941 to date is figured at (N-H ADD 15%)

HOW TO FIND YOUR STAMP

This new stamp catalog takes the confusion out of finding and identifying individual stamps. A complete new FULL-COLOR–FAST FIND PHOTO INDEX is illustrated on the following pages. All of the stamp photographs are arranged in Scott numerical order and date of issue. Below each stamp picture is the Scott number and the page number the stamp listing appears on.

GENERAL ISSUE—SCOTT NO. 1–116 (1847–1869)

| 1, 39, 48a
PG 21 | 2, 4, 948b
PG 21 | 5, 9, 18–24, 40
PG 21 | 10, 11, 25, 26
41–PG 21 | 12, 27–30A
42–PG 21 |

| 13–16, 31–35,
43–PG 21 | 17, 36, 44
PG 21 | 37, 45
PG 22 | 38, 46
PG 22 | 39, 47
PG 22 |

| 56, 63, 85, 86
92, 102–PG 22 | 64–66, 74, 79, 88
94, 104–PG 22 | 57–67, 75, 76, 80
95, 195–PG 22 | 58–62B, 68, 85D,
89, 96, 106–PG 22 | 59, 69, 85E, 90
97, 107–PG 22 |

| 60, 70, 78, 99
109–PG 22 | 61, 71, 81, 100,
110–PG 22 | 62, 72, 101,
111–PG 22 | 73, 84, 85B, 87,
93, 103–PG 22 | 77, 85F, 91, 98,
108–PG 22 |

| 112, 123, 133
PG 24 | 113, 124
PG 24 | 114, 125
PG 24 | 115, 126
PG 24 | 116, 127
PG 24 |

GENERAL ISSUE—SCOTT NO. 117–222 (1869–1890)

117, 128
PG 24

118, 119, 129
PG 24

120, 130
PG 24

121, 131
PG 24

122, 132
PG 24

134, 156, 167
182, 206–PG 24

135, 157, 168
203–PG 24

136, 158, 169
214–PG 24

137, 148, 159
195, 208–PG 24

138, 149, 160
171, 196–PG 24

139, 150, 161,
197, 209–PG 24

140–151, 162,
173, 198–PG 24

141, 152, 163,
189, 199–PG 24

142, 153, 164,
175, 200–PG 24

143, 154, 165,
201, 2117–PG 24

144, 155, 166,
202, 218–PG 24

179, 181, 185,
204–PG 25

205, 205C, 216
PG 25

210, 211B, 213,
PG 26

211, 211D, 215
PG 26

212–PG 26

219–PG 26

219D, 220–PG 26

221–PG 26

222–PG 26

223–PG 26

224–PG 26

225–PG 26

226–PG 26

227–PG 26

228–PG 26

229–PG 26

230–PG 26

231–PG 26

232–PG 26

233–PG 26

234–PG 26

235–PG 26

236–PG 26

237–PG 26

238–PG 26

239–PG 27

240–PG 27

241–PG 27

242–PG 27

243–PG 27

244–PG 27

245–PG 27

246, 247, 264,
279–PG 27

248–252, 265–267,
279B–PG 27

253, 268
PG 27

254, 269, 280
PG 27

255, 270, 281
PG 27

256, 271, 282
PG 27

257, 272
PG 27

258, 273, 262C,
283–PG 27

259, 273, 284
PG 27

260, 275
PG 27

261–261A, 276,
276A–PG 27

262, 277
PG 27

263, 278–PG 27

285–PG 28

286–PG 28

287–PG 28

288–PG 28

289–PG 28

290–PG 28

291–PG 28

292–PG 28

293–PG 28

294–PG 28

295–PG 28

296–PG 28

297–PG 28

298–PG 28

299–PG 28

300, 314, 316,
318–PG 28

301–PG 28

302–PG 28

303, 314A
PG 28

304, 315, 317
PG 28

305–PG 28

306–PG 28

307–PG 28

308–PG 28

GENERAL ISSUE—SCOTT NO. 309–398 (1903–1913)

309–PG 28

310–PG 28

311–PG 28

312, 479
PG 28

313, 480
PG 28

319–322
PG 29

323–PG 29

324–PG 29

325–PG 29

326–PG 29

327–PG 29

328–PG 29

329–PG 29

330–PG 29

331, 392
PG 29

332–393, 519
PG 29

333–541
PG 29

367, 369
PG 30

370, 371–PG 30

372, 373–PG 30

397, 401–PG 31

398, 402–PG 31

399, 403
PG 31

400, 400A, 404
PG 31

405–545
PG 32

406–546
PG 32

414–518
PG 32

523, 524, 547
PG 35

537–PG 36

548–PG 37

549–PG 37

550–PG 37

551, 653
PG 37

552, 575, 578,
604, 632–PG 37

553, 576, 598,
605, 633–PG 37

583, 599–99A
634–34A–PG 38

555, 584, 600,
635–PG 37

556–585, 601
636–PG 37

557, 586, 602,
637–PG 37

558, 587, 638,
723–PG 37

559, 588, 639
PG 37

560, 589, 640
PG 37

561, 590, 641
PG 37

562, 591, 603,
641–PG 37

563, 692
PG 37

564, 693
PG 37

565, 695–PG 37   566–696–PG 37   567, 698–PG 37   568, 699–PG 37   569, 700–PG 37

570, 701–PG 37   571–PG 37   572–PG 37   573–PG 37   610–613–PG 38

614–PG 38   615–PG 38   616–PG 38

617–PG 39   618–PG 39   619–PG 39

620–PG 39   621–PG 39   622, 694–PG 39   623, 697–PG 39

627–PG 39 628–PG 39 629–PG 39 643–PG 39

644–PG 39 645–PG 39 646–PG 39 647–PG 40 648–PG 40

649–PG 40 650–PG 40 651–PG 40

654–656–PG 40 657–PG 40 680–PG 41 681–PG 41 682–PG 41

683–PG 41 684, 686–PG 41 685, 687–PG 41 688–PG 41 689–PG 41

690–PG 41   702–PG 42   703–PG 42   704–PG 42   705–PG 42

706–PG 42   707–PG 42   708–PG 42   709–PG 42   710–PG 42   711–PG 42

712–PG 42   713–PG 42   714–PG 42   715–PG 42   716–PG 42

717–PG 42   718–PG 42   719–PG 42   720–722   724–PG 43   725–PG 43
PG 42

726–PG 43   727, 752   728, 730, 766   729, 731, 767   732–PG 43
PG 43   PG 43   PG 43

733, 735, 753
PG 43

734–PG 43

736–PG 43

737, 738, 754–PG 44

739, 755–PG 44

740, 751, 756,
769–PG 44

741, 757–PG 44

742, 750, 758, 770–PG 44

743, 759–PG 44

744, 760–PG 44

745, 761–PG 44

746, 762–PG 44

747, 763–PG 44

748, 764–PG 44

749, 765, 797–PG 44

772, 778A–PG 45

773, 778B–PG 45

774–PG 45

775, 778C–PG 45

776, 778D–PG 45

777–PG 45

782–PG 45

783–PG 46

784–PG 46

785–PG 46

786–PG 46

787–PG 46

788–PG 46

789–PG 46

790–PG 46

791–PG 46

792–PG 46

793–PG 46

794–PG 46

795–PG 46

796–PG 46

798–PG 46

799–PG 46

800–PG 46

801–PG 46

802–PG 46

GENERAL ISSUE—SCOTT NO. 803-836 (1938)

803–PG 46   804, 848–PG 46   805, 849–PG 46   806–PG 46   807–PG 46   808, 843–PG 46

809, 844–PG 46   810, 845–PG 47   811, 846–PG 47   812–PG 47   813–PG 47   814–PG 47

815, 847–PG 47   816–PG 47   817–PG 47   818–PG 47   819–PG 47   820–PG 47

821–PG 47   822–PG 47   823–PG 47   824–PG 47   825–PG 47   826–PG 47

827–PG 47   828–PG 47   829–PG 47   830–PG 47   831–PG 47   832–PG 47

833–PG 47

834–PG 47

835–PG 47

836–PG 47

837–PG 47

838–PG 47

852–PG 48

853–PG 48

854–PG 48

855–PG 48

856–PG 48

857–PG 48

858–PG 48

859–PG 48

860–PG 48

861–PG 48

862–PG 48

863–PG 48

864–PG 49

865–PG 49

866–PG 49

867–PG 49

868–PG 49

869–PG 49

870–PG 49

871–PG 49

872–PG 49

873–PG 49

874–PG 49

875–PG 49

876–PG 49

877–PG 49

878–PG 49

879–PG 49

880–PG 49

881–PG 49

882–PG 49

883–PG 49

884–PG 49

885–PG 49

886–PG 49

887–PG 49

888–PG 49

889–PG 49

890–PG 49

891–PG 49

892–PG 49

893–PG 49

894–PG 49

895–PG 49

896–PG 50

897–PG 50

898–PG 50

899–PG 50

900–PG 50

901–PG 50

902–PG 50

903–PG 50

904–PG 50

905–PG 50

906–PG 50

907–PG 50

908-PG 50   909-PG 50   921-PG 51

922-PG 51   923-PG 51   924-PG 51

925-PG 51   926-PG 51   927-PG 51

928-PG 51   929-PG 51   930-PG 51

931-PG 51   932-PG 51   933-PG 51

934–PG 51

935–PG 51

936–PG 51

937–PG 51

938–PG 51

939–PG 52

940–PG 52

941–PG 52

942–PG 52

943–PG 52

944–PG 52

945–PG 52

946–PG 52

947–PG 52

948-PG 52

949-PG 52

950-PG 52

951-PG 52

952-PG 52

953-PG 52

954-PG 52

955-PG 52

956-PG 53

957-PG 53

958-PG 53

959–PG 53

960–PG 53

961–PG 53

962–PG 53

963–PG 53

964–PG 53

965–PG 53

966–PG 53

967–PG 53

969–PG 53

970–PG 53

971–PG 53

972–PG 53

973–PG 53

974–PG 53

968–PG 53

975–PG 54 976–PG 54 977–PG 54 978–PG 54

979–PG 54 980–PG 54 981–PG 54 982–PG 54

983–PG 54 984–PG 54 985–PG 54

986–PG 54 987–PG 54 988–PG 54 989–PG 54

990–PG 54 991–PG 54 992–PG 54

993–PG 54

994–PG 54

995–PG 55

996–PG 55

997–PG 55

998–PG 55

999–PG 55

1000–PG 55

1001–PG 55

1002–PG 55

1003–PG 55

1004–PG 55

1005–PG 55

1006–PG 55

1007–PG 55

1008–PG 55

1009–PG 55

1010–PG 55

1011–PG 55

1012–PG 55

1013–PG 56

1014–PG 56

1015–PG 56

1016–PG 56

1017–PG 56

1018–PG 56

1019–PG 56

1020–PG 56

1021–PG 56

1022–PG 56

1023–PG 56

1024–PG 56

1025–PG 56

1026–PG 56

1027–PG 56

1028–PG 56

1029–PG 56

1030–PG 56

1031, 1054–PG 56

1031A, 1054A–PG 56

1032–PG 57

1033, 1055–PG 57

1034, 1056–PG 57

1035–1075–PG 57

1036–1058–PG 57

1037, 1059–PG 57

1038–PG 57

1039–PG 57

1040–PG 57

1041, 1075B–PG 57

1042A–PG 57

1043–PG 57

1044A–PG 57

1044–PG 57

1045–PG 57

1046–PG 57

1047–PG 57

1048–PG 57

1049–PG 57

1050–PG 57

1051–PG 57   1052–PG 57   1053–PG 57   1060–PG 57

1061–PG 57   1062–PG 57   1063–PG 58   1064–PG 58

1065–PG 58   1066–PG 58   1067–PG 58

1068–PG 58   1069–PG 58   1070–PG 58

1071–PG 58   1072–PG 58

1073–PG 58

1074–PG 58

1075–PG 58

1076–PG 58

1077–PG 58

1078–PG 58

1079–PG 58

GENERAL ISSUE—SCOTT NO. 1080–1093 (1956–1957)

1080–PG 58

1081–PG 58

1082–PG 59

1083–PG 59

1084–PG 59

1085–PG 59

1086–PG 59

1087–PG 59

1088–PG 59

1089–PG 59

1090–PG 59

1091–PG 59

1092–PG 59

1093–PG 59

109

1094–PG 59   1095–PG 59   1096–PG 59   1097–PG 59

1098–PG 59   1099–PG 59   1100–PG 60   1104–PG 60

1105–PG 60   1106–PG 60   1107–PG 60

1108–PG 60   1109–PG 60   1110–PG 60   1111–PG 60

1112–PG 60   1113–PG 60   1114–PG 60   1115–PG 60

1116–PG 60   1117–PG 60   1118–PG 60   1119–PG 60

1120–PG 60   1121–PG 60   1122–PG 60   1123–PG 60

1124–PG 61   1125–PG 61   1126–PG 61   1127–PG 61

1128–PG 61

1129–PG 61

1130–PG 61

1131–PG 61

1132–PG 61

1133–PG 61

1134–PG 61

1135–PG 61

1136–PG 61

1137–PG 61

1138–PG 61

1139–PG 61

1140–PG 61

1141–PG 61

1142–PG 61

1143–PG 61

1144–PG 61   1145–PG 61   1146–PG 62   1147–PG 62

1148–PG 62   1149–PG 62   1150–PG 62   1151–PG 62

1152–PG 62   1153–PG 62   1154–PG 62   1155–PG 62

1156–PG 62   1157–PG 62   1158–PG 62   1159–PG 62   1160–PG 62

113

1161–PG 62

1162–PG 62

1163–PG 62

1164–PG 62

1165–PG 62

1166–PG 62

1167–PG 63

1168–PG 63

1169–PG 63

1170–PG 63

1171–PG 63

1172–PG 63

1173–PG 63

1174–PG 63

1175–PG 63

1176–PG 63

1177–PG 63

1178–PG 63

1179–PG 63

1180–PG 63

1181–PG 63

1182–PG 63

1183–PG 63

1184–PG 63

1185–PG 63

1186–PG 64

1187–PG 64

1188–PG 64

1189–PG 64

1190–PG 64

1191–PG 64

1192–PG 64

1193–PG 64

1194–PG 64

1195–PG 64

1196–PG 64

1197–PG 64

1198–PG 64

1199–PG 64

1200–PG 64

1202–PG 64

1201–PG 64

1203–PG 64

1204–PG 64

1205–PG 65

1206–PG 65

1207–PG 65

1208–PG 65

1209, 1225–PG 65

1213–PG 65

1230–PG 65

GENERAL ISSUE—SCOTT NO. 1231–1244 (1963–1964)

1231–PG 65

1232–PG 65

1233–PG 65

1234–PG 65

1235–PG 65

1236–PG 65

1237–PG 65

1238–PG 65

1239–PG 66

1240–PG 66

1241–PG 66

1242–PG 66

1243–PG 66

1244–PG 66

1245–PG 66

1246–PG 66

1247–PG 66

1248–PG 66

1249–PG 66

1250–PG 66

1251–PG 66

1252–PG 66

1253–PG 66

1254–PG 66

1255–PG 66

1256–PG 66

1257–PG 66

1258–PG 66

1259–PG 67

1260–PG 67

1261–PG 67

GENERAL ISSUE—SCOTT NO. 1262–1278 (1965)

1262–PG 67

1263–PG 67

1264–PG 67

1265–PG 67

1266–PG 67

1267–PG 67

1268–PG 67

1269–PG 67

1270–PG 67

1271–PG 67

1272–PG 67

1273–PG 67

1274–PG 67

12/5–PG 67

1276–PG 67

1278–PG 68

1279–PG 68

1280–PG 68

1281 1297–PG 68

1282 1303–PG 68

1283 1304–PG 68

1283B–PG 68

1284 1298–PG 68

1285–PG 68

1286–PG 68

1286A–PG 68

1287–PG 68

1288–PG 68

1289–PG 68

1290–PG 68

1291–PG 68

1292–PG 68

1293–PG 68

1294 1305C–PG 68

1295–PG 68

1305–PG 68

1306–PG 68

1307–PG 68

1308–PG 68

1309–PG 69

1310–PG 69

1311–PG 69

1312–PG 69

1313–PG 69

1314–PG 69

1315–PG 69

1316–PG 69

1317–PG 69

1318–PG 69

GENERAL ISSUE—SCOTT NO. 1319–1334 (1966–1967)

1319–PG 69   1320–PG 69   1321–PG 69   1322–PG 69   1323–PG 69

1324–PG 69   1325–PG 69   1326–PG 69

1327–PG 69   1328–PG 70   1329–PG 70   1330–PG 70

1331–PG 70   1332–PG 70   1333–PG 70   1334–PG 70

1335—PG 70

1336—PG 70

1337—PG 70

1338, 1338A
PG 70

1338F, G—PG 70

1339—PG 70

1340—PG 70

1341—PG 70

1342—PG 70

1343—PG 70

1344—PG 70

1345—PG 70

1354—PG 71

1355—PG 71

1356—PG 71

1357–PG 71

1358–PG 71

1359–PG 71

1360–PG 71

1361–PG 71

1362–PG 71

1363–PG 71

1364–PG 71

PLANT for more BEAUTIFUL CITIES PLANT for more BEAUTIFUL PARKS

PLANT for more BEAUTIFUL HIGHWAYS PLANT for more BEAUTIFUL STREETS

1365–1368–PG 71

1369–PG 71

1370–PG 71

1371–PG 71

GENERAL ISSUE—SCOTT NO. 1372–1384 (1969)

1372-PG 72

1373-PG 72

1374-PG 72

1375-PG 72

1376–1379-PG 72

1380-PG 72

1381-PG 72

1382-PG 72

1383-PG 72

1384-PG 72

1385–PG 72

1386–PG 72

1387–1390–PG 72

1391–PG 72

1392–PG 72

1393–PG 72

1393D–PG 72

1394–PG 73

1395–PG 73

1396–PG 73

1397–PG 73

1398–PG 73

1399–PG 73

1400–PG 73

1405–PG 73

1406–PG 73

GENERAL ISSUE—SCOTT NO. 1407–1424 (1970–1971)

1407–PG 73

1408–PG 73

1409–PG 73

1410–1413–PG 73

1414–PG 73

1415–1418–PG 73

1419–PG 74

1420–PG 74

1421–PG 74

1422–PG 74

1423–PG 74

1424–PG 74

1425–PG 74

1426–PG 74

1427–1430–PG 74

1431–PG 74

1432–PG 74

1433–PG 74

1434–PG 74   1435–PG 74

1436–PG 74

1437–PG 74

1438–PG 74

1439–PG 74

HISTORIC PRESERVATION

HISTORIC PRESERVATION

HISTORIC PRESERVATION

HISTORIC PRESERVATION

1440–1443–PG 74

1444–PG 75

1445–PG 75

1446–PG 75

1447–PG 75

1448–1451–PG 75

1452–PG 75

1453–PG 75

1454–PG 75

1455–PG 75

1456-1459–PG 75

1460–PG 75

1461–PG 75

1462–PG 75

1464-1467–PG 75

1463–PG 75

1468–PG 75

1469–PG 76

1470–PG 76

1471–PG 76

1472–PG 76

1473–PG 76

1474–PG 76

1475–PG 76

1476–PG 76

1477–PG 76

1478–PG 76

1479–PG 76

1480–1483–PG 76

1484–PG 76

1485–PG 76

1486–PG 76

1487–PG 76

1488–PG 76

1489–PG 76

1490–PG 76

1491–PG 76

1492–PG 76

1493–PG 76

1494–PG 76

1495–PG 77

1496–PG 77

1497–PG 77

1498–PG 77

1499–PG 77

1500–PG 77

1501–PG 77

1502–PG 77

1503–PG 77

1504–PG 77

1505–PG 77

1506F–PG 77

1507–PG 77

1508–PG 77

1509, 1519–PG 77

1510–PG 77

1511–PG 77

1518–PG 77

1525–PG 77

1526–PG 77

1527–PG 77

1528–PG 78

1529–PG 78

1530–PG 78   1531–PG 78   1532–PG 78   1533–PG 78   1534–PG 78

1535–PG 78   1536–PG 78

1538–1539–PG 78
1540–1541–PG 78

1537–PG 78

1543–1546–PG 78

1542–PG 78

1547–PG 78

1548–PG 78

1549–PG 78

1550–PG 78

1551–PG 78

1552–PG 78

1553–PG 78

1554–PG 78

1555–PG 79

1556–PG 79

1557–PG 79

1558–PG 79

1559–PG 79

1560–PG 79

1561–PG 79

1562–PG 79

1563–PG 79

1564–PG 79

1565–PG 79

1566–PG 79

1567–PG 79

1568–PG 79

1569–PG 79

1570–PG 79

1571–PG 79

1572–PG 79

1573–PG 79

1574–PG 79

GENERAL ISSUE—SCOTT NO. 1575–1608 (1975)

1575–PG 79

1577–1578–PG 79

1576–PG 79

1581–PG 80

1582–PG 80

1584–PG 80

1585–PG 80

1579–PG 79

1580–PG 79

1590–PG 80

1592–PG 80

1593–PG 80

1594–PG 80

1595–PG 80

1596–PG 80

1597–1598–PG 80

1599–PG 80

1603–PG 80

1604–PG 80

1605–PG 80

1606–PG 80

1608–PG 80

GENERAL ISSUE—SCOTT NO. 1610–1687 (1975–1976)

1610–PG 80

1611–PG 80

1612–PG 80

1613–PG 80

1614–PG 80

1615–PG 80

1615C–PG 80

1629–1630–1631–PG 171

1622–PG 80

1623–PG 80

1632–PG 171

1633–1682–PG 171

1683–PG 171

1684–PG 171

1685–PG 171

1686–PG 171

1687–PG 171

1688–PG 172

1689–PG 172

1690–PG 172

1691-1692-1693-1694–PG 172

1695–PG 172

1696–PG 172

1697–PG 172

1698–PG 172

1699–PG 172

1701–PG 172

1702-1703–PG 172

Adolph S. Ochs
PUBLISHER

13c USA

1700–PG 172

Washington at Princeton 1777 by Peale
US Bicentennial 13c

1704–PG 172

CENTENNIAL
OF SOUND RECORDING
USA 13¢

1705–PG 172

Zia: Museum of New Mexico
Pueblo Art USA 13c

1706–PG 172

San Ildefonso: Denver Art Museum
Pueblo Art USA 13c

1707–PG 172

Hopi: Heard Museum Phoenix
Pueblo Art USA 13c

1708–PG 172

Acoma: School of American Research
Pueblo Art USA 13c

1709–PG 172

USA 13¢
50th Anniversary Solo Transatlantic Flight

1710–PG 173

COLORADO
13c USA
THE CENTENNIAL STATE

1711–PG 173

Swallowtail
USA 13¢ Papilio oregonius

1712–PG 173

Checkerspot
USA 13¢ Euphydryas phaeton

1713–PG 173

Dogface
USA 13¢ Colias eurydice

1714–PG 173

Orange-Tip
USA 13¢ Anthocaris midea

1715–PG 173

Lafayette
US Bicentennial 13c

1716–PG 173

the SEAMSTRESS
for INDEPENDENCE USA 13¢

1717–PG 173

the BLACKSMITH
for INDEPENDENCE USA 13¢

1718–PG 173

1719–PG 173

1720–PG 173

1721–PG 173

1722–PG 173

1723–PG 173

1724–PG 173

1725–PG 173

1726–PG 173

1727–PG 173

1728–PG 173

1729–PG 173

1730–PG 173

1731–PG 173

1732–PG 173

1733–PG 173

1734–PG 174

1735–PG 174

1737–PG 174

1738–1739–1740–1741–1742–PG 174

1744–PG 174

1745–PG 174

1746–PG 174

1747–PG 174

1748–PG 174

1749–PG 174

1750–PG 174

1751–PG 174

1752–PG 174

1753–PG 174

1754–PG 174

1755–PG 174

1756–PG 174

1757–PG 174

1758–PG 174

1759–PG 175

1760–PG 175

1761–PG 175

1762–PG 175

1763–PG 175

1764–PG 175

1765–PG 175

1766–PG 175

1767–PG 175

1768–PG 175

1769–PG 175

1770–PG 175

1771–PG 175

1772–PG 175

1773–PG 175

1774–PG 175

1775–PG 175

1776–PG 175

1777–PG 175

1778–PG 175

1779–PG 175

1780–PG 175

1781–PG 175

1782–PG 175

1783–PG 175

1785–PG 175

1784–PG 175

1786–PG 175

1787–PG 175

1788–PG 176

1789–PG 176

1790–PG 176

1791–PG 176

1792–PG 176

1794–PG 176

1793–PG 176

1795–PG 176

1796–PG 176

1797–PG 176

1798–PG 176

1799–PG 176

1800–PG 176

1801–PG 176   1802–PG 176   1803–PG 176   1804–PG 176

1805–1806 PG 176   1807–1808 PG 177   1809–1810 PG 177   1811–PG 177   1813–PG 177

1818–PG 177   1821–PG 177   1822 PG 177   1823–PG 177   1824–PG 177

1825–PG 177

1826–PG 177

1827–PG 177

1828–PG 177

1829–PG 177

1830–PG 177

1831–PG 177

1832–PG 177

1833–PG 177

1834–PG 178

1835–PG 178

1836–PG 178

1837–PG 178

1838–PG 178

1839–PG 178

1840–PG 178

Architecture USA 15c

1841–PG 178

Christmas USA 15c

1842–PG 178

USA15c Season's Greetings

1843–PG 178

Dorothea Dix USA 1c

1844–PG 178

Igor Stravinsky USA 2c

1845–PG 178

Henry Clay USA 3c

1846–PG 178

Carl Schurz 4c USA

1847–PG 178

Pearl Buck USA 5c

1848–PG 178

Walter Lippmann 6 USA

1849–PG 178

Abraham Baldwin USA 7

1850–PG 178

Henry Knox USA 8

1851–PG 178

Sylvanus Thayer 9

1852–PG 178

Richard Russell USA 10c

1853–PG 178

Alden Partridge USA 11

1854–PG 178

USA 8c Crazy Horse

1855–PG 178

Sinclair Lewis USA 14

1856–PG 178

Rachel Carson USA 17c

1857–PG 179

George Mason USA 18c

1858–PG 179

USA 19c Sequoyah

1859–PG 179

Ralph Bunche
USA 20c
1860–PG 179

Thomas H. Gallaudet
USA 20c
1861–PG 179

Harry S Truman
USA 20c
1862–PG 179

John J. Audubon
USA 22
1863–PG 179

Frank C. Laubach
USA 30c
1864–PG 179

Charles R Drew MD
USA 35c
1865–PG 179

Robert Millikan
37c USA
1866–PG 179

Grenville Clark
USA 39
1867–PG 179

Lillian M. Gilbreth
USA 40c
1868–PG 179

Chester W. Nimitz
USA 50
1869–PG 179

Rose USA 18c
1876–PG 179

Camellia USA 18c
1877–PG 179

USA 15c
Everett Dirksen
1874–PG 179

Whitney Moore Young
Black Heritage USA 15
1875–PG 179

Dahlia USA 18c
1878–PG 179

Lily USA 18c
1879–PG 179

USA 18c
1880–PG 179

USA 18c
1881–PG 179

USA 18c
1882–PG 179

USA 18c
1886–PG 180

1887–PG 180

USA 18c
1883–PG 179

USA 18c
1884–PG 180

1885–PG 180

USA 18c
1888–PG 180

USA 18c
1889–PG 180

USA 18c
... for amber waves of grain
1890–PG 180

USA 18c
... from sea to shining sea
1891–PG 180

1892–PG 180

1893–PG 180

1894–PG 180

1900–PG 180

1902–PG 180

1905–PG 180

1906–PG 180

1907–PG 180

1910–PG 180

1911–PG 180

1920–PG 180

1912–1916–PG 180
1917–1919–PG 180

GENERAL ISSUE—SCOTT NO. 1921-1933 (1981)

1921–PG 181

1922–PG 181

1923–PG 181

1924–PG 181

1925–PG 181

1926–PG 181

1927–PG 181

1928–PG 181

1929–PG 181

1930–PG 181

1931–PG 181

1932–PG 181

1933–PG 181

1934–PG 181

1935–PG 181

1936–PG 181

1937–PG 181   1938–PG 181

1939–PG 181

1949–PG 182

1940–PG 181

1941–PG 181

1946–1948–PG 182

1950–PG 182

1942–1945–PG 181

152

1951-PG 182

1952-PG 182

2003-PG 182

2004-PG 182

2005-PG 182

1953-2002-PG 182

2006–2009–PG 182

2010–PG 182

2011–PG 182

2012–PG 182

2013–PG 182

International Peace Garden

2014–PG 183

2015–PG 183

2017–PG 183

2016–PG 183

2018–PG 183

2023–PG 183

2019–2022–PG 183

2024–PG 183

2025–PG 183

2026–PG 183

2027–2030–PG 183

2031–PG 183

2032-2035–PG 184

2036–PG 184

2037–PG 184

2038–PG 184

2039–PG 184

2040–PG 184

2041–PG 184

2042–PG 184

2043–PG 184

2044–PG 184

2045–PG 184

2046–PG 184

2048–2051–PG 184

2047–PG 184

2052–PG 185

2053–PG 185

2054–PG 185

2055–PG 185

Charles Steinmetz

Edwin Armstrong

2056–PG 185

Nikola Tesla

2057–PG 185

Philo T. Farnsworth

2058–PG 185

2059–PG 185

Early electric streetcar, Montgomery, Ala. 1886

2060–PG 185

"Bobtail" horsecar, Sulphur Rock, Ark. 1926

2061–PG 185

St. Charles streetcar, New Orleans, La. 1923

2062–PG 185

Christmas USA 20c

Raphael, 1483-1483, National Gallery

2063–PG 185

Martin Luther

1483-1983 USA 20c

2065–PG 185

2067-2070–PG 185

Season's Greetings USA 20c

2064–PG 185

USA 20c

1959-1984
Alaska Statehood

2066–PG 185

FEDERAL DEPOSIT
INSURANCE
CORPORATION

2071–PG 186

LOVE
LOVE
LOVE
LOVE
LOVE
USA 20c

2072–PG 186

Carter G. Woodson

Black Heritage USA 20c

2073–PG 186

SOIL AND WATER
CONSERVATION

2074–PG 186

2075–PG 186

2080–PG 186

2082–2085–PG 186

2076–2079–PG 186

2081–PG 186

2086–PG 186

2088–PG 186

2089–PG 187

2090–PG 187

2087–PG 186

2091–PG 187

2092–PG 187

2093–PG 187

2094–PG 187

2095–PG 187

2096–PG 187

2097–PG 187

2098–PG 187

2099–PG 187

2100–PG 187

2101–PG 187

2102–PG 187

2103–PG 187

2104–PG 187

2105–PG 187

2106–PG 187

2107–PG 187

2108–PG 188

GENERAL ISSUE—SCOTT NO. 2109-2136 (1984-1986)

Vietnam Veterans Memorial USA 20c

2109–PG 188

JEROME KERN
Performing Arts USA

2110–PG 188

Domestic Mail
D
US Postage

2111–2113–PG 188

USA 22

2114–2116–PG 188

USA $10.75

2122–PG 188

School Bus 1920s
3.4 USA

2123–PG 188

Buckboard 1880s
USA 4.9

2125–PG 188

Star Route Truck
5.5 USA 1910s

2126–PG 188

Tricycle 1880s
6 USA

2127–PG 189

Stanley Steamer 1909
USA 12

2131–PG 189

Pushcart 1880s
12.5
USA

2132–PG 189

Ambulance 1860s
8.3 USA

2128–PG 189

Oil Wagon 1890s
10.1 USA

2129–PG 189

Stutz Bearcat 1933
11 USA

2130–PG 189

Iceboat 1880s
USA 14

2134–PG 189

USA 22
Frilled Dogwinkle

USA 22
Reticulated Helmet

USA 22
New England Neptune

USA 22
Calico Scallop

USA 22
Lightning Whelk

2117–2121–PG 188

Dog Sled 1920s
17 USA

2135–PG 189

Bread Wagon 1880s
25 USA

2136–PG 189

161

2138-2141-PG 189

2142-PG 189

2137-PG 189

2144-PG 189

2145-PG 189

2146-PG 190

2143-PG 189

2147-PG 190

2149-PG 190

2150-PG 190

2152-PG 190

2153-PG 190

2154-PG 190

2155-2158-PG 190

2159-PG 190

YMCA Youth Camping USA — Boy Scouts USA — Big Brothers/Big Sisters USA — Camp Fire USA

2160-2163-PG 190

Help End Hunger USA 22

2164-PG 190

Season's Greetings USA 22

2166-PG 191

CHRISTMAS
USA 22

2165-PG 190

Arkansas Statehood
USA 22

2167-PG 191

Margaret Mitchell USA 1

2168-PG 191

Mary Lyon USA 2

2169-PG 191

Paul Dudley White MD USA 3

2170-PG 191

Father Flanagan USA 4

2171-PG 191

Hugo L. Black 5 USA

2172-PG 191

14 USA
Julia Ward Howe

2177-PG 191

Belva Ann Lockwood
USA 17

2179-PG 191

USA 25
Jack London

2183-PG 191

John Harvard USA 56

2191-PG 191

Bernard Revel USA $1

2194-PG 191

Bryan $2 USA
William Jennings

2195-PG 191

Bret Harte USA $5

2196-PG 191

2198–2201–PG 191

2202–PG 192

2203–PG 192

2204–PG 192

2210–PG 192

2211–PG 192

2205–2209–PG 192

2216–PG 192

2217–PG 192

2218–PG 192

2219–PG 192

2220–2223–PG 192

2224–PG 193

Navajo Art USA 22

2240–2243–PG 193

2239–PG 193

2235–2238–PG 193

2244–PG 193

2245–PG 193

2246–PG 193

2247–PG 193

2248–PG 193

2249–PG 193

2250–PG 193

166

2251–PG 193

2275– PG 194

2276–PG 194

2286–2335–PG 194

2336–PG 194

2337–PG 194

2338–PG 194

2349–PG 194

2350–PG 194

2351–2354–PG 194

2355–2359 – PG 194

2360–PG 194

2361–PG 194

2367–PG 194

2368–PG 194

2369–PG 195

2370–PG 195

2371–PG 195

2372–2375–PG 195

2376–PG 195

2377–PG 195

2378–PG 195

2379–PG 195

2380–PG 195

2381–2385
PG 195

2399–PG 195

2400–PG 195

2401–PG 196

2402–PG 196

2403–PG 196

2404–PG 196

Scott No.		Mint Sheet	Plate Block	Fine Unused Each	Fine Used Each
1976. COMMEMORATIVES—AMERICAN BICENTENNIAL					
1976. SPIRIT OF '76					
☐ 1629	13¢ Multicolored	—	—	.35	.12
☐ 1630	13¢ Multicolored	—	—	.35	.12
☐ 1631	13¢ Multicolored	—	—	.35	.12
1976. INTERPHIL '76					
☐ 1632	13¢ Dark Blue, Red, Ultramarine	14.75	1.75	.35	.12
1976. STATE FLAGS					
☐	13¢ All 50 States	25.00	7.50	—	—
☐	13¢ Individual States	—	—	.75	.50

☐ 1633 Delaware	1650 Louisiana	1667 West Virginia	
☐ 1634 Pennsylvania	1651 Indiana	1668 Nevada	
☐ 1635 New Jersey	1652 Mississippi	1669 Nebraska	
☐ 1636 Georgia	1653 Illinois	1670 Colorado	
☐ 1637 Connecticut	1654 Alabama	1671 North Dakota	
☐ 1638 Massachusetts	1655 Maine	1672 South Dakota	
☐ 1639 Maryland	1656 Missouri	1673 Montana	
☐ 1640 South Carolina	1657 Arkansas	1674 Washington	
☐ 1641 New Hampshire	1658 Michigan	1675 Idaho	
☐ 1642 Virginia	1659 Florida	1676 Wyoming	
☐ 1643 New York	1660 Texas	1677 Utah	
☐ 1644 North Carolina	1661 Iowa	1678 Oklahoma	
☐ 1645 Rhode Island	1662 Wisconsin	1679 New Mexico	
☐ 1646 Vermont	1663 California	1680 Arizona	
☐ 1647 Kentucky	1664 Minnesota	1681 Alaska	
☐ 1648 Tennessee	1665 Oregon	1682 Hawaii	
☐ 1649 Ohio	1666 Kansas		

Scott No.		Mint Sheet	Plate Block	Fine Unused Each	Fine Used Each
1976. TELEPHONE CENTENNIAL					
☐ 1683	13¢ Black, Purple, Red	14.00	1.50	.35	.12
1976. COMMERCIAL AVIATION					
☐ 1684	13¢ Multicolored	14.50	3.60	.35	.12
1976. CHEMISTRY					
☐ 1685	13¢ Multicolored	14.50	3.75	.35	.12
1976. BICENTENNIAL SOUVENIR SHEETS					
☐ 1686	65¢ Sheet of 5	—	—	4.60	4.00
☐ 1686a	13¢ Multicolored	—	—	1.20	1.00
☐ 1686b	13¢ Multicolored	—	—	1.20	1.00
☐ 1686c	13¢ Multicolored	—	—	1.20	1.00
☐ 1686d	13¢ Multicolored	—	—	1.20	1.00
☐ 1686e	13¢ Multicolored	—	—	1.20	1.00
☐ 1687	90¢ Sheet of 5	—	—	6.30	5.20
☐ 1687a	18¢ Multicolored	—	—	1.65	1.25
☐ 1687b	18¢ Multicolored	—	—	1.65	1.25
☐ 1687c	18¢ Multicolored	—	—	1.65	1.25
☐ 1687d	18¢ Multicolored	—	—	1.65	1.25

*No hinge pricing from 1941 to date is figured at (N-H ADD 15%)

Scott No.		Mint Sheet	Plate Block	Fine Unused Each	Fine Used Each
☐ 1687e	18¢ Multicolored	—	—	1.75	1.40
☐ 1688	1.20 Sheet of 5	—	—	9.25	7.50
☐ 1688a	24¢ Multicolored	—	—	2.40	1.80
☐ 1688b	24¢ Multicolored	—	—	2.40	1.80
☐ 1688c	24¢ Multicolored	—	—	2.40	1.80
☐ 1688d	24¢ Multicolored	—	—	2.40	1.80
☐ 1688e	24¢ Multicolored	—	—	2.40	1.80
☐ 1689	1.55 Sheet of 5	—	—	11.00	9.50
☐ 1689a	31¢ Multicolored	—	—	2.75	2.20
☐ 1689b	31¢ Multicolored	—	—	2.75	2.20
☐ 1689c	31¢ Multicolored	—	—	2.75	2.20
☐ 1689d	31¢ Multicolored	—	—	2.75	2.20
☐ 1689e	31¢ Multicolored	—	—	2.75	2.20

1976. BENJAMIN FRANKLIN
☐ 1690	13¢ Blue & Multicolored	12.50	1.50	.35	.12

1976. DECLARATION OF INDEPENDENCE
☐ 1691	13¢ Multicolored	—	—	.35	.15
☐ 1692	13¢ Multicolored	—	—	.35	.15
☐ 1693	13¢ Multicolored	—	—	.35	.15
☐ 1694	13¢ Multicolored	—	—	.35	.15

1976. OLYMPIC GAMES
☐ 1695	13¢ Multicolored	—	—	.58	.15
☐ 1696	13¢ Multicolored	—	—	.58	.15
☐ 1697	13¢ Multicolored	—	—	.58	.15
☐ 1698	13¢ Multicolored	—	—	.58	.15

1976. CLARA MAASS
☐ 1699	13¢ Multicolored	10.70	4.00	.34	.12

1976. ADOLPH S. OCHS
☐ 1700	13¢ Black, Green & White	8.75	1.45	.42	.12

1976. CHRISTMAS
☐ 1701	13¢ Multicolored	12.50	3.90	.28	.12
☐ 1702	13¢ Multicolored	12.50	3.65	.28	.12
☐ 1703	13¢ Multicolored	12.50	6.60	.28	.12

1977. COMMEMORATIVES

1977. WASHINGTON
☐ 1704	13¢ Multicolored	10.90	3.40	.30	.10

1977. SOUND RECORDING CENTENARY
☐ 1705	13¢ Multicolored	13.10	1.35	.30	.10

1977. PUEBLO ART
☐ 1706	13¢ Multicolored	—	—	.25	.12
☐ 1707	13¢ Multicolored	—	—	.25	.12
☐ 1708	13¢ Multicolored	—	—	.25	.12
☐ 1709	13¢ Multicolored	—	—	.25	.12

*No hinge pricing from 1941 to date is figured at (N-H ADD 15%)

Scott No.		Mint Sheet	Plate Block	Fine Unused Each	Fine Used Each
1977. TRANSATLANTIC FLIGHT					
☐ 1710	13¢ Multicolored	12.90	4.00	.29	.10
1977. COLORADO					
☐ 1711	13¢ Multicolored	12.90	4.00	.29	.10
1977. BUTTERFLIES					
☐ 1712	13¢ Multicolored	—	—	.30	.11
☐ 1713	13¢ Multicolored	—	—	.30	.11
☐ 1714	13¢ Multicolored	—	—	.30	.11
☐ 1715	13¢ Multicolored	—	—	.30	.11
1977. LAFAYETTE					
☐ 1716	13¢ Multicolored	11.20	1.70	.30	.13
1977. SKILLED HANDS					
☐ 1717	13¢ Multicolored	—	—	.38	.13
☐ 1718	13¢ Multicolored	—	—	.38	.13
☐ 1719	13¢ Multicolored	—	—	.38	.13
☐ 1720	13¢ Multicolored	—	—	.38	.13
1977. PEACE BRIDGE					
☐ 1721	13¢ Blue & White	13.50	1.60	.30	.10
1977. BATTLE OF ORISKANY					
☐ 1722	13¢ Multicolored	11.20	3.60	.29	.11
1977. ENERGY CONSERVATION AND DEVELOPMENT					
☐ 1723	13¢ Multicolored	—	—	.32	.10
☐ 1724	13¢ Multicolored	—	—	.32	.10
1977. ALTA. CALIFORNIA BICENTENNIAL					
☐ 1725	13¢ Multicolored	13.00	1.50	.33	.11
1977. ARTICLES OF CONFEDERATION					
☐ 1726	13¢ Red & Brown on Tan	13.00	1.60	.30	.11
1977. TALKING PICTURES					
☐ 1727	13¢ Multicolored	13.10	1.60	.31	.12
1977. SURRENDER AT SARATOGA					
☐ 1728	13¢ Multicolored	11.00	4.10	.31	.12
1977. CHRISTMAS					
☐ 1729	13¢ Multicolored	29.00	8.00	.30	.11
☐ 1730	13¢ Multicolored	27.00	8.00	.30	.11
1978. CARL SANDBURG					
☐ 1731	13¢ Brown, Black, White	12.50	1.70	.30	.11
1978. CAPTAIN COOK ISSUES					
☐ 1732	13¢ Dark Blue	—	1.70	.30	.10
☐ 1733	13¢ Green	—	1.70	.30	.10

*No hinge pricing from 1941 to date is figured at (N-H ADD 15%)

Scott No.		Mint Sheet	Plate Block	Fine Unused Each	Fine Used Each
1978. INDIAN HEAD PENNY					
☐ 1734	13¢ Brown & Blue Green	41.00	3.30	.35	.15
1978. NONDENOMINATED "A"					
☐ 1735	15¢ Orange	33.00	1.90	.37	.11
1978. ROSES					
☐ 1737	15¢ Multicolored	—	—	.41	.10
1980. WINDMILL—VIRGINIA					
☐ 1738	15¢ Black	—	—	.41	.10
1980. WINDMILL—RHODE ISLAND					
☐ 1739	15¢ Black	—	—	.51	.10
1980. WINDMILL—MASSACHUSETTS					
☐ 1740	15¢ Black	—	—	.51	.10
1980. WINDMILL—ILLINOIS					
☐ 1741	15¢ Black	—	—	.51	.10
1980. WINDMILL—TEXAS					
☐ 1742	15¢ Black	—	—	.51	.10
1978. HARRIET TUBMAN					
☐ 1744	13¢ Multicolored	13.60	4.00	.35	.11
1978. AMERICAN FOLK ART ISSUE					
☐ 1745	13¢ Multicolored	—	—	.40	.14
☐ 1746	13¢ Multicolored	—	—	.40	.14
☐ 1747	13¢ Multicolored	—	—	.40	.14
☐ 1748	13¢ Multicolored	—	—	.40	.14
1978. AMERICAN DANCE ISSUE					
☐ 1749	13¢ Multicolored	—	—	.38	.14
☐ 1750	13¢ Multicolored	—	—	.38	.14
☐ 1751	13¢ Multicolored	—	—	.38	.14
☐ 1752	13¢ Multicolored	—	—	.38	.14
1978. FRENCH ALLIANCE					
☐ 1753	13¢ Blue, Black & Red	11.00	1.70	.31	.10
1978. EARLY CANCER DETECTION					
☐ 1754	13¢ Brown	14.00	1.75	.28	.10
1978. JIMMIE RODGERS					
☐ 1755	13¢ Multicolored	14.00	4.00	.33	.10
1978. GEORGE M. COHAN					
☐ 1756	13¢ Multicolored	16.00	4.40	.41	.12
1978. "CAPAX" '78 SOUVENIR SHEET					
☐ 1757	13¢ Multicolored, set of 6	12.90	—	2.70	2.60
1978. PHOTOGRAPHY					
☐ 1758	15¢ Multicolored	12.70	4.80	.43	.10

*No hinge pricing from 1941 to date is figured at (N-H ADD 15%)

Scott No.		Mint Sheet	Plate Block	Fine Unused Each	Fine Used Each
1978. VIKING MISSION TO MARS					
☐ 1759	15¢ Multicolored	17.50	2.25	.43	.11
1978. AMERICAN OWL ISSUE					
☐ 1760	15¢ Multicolored	—	—	.49	.13
☐ 1761	15¢ Multicolored	—	—	.49	.13
☐ 1762	15¢ Multicolored	—	—	.49	.13
☐ 1763	15¢ Multicolored	—	—	.49	.13
1978. AMERICAN TREES ISSUE					
☐ 1764	15¢ Multicolored	—	—	.49	.13
☐ 1765	15¢ Multicolored	—	—	.49	.13
☐ 1766	15¢ Multicolored	—	—	.49	.13
☐ 1767	15¢ Multicolored	—	—	.49	.13
1978. CHRISTMAS ISSUES					
☐ 1768	15¢ Multicolored	29.00	—	.41	.11
☐ 1769	15¢ Multicolored	29.00	—	.41	.11
1979. ROBERT F. KENNEDY ISSUE					
☐ 1770	15¢ Blue	15.70	1.95	.37	.09
1979. MARTIN LUTHER KING ISSUE					
☐ 1771	15¢ Multicolored	16.70	4.70	.37	.09
1979. INTERNATIONAL YEAR OF THE CHILD					
☐ 1772	15¢ Light Brown	16.70	2.11	.37	.09
1979. JOHN STEINBECK ISSUE					
☐ 1773	15¢ Dark Blue	16.70	2.12	.37	.09
1979. ALBERT EINSTEIN ISSUE					
☐ 1774	15¢ Brown	16.70	2.11	.37	.09
1979. PENNSYLVANIA TOLEWARE ISSUE					
☐ 1775	15¢ Multicolored	—	—	.40	.09
☐ 1776	15¢ Multicolored	—	—	.40	.09
☐ 1777	15¢ Multicolored	—	—	.40	.09
☐ 1778	15¢ Multicolored	—	—	.40	.09
1979. ARCHITECTURE U.S.A. ISSUE					
☐ 1779	15¢ Light Blue & Brown	—	—	.45	.11
☐ 1780	15¢ Light Blue & Brown	—	—	.45	.11
☐ 1781	15¢ Light Blue & Brown	—	—	.45	.11
☐ 1782	15¢ Light Blue & Brown	—	—	.45	.11
1979. ENDANGERED FLORA ISSUE					
☐ 1783	15¢ Multicolored	—	—	.45	.11
☐ 1784	15¢ Multicolored	—	—	.45	.11
☐ 1785	15¢ Multicolored	—	—	.45	.11
☐ 1786	15¢ Multicolored	—	—	.45	.11
1979. SEEING FOR ME ISSUE					
☐ 1787	15¢ Multicolored	16.10	7.20	.42	.11

*No hinge pricing from 1941 to date is figured at (N-H ADD 15%)

Scott No.	Mint Sheet	Plate Block	Fine Unused Each	Fine Used Each
1979. SPECIAL OLYMPICS				
☐ 1788 15¢ Multicolored	16.50	4.10	.39	.11
1979. JOHN PAUL JONES				
☐ 1789 15¢ Multicolored	19.00	5.25	.44	.12
1979. OLYMPIC DECATHLON				
☐ 1790 10¢ Multicolored	16.50	5.00	.35	.20
1979. OLYMPIC RUNNERS				
☐ 1791 15¢ Multicolored	—	—	.47	.15
1979. OLYMPIC SWIMMERS				
☐ 1792 15¢ Multicolored	—	—	.47	.15
1979. OLYMPIC ROWERS				
☐ 1793 15¢ Multicolored	—	—	.47	.15
1979. OLYMPIC EQUESTRIAN				
☐ 1794 15¢ Multicolored	—	—	.47	.15
1979. OLYMPIC SKATER				
☐ 1795 15¢ Multicolored	—	—	.55	.13
1979. OLYMPIC SKIER				
☐ 1796 15¢ Multicolored	—	—	.55	.13
1979. OLYMPIC SKI JUMPER				
☐ 1797 15¢ Multicolored	—	—	.55	.13
1979. OLYMPIC GOALTENDER				
☐ 1798 15¢ Multicolored	—	—	.55	.13
1979. MADONNA				
☐ 1799 15¢ Multicolored	32.00	4.60	.40	.11
1979. CHRISTMAS				
☐ 1800 15¢ Multicolored	32.00	4.60	.40	.11
1979. WILL ROGERS				
☐ 1801 15¢ Multicolored	17.50	4.80	.40	.11
1979. VIETNAM VETERANS				
☐ 1802 15¢ Multicolored	17.00	4.50	.40	.11
1980. W.C. FIELDS				
☐ 1803 15¢ Multicolored	17.00	4.80	.40	.11
1980. BENJAMIN BANNEKER				
☐ 1804 15¢ Multicolored	17.00	4.80	.40	.11
1980. LETTERS PRESERVE MEMORIES				
☐ 1805 15¢ Violet & Bistre	—	—	.41	.10
1980. PRESERVE MEMORIES—P.S. WRITE SOON				
☐ 1806 15¢ Violet & Pink	—	—	.41	.10

*No hinge pricing from 1941 to date is figured at (N-H ADD 15%)

Scott No.	Mint Sheet	Plate Block	Fine Unused Each	Fine Used Each
1980. LETTERS LIFT SPIRITS				
☐ 1807 15¢ Green & Pink & Orange	—	—	.43	.10
1980. LIFT SPIRITS—P.S. WRITE SOON				
☐ 1808 15¢ Green & Yellow Green	—	—	.43	.10
1980. LETTERS SHAPE OPINIONS				
☐ 1809 15¢ Scarlet & Blue	—	—	.43	.10
1980. SHAPE OPINIONS—P.S. WRITE SOON				
☐ 1810 15¢ Scarlet & Blue	—	—	.43	.10
1980. AMERICANA SERIES				
☐ 1811 1¢ Dark Blue & Green	—	—	.43	.08
☐ 1813 3.5¢ Purple & Yellow	—	—	.13	.08
1980. NONDENOMINATED "B"				
☐ 1818 18¢ Purple	—	—	.32	.09
1980. FRANCIS PERKINS				
☐ 1821 15¢ Blue	16.50	1.80	.40	.11
1980. DOLLY MADISON				
☐ 1822 15¢ Multicolored	52.00	2.70	40	.11
1980. EMILY BISSELL				
☐ 1823 15¢ Scarlet & Black	16.50	1.80	.40	.11
1980. HELEN KELLER—ANNE SULLIVAN				
☐ 1824 15¢ Multicolored	16.50	1.80	.40	.11
1980. VETERANS ADMINISTRATION				
☐ 1825 15¢ Carmine & Blue	—	—	.40	.11
1980. GENERAL BERNARDO de G'ALVEZ				
☐ 1826 15¢ Multicolored	—	—	.40	.11
1980. CORAL REEFS—VIRGIN ISLANDS				
☐ 1827 15¢ Multicolored	—	—	.41	.12
1980. CORAL REEFS—FLORIDA				
☐ 1828 15¢ Multicolored	—	—	.41	.12
1980. CORAL REEFS—AMERICAN SAMOA				
☐ 1829 15¢ Multicolored	—	—	.41	.12
1980. CORAL REEFS—HAWAII				
☐ 1830 15¢ Multicolored	—	—	.41	.11
1980. ORGANIZED LABOR				
☐ 1831 15¢ Multicolored	16.50	4.30	.38	.11
1980. EDITH WHARTON				
☐ 1832 15¢ Violet	16.50	4.30	.38	.11
1980. EDUCATION				
☐ 1833 15¢ Multicolored	16.50	2.60	.38	.11

*No hinge pricing from 1941 to date is figured at (N-H ADD 15%)

Scott No.		Mint Sheet	Plate Block	Fine Unused Each	Fine Used Each
1980. INDIAN ARTS					
☐ 1834	15¢ Multicolored	—	5.20	.43	.11
☐ 1835	15¢ Multicolored	—	5.20	.43	.11
☐ 1836	15¢ Multicolored	—	5.20	.43	.11
☐ 1837	15¢ Multicolored	—	5.20	.43	.11
1980. ARCHITECTURE					
☐ 1838	15¢ Black & Red	—	2.30	.47	.13
☐ 1839	15¢ Black & Red	—	2.30	.47	.13
☐ 1840	16¢ Black & Red	—	2.30	.47	.13
☐ 1841	15¢ Black & Red	—	2.30	.47	.13
1980. CHRISTMAS ISSUE					
☐ 1842	15¢ Multicolored	12.00	5.40	.40	.11
☐ 1843	15¢ Multicolored	12.00	7.50	1.10	.11
1982. DOROTHEA DIX					
☐ 1844	1¢ Black	2.10	.26	.07	.05
1983. IGOR STRAVINSKY					
☐ 1845	2¢ Brown	2.90	.28	.07	.05
1983. HENRY CLAY					
☐ 1846	3¢ Green	4.20	.32	.07	.05
1983. CARL SCHURZ					
☐ 1847	4¢ Purple	6.20	.51	.09	.05
1983. PEARL BUCK					
☐ 1848	5¢ Reddish Brown	8.40	.73	.13	.07
1985. WALTER LIPPMANN					
☐ 1849	6¢ Orange	10.50	.82	.13	.07
1985. ABRAHAM BALDWIN					
☐ 1850	7¢ Red	12.50	.84	.14	.07
1985. HENRY KNOX					
☐ 1851	8¢ Black	12.60	.96	.13	.07
1985. SYLVANUS THAYER					
☐ 1852	9¢ Green	15.00	1.40	.15	.07
1984. RICHARD RUSSELL					
☐ 1853	10¢ Blue	16.50	1.50	.17	.07
1985. ALDEN PARTRIDGE					
☐ 1854	11¢ Blue	18.50	1.65	.19	.07
1982. CRAZY HORSE					
☐ 1855	13¢ Brown	20.00	1.70	.19	.07
1985. SINCLAIR LEWIS					
☐ 1856	14¢ Green	21.50	1.72	.19	.07

*No hinge pricing from 1941 to date is figured at (N-H ADD 15%)

Scott No.		Mint Sheet	Plate Block	Fine Unused Each	Fine Used Each
1981. RACHEL CARSON					
☐ 1857	17¢ Blue Green	25.00	1.73	.23	.09
1981. GEORGE MASON					
☐ 1858	18¢ Dark Blue	28.00	1.73	.25	.11
1980. SEQUOYAH					
☐ 1859	19¢ Light Brown	31.00	1.73	.30	.11
1982. RALPH BUNCHE					
☐ 1860	20¢ Carmine	34.00	1.73	.33	.11
1983. THOMAS H. GALLAUDET					
☐ 1861	20¢ Green	32.00	1.73	.33	.11
1984. HARRY S. TRUMAN					
☐ 1862	20¢ Black & White	32.00	1.73	.33	.11
1985. JOHN J. AUDUBON					
☐ 1863	22¢ Blue	36.00	1.73	.36	.11
1984. FRANK C. LAUBACH					
☐ 1864	30¢ Dark Green	45.00	2.00	.45	.11
1981. CHARLES DREW					
☐ 1865	35¢ Gray	50.00	2.30	.51	.11
1982. ROBERT MILLIKAN					
☐ 1866	37¢ Blue	55.00	2.30	.51	.11
1985. GRENVILLE CLARK					
☐ 1867	39¢ Reddish Purple	57.00	2.60	.62	.11
1984. LILLIAN M. GILBRETH					
☐ 1868	40¢ Green	63.00	2.60	.72	.11
1985. CHESTER W. NIMITZ					
☐ 1869	50¢ Dark Brown	68.00	4.10	.85	.19
1981. EVERETT M. DIRKSEN					
☐ 1874	15¢ Dark Green	17.10	2.30	.40	.11
1981. WHITNEY M. YOUNG					
☐ 1875	15¢ Multicolored	17.00	2.00	.40	.11
1981. FLOWERS					
☐ 1876	18¢ Multicolored	—	—	.45	.13
☐ 1877	18¢ Multicolored	—	—	.45	.13
☐ 1878	18¢ Multicolored	—	—	.45	.13
☐ 1879	18¢ Multicolored	—	—	.45	.13
1981. AMERICAN WILDLIFE					
☐ 1880	18¢ Light Brown	—	—	.58	.14
☐ 1881	18¢ Light Brown	—	—	.58	.14
☐ 1882	18¢ Light Brown	—	—	.58	.14
☐ 1883	18¢ Light Brown	—	—	.58	.14

*No hinge pricing from 1941 to date is figured at (N-H ADD 15%)

Scott No.		Mint Sheet	Plate Block	Fine Unused Each	Fine Used Each
☐ 1884	18¢ Light Brown	—	—	.59	.14
☐ 1885	18¢ Light Brown	—	—	.59	.14
☐ 1886	18¢ Light Brown	—	—	.59	.14
☐ 1887	18¢ Light Brown	—	—	.59	.14
☐ 1888	18¢ Light Brown	—	—	.59	.14
☐ 1889	18¢ Light Brown	Booklet	5.60	—	—

1981. FLAG—FOR AMBER WAVES OF GRAIN

☐ 1890	18¢ Multicolored	41.00	10.00	.45	.11

1981. FLAG—FROM SEA TO SHINING SEA

☐ 1891	18¢ Multicolored	—PR.	4.20	.50	.11

1981. U.S.A.

☐ 1892	6¢ Carmine & Dark Blue	—	—	.38	.14

1981. FLAG—FOR PURPLE MOUNTAIN MAJESTIES

☐ 1893	18¢ Multicolored	—	—	.43	.12

1982. FLAG OVER SUPREME COURT

☐ 1894	20¢ Carmine & Dark blue	33.00	2.70	.36	.16

1982. MAIL WAGON

☐ 1900	9.3¢ Carmine	—	—	.22	.13

1984. RAILROAD CABOOSE

☐ 1902	11¢ Red, coil	—	—	.22	.09

1981. ELECTRIC CAR

☐ 1905	17¢ Blue	—LP.	2.00	.32	.08

1981. SURREY

☐ 1906	18¢ Brown	—LP.	2.00	.32	.08

1982. FIRE PUMPER

☐ 1907	20¢ Red Orange	—	—	.37	.19

1981. AMERICAN RED CROSS

☐ 1910	18¢ Multicolored	19.50	2.00	.45	.10

1981. SAVINGS AND LOAN

☐ 1911	18¢ Multicolored	19.50	2.00	.45	.10

1981. SPACE ACHIEVEMENT

☐ 1912	18¢ Multicolored	—	5.00	.53	.17
☐ 1913	18¢ Multicolored	—	5.00	.53	.17
☐ 1914	18¢ Multicolored	—	5.00	.53	.17
☐ 1915	18¢ Multicolored	—	5.00	.53	.17
☐ 1916	18¢ Multicolored	—	5.00	.53	.17
☐ 1917	18¢ Multicolored	—	5.00	.53	.17
☐ 1918	18¢ Multicolored	—	5.00	.53	.17
☐ 1919	18¢ Multicolored	—	5.00	.53	.17

1981. PROFESSIONAL MANAGEMENT

☐ 1920	18¢ Dark Blue & Black	20.00	2.40	.53	.12

*No hinge pricing from 1941 to date is figured at (N-H ADD 15%)

Scott No.		Mint Sheet	Plate Block	Fine Unused Each	Fine Used Each
1981. PRESERVATION OF WILDLIFE HABITATS					
☐ 1921	18¢ Multicolored	—	2.40	.52	.12
☐ 1922	18¢ Multicolored	—	2.40	.52	.12
☐ 1923	18¢ Multicolored	—	2.40	.52	.12
☐ 1924	18¢ Multicolored	—	2.40	.52	.12
1981. DISABLED PERSONS					
☐ 1925	18¢ Multicolored	21.00	2.40	.53	.12
1981. EDNA ST. VINCENT MILLAY					
☐ 1926	18¢ Multicolored	20.00	2.40	.53	.12
1981. ALCOHOLISM					
☐ 1927	18¢ Dark Blue	29.00	16.00	.47	.10
1981. ARCHITECTURE					
☐ 1928	18¢ Brown & Black	—	2.40	.50	.12
☐ 1929	18¢ Brown & Black	—	2.40	.50	.12
☐ 1930	18¢ Brown & Black	—	2.40	.50	.12
☐ 1931	18¢ Brown & Black	—	2.40	.50	.12
1981. BABE ZAHARIAS					
☐ 1932	18¢ Purple	—	2.30	.53	.12
1981. BOBBY JONES					
☐ 1933	18¢ Dark Green	—	2.30	.53	.12
1981. FREDERIC REMINGTON					
☐ 1934	18¢ Light Brown & Green	21.00	2.30	.51	.12
1981. JAMES HOBAN					
☐ 1935	18¢ Multicolored	23.00	2.90	.51	.12
1981. JAMES HOBAN					
☐ 1936	20¢ Multicolored	22.00	2.60	.51	.11
1981. YORKTOWN MAP					
☐ 1937	18¢ Multicolored	—	—	.51	.11
1981. VIRGINIA CAPES MAP					
☐ 1938	18¢ Multicolored	—	—	.51	.11
1981. CHRISTMAS—BOTTICELLI					
☐ 1939	20¢ Multicolored	45.00	2.40	.51	.11
1981. SEASONS GREETINGS					
☐ 1940	20¢ Multicolored	22.00	2.40	.51	.11
1981. JOHN HANSON					
☐ 1941	20¢ Multicolored	22.00	2.40	.51	.11
1981. DESERT PLANTS					
☐ 1942	Multicolored	—	2.50	.51	.11
☐ 1943	Multicolored	—	2.50	.51	.11

*No hinge pricing from 1941 to date is figured at (N-H ADD 15%)

Scott No.		Mint Sheet	Plate Block	Fine Unused Each	Fine Used Each
☐ 1944	Multicolored	—	2.50	.51	.11
☐ 1945	Multicolored	—	2.50	.51	.11

1981. "C" EAGLE—SINGLE
| ☐ 1946 | 20¢ Light Brown | 43.00 | 2.70 | .51 | .11 |

1981. "C" EAGLE—COIL SINGLE
| ☐ 1947 | 20¢ Light Brown | — | — | .51 | .11 |

1981. "C" EAGLE—BOOKLET SINGLE
| ☐ 1948 | 20¢ Light Brown | — | — | .51 | .11 |

1981. BIGHORN SHEEP
| ☐ 1949 | 20¢ Dark Blue | — | — | .51 | .11 |

1982. FRANKLIN ROOSEVELT
| ☐ 1950 | 20¢ Dark Blue | 20.00 | 2.30 | .51 | .11 |

1982. "LOVE" FLOWERS
| ☐ 1951 | 20¢ Multicolored | 21.50 | 2.30 | .51 | .11 |

1982. GEORGE WASHINGTON
| ☐ 1952 | 20¢ Multicolored | 21.50 | 2.30 | .51 | .11 |

1982. BIRDS AND FLOWERS
| ☐ 1953-2002 | 20¢ Multicolored | 21.50 | — | .51 | .11 |

1982. THE NETHERLANDS
| ☐ 2003 | 20¢ Dark Blue & Red | 21.50 | 2.30 | .51 | .11 |

1982. LIBRARY OF CONGRESS
| ☐ 2004 | 20¢ Rose & Dark Gray | 21.50 | 2.30 | .51 | .11 |

1982. CONSUMER EDUCATION
| ☐ 2005 | 20¢ Light Blue & Dark Blue | — | — | .51 | .11 |

1982. KNOXVILLE WORLD'S FAIR
☐ 2006	20¢ Multicolored	—	2.30	.51	.11
☐ 2007	20¢ Multicolored	—	2.30	.51	.11
☐ 2008	20¢ Multicolored	—	2.30	.51	.11
☐ 2009	20¢ Multicolored	—	2.30	.51	.11

1982. HORATIO ALGER
| ☐ 2010 | 20¢ Carmine & Black | 21.50 | 2.30 | .51 | .11 |

1982. AGING TOGETHER
| ☐ 2011 | 20¢ Light Rose | 21.50 | 2.30 | .51 | .11 |

1982. THE BARRYMORES
| ☐ 2012 | 20¢ Multicolored | 21.50 | 2.30 | .46 | .11 |

1982. DR. MARY WALKER
| ☐ 2013 | 20¢ Multicolored | 21.50 | 2.30 | .46 | .11 |

*No hinge pricing from 1941 to date is figured at (N-H ADD 15%)

Scott No.	Mint Sheet	Plate Block	Fine Unused Each	Fine Used Each
1982. INTERNATIONAL PEACE GARDEN				
☐ 2014 20¢ Multicolored	20.50	2.30	.41	.11
1982. AMERICA'S LIBRARIES				
☐ 2015 20¢ Orange-Red & Black	20.50	2.30	.41	.11
1982. JACKIE ROBINSON				
☐ 2016 20¢ Multicolored	20.50	2.30	.41	.11
1982. TOURO SYNAGOGUE				
☐ 2017 20¢ Multicolored	20.50	2.30	.41	.11
1982. WOLF TRAP FARM PARK				
☐ 2018 20¢ Multicolored	20.50	2.30	.41	.11
1982. ARCHITECTURAL—WRIGHT				
☐ 2019 20¢ Black and Brown	—	—	.41	.11
1982. ARCHITECTURE—VAN DER ROHE				
☐ 2020 20¢ Black and Brown	—	—	.41	.11
1982. ARCHITECTURE—GROPIUS				
☐ 2021 20¢ Black and Brown	—	—	.41	.11
1982. ARCHITECTURE—SAARINEN				
☐ 2022 20¢ Black and Brown	—	—	.41	.11
☐ Architecture, above four attached	20.50	2.30	.41	.11
1982. FRANCIS OF ASSISI				
☐ 2023 20¢ Multicolored	20.50	2.30	.41	.11
1982. PONCE DE LEON				
☐ 2024 20¢ Multicolored	20.50	2.30	.41	.11
1982. CHRISTMAS ISSUE, CAT AND DOG				
☐ 2025 13¢ Multicolored	14.00	2.30	.41	.11
1982. CHRISTMAS ISSUE, TIEPOLO'S "MADONNA AND CHILD"				
☐ 2026 20¢ Multicolored	21.50	2.20	.41	.11
1982. SEASON'S GREETINGS, SLEDDING				
☐ 2027 20¢ Multicolored	21.50	—	.41	.11
1982. SEASON'S GREETINGS, BUILDING SNOWMAN				
☐ 2028 20¢ Multicolored	—	—	.41	.11
1982. SEASON'S GREETINGS, ICE SKATING				
☐ 2029 20¢ Multicolored	—	—	.41	.11
1982. SEASON'S GREETINGS, TRIMMING TREE				
☐ 2030 20¢ Multicolored	—	—	.41	.11
☐ Season's Greetings, above four attached.............	21.50	2.25	.41	.11
1982. SCIENCE AND INDUSTRY				
☐ 2031 20¢ Multicolored	21.50	2.25	.41	.11

*No hinge pricing from 1941 to date is figured at (N-H ADD 15%)

Scott No.	Mint Sheet	Plate Block	Fine Unused Each	Fine Used Each
1983. BALLOONING				
☐ 2032 20¢ Multicolored	—	—	.46	.11
1982. BALLOONING				
☐ 2033 20¢ Multicolored	—	—	.44	.11
1982. BALLOONING				
☐ 2034 20¢ Multicolored	—	—	.44	.11
1982. BALLOONING				
☐ 2035 20¢ Multicolored	—	—	.44	.11
☐ Ballooning, above four attached	18.00	2.20	.44	.11
1983. TREATY OF AMITY				
☐ 2036 20¢ Blue and Black	20.50	2.20	.44	.11
1983. CIVILIAN CONSERVATION CORPS				
☐ 2037 20¢ Multicolored	20.50	2.20	.44	.11
1983. JOSEPH PRIESTLEY				
☐ 2038 20¢ Rust Brown	20.50	2.20	.44	.11
1983. VOLUNTEER				
☐ 2039 20¢ Black and Red	20.50	2.20	.44	.11
1983. CONCORD				
☐ 2040 20¢ Beige	20.50	2.20	.44	.11
1983. BROOKLYN BRIDGE				
☐ 2041 20¢ Blue	20.50	2.20	.44	.11
1983. TENNESSEE VALLEY AUTHORITY				
☐ 2042 20¢ Multicolored	20.50	2.20	.44	.11
1983. PHYSICAL FITNESS				
☐ 2043 20¢ Multicolored	20.50	2.20	.44	.11
1982. SCOTT JOPLIN				
☐ 2044 20¢ Multicolored	20.50	2.20	.44	.11
1983. MEDAL OF HONOR				
☐ 2045 20¢ Multicolored	19.00	2.20	.44	.11
1983. BABE RUTH				
☐ 2046 20¢ Blue	20.50	2.20	.44	.11
1983. NATHANIEL HAWTHORNE				
☐ 2047 20¢ Multicolored	20.50	2.20	.44	.11
1983. SUMMER OLYMPICS 1984				
☐ 2048 13¢ Multicolored	—	—	.30	.11
1983. SUMMER OLYMPICS 1984				
☐ 2049 13¢ Multicolored	—	—	.30	.11
1983. SUMMER OLYMPICS 1984				
☐ 2050 13¢ Multicolored	—	—	.30	.11

*No hinge pricing from 1941 to date is figured at (N-H ADD 15%)

Scott No.	Mint Sheet	Plate Block	Fine Unused Each	Fine Used Each
1983. SUMMER OLYMPICS 1984				
☐ 2051 13¢ Multicolored	—	—	.30	.11
1983. TREATY OF PARIS				
☐ 2052 20¢ Multicolored	20.50	2.20	.43	.11
1983. CIVIL SERVICE				
☐ 2053 20¢ Multicolored	20.50	2.20	.43	.11
1983. METROPOLITAN OPERA				
☐ 2054 20¢ Yellow and Brown	20.50	2.20	.43	.11
1983. INVENTORS				
☐ 2055 20¢ Multicolored	—	—	.43	.11
1983. INVENTORS				
☐ 2056 20¢ Multicolored	—	—	.43	.11
1983. INVENTORS				
☐ 2057 20¢ Multicolored	—	—	.43	.11
1983. INVENTORS				
☐ 2058 20¢ Multicolored	—	—	.43	.11
1983. STREETCARS				
☐ 2059 20¢ Multicolored	—	—	.43	.11
1983. STREETCARS				
☐ 2060 20¢ Multicolored	—	—	.43	.11
1983. STREETCARS				
☐ 2061 20¢ Multicolored	—	—	.43	.11
1983. STREETCARS				
☐ 2062 20¢ Multicolored	—	—	.43	.11
1983. CHRISTMAS, MADONNA				
☐ 2063 20¢ Multicolored	20.50	2.20	.43	.11
1983. CHRISTMAS, SEASON'S GREETINGS				
☐ 2064 20¢ Multicolored	20.50	2.20	.43	.11
1983. MARTIN LUTHER				
☐ 2065 20¢ Multicolored	20.50	2.20	.43	.11
1984. ALASKA STATEHOOD				
☐ 2066 20¢ Multicolored	20.50	2.20	.43	.11
1984. WINTER OLYMPICS 1984				
☐ 2067 20¢ Multicolored	—	—	.43	.11
1984. WINTER OLYMPICS 1984				
☐ 2068 20¢ Multicolored	—	—	.43	.11
1984. WINTER OLYMPICS 1984				
☐ 2069 20¢ Multicolored	—	—	.43	.11

*No hinge pricing from 1941 to date is figured at (N-H ADD 15%)

Scott No.	Mint Sheet	Plate Block	Fine Unused Each	Fine Used Each
1984. WINTER OLYMPICS 1984				
☐ 2070　20¢ Multicolored	—	—	.42	.11
1984. FEDERAL DEPOSIT INSURANCE CORPORATION				
☐ 2071　20¢ Red & Yellow	17.70	1.80	.42	.11
1984. LOVE				
☐ 2072　20¢ Multicolored	17.70	1.80	.42	.11
1984. CARTER G. WOODSON				
☐ 2073　20¢ Multicolored	17.70	1.80	.42	.11
1984. SOIL AND WATER CONSERVATION				
☐ 2074　20¢ Multicolored	17.70	1.80	.42	.11
1984. CREDIT UNION				
☐ 2075　20¢ Multicolored	17.70	1.80	.42	.11
1984. ORCHIDS				
☐ 2076　20¢ Multicolored	—	—	.42	.11
1984. ORCHIDS				
☐ 2077　20¢ Multicolored	—	—	.42	.11
1984. ORCHIDS				
☐ 2078　20¢ Multicolored	—	—	.42	.11
1984. ORCHIDS				
☐ 2079　20¢ Multicolored	—	—	.42	.11
1984. HAWAII STATEHOOD				
☐ 2080　20¢ Blue & Yellow	17.70	1.80	.42	.11
1984. NATIONAL ARCHIVES				
☐ 2081　20¢ Brown & Black	17.70	1.80	.42	.11
1984. SUMMER OLYMPICS 1984				
☐ 2082　20¢ Multicolored	—	—	.42	.11
1984. SUMMER OLYMPICS 1984				
☐ 2083　20¢ Multicolored	—	—	.42	.11
1984. SUMMER OLYMPICS 1984				
☐ 2084　20¢ Multicolored	—	—	.42	.11
1984. SUMMER OLYMPICS 1984				
☐ 2085　20¢ Multicolored	—	—	.42	.11
1984. LOUISIANA WORLD'S FAIR				
☐ 2086　20¢ Multicolored	17.70	1.80	.42	.11
1984. HEALTH RESEARCH				
☐ 2087　20¢ Multicolored	17.70	1.80	.42	.11
1984. DOUGLAS FAIRBANKS				
☐ 2088　20¢ Black & White	17.70	1.80	.42	.11

*No hinge pricing from 1941 to date is figured at (N-H ADD 15%)

Scott No.	Mint Sheet	Plate Block	Fine Unused Each	Fine Used Each
1984. JIM THORPE				
☐ 2089 20¢ Black & White	17.70	1.80	.40	.11
1984. JOHN McCORMACK				
☐ 2090 20¢ Multicolored	17.70	1.80	.40	.11
1984. ST. LAWRENCE SEAWAY				
☐ 2091 20¢ Multicolored	17.70	1.80	.40	.11
1984. WATERFOWL PRESERVATION				
☐ 2092 20¢ Multicolored	17.70	1.80	.40	.11
1984. ROANOKE VOYAGES 1584				
☐ 2093 20¢ Multicolored	17.70	1.80	.40	.11
1984. HERMAN MELVILLE				
☐ 2094 20¢ Green	17.70	1.80	.40	.11
1984. HORACE MOSES				
☐ 2095 20¢ Orange & Brown	17.70	1.80	.40	.11
1984. SMOKEY THE BEAR				
☐ 2096 20¢ Multicolored	17.70	1.80	.40	.11
1984. ROBERTO CLEMENTE				
☐ 2097 20¢ Multicolored	17.70	1.80	.40	.11
1984. DOGS: BEAGLE				
☐ 2098 20¢ Multicolored	—	—	.42	.11
1984. DOGS: RETRIEVER				
☐ 2099 20¢ Multicolored	—	—	.42	.11
1984. DOGS: MALAMUTE				
☐ 2100 20¢ Multicolored	—	—	.42	.11
1984. DOGS: COONHOUND				
☐ 2101 20¢ Multicolored	—	—	.42	.11
1984. CRIME PREVENTION				
☐ 2102 20¢ Multicolored	17.70	1.82	.42	.11
1984. HISPANIC AMERICANS				
☐ 2103 20¢ Multicolored	17.70	1.82	.42	.11
1984. FAMILY UNITY				
☐ 2104 20¢ Multicolored	17.80	1.82	.42	.11
1984. ELEANOR ROOSEVELT				
☐ 2105 20¢ Blue	17.70	1.82	.42	.11
1984. NATION OF READERS				
☐ 2106 20¢ Brown & Maroon	17.70	1.82	.42	.11
1984. MADONNA AND CHILD				
☐ 2107 20¢ Multicolored	17.70	1.82	.42	.11

*No hinge pricing from 1941 to date is figured at (N-H ADD 15%)

Scott No.		Mint Sheet	Plate Block	Fine Unused Each	Fine Used Each
1984. SANTA CLAUS					
☐ 2108	20¢ Multicolored	17.70	1.80	.42	.11
1984. VIETNAM MEMORIAL					
☐ 2109	20¢ Multicolored	17.70	1.80	.42	.11
1985. JEROME KERN					
☐ 2110	22¢ Multicolored	18.50	2.10	.42	.11
1985. "D" NON-DENOMINATIONAL					
☐ 2111	22¢ Green	36.00	2.10	.42	.11
1985. "D" NON-DENOMINATIONAL COIL					
☐ 2112	22¢ Green	—	—	.42	.11
1985. "D" NON-DENOMINATIONAL BOOKLET					
☐ 2113	22¢ Green	—	—	.42	.11
1985. FLAG OVER DOME					
☐ 2114	22¢ Multicolored	35.20	2.00	.42	.11
1985. FLAG OVER DOME COIL					
☐ 2115	22¢ Multicolored	—	—	.42	.11
1985. FLAG OVER DOME BOOKLET					
☐ 2116	22¢ Multicolored	—	—	.42	.11
1985. SEASHELLS: DOGWINKLE					
☐ 2117	22¢ Brown	—	—	.42	.11
1985. SEASHELLS: HELMET					
☐ 2118	22¢ Brown	—	—	.42	.11
1985. SEASHELLS: NEPTUNE					
☐ 2119	22¢ Brown	—	—	.42	.11
1985. SEASHELLS: SCALLOP					
☐ 2120	22¢ Pink	—	—	.42	.11
1985. SEASHELLS: WHELK					
☐ 2121	22¢ Brown	—	—	.42	.11
1985. EXPRESS MAIL U.S.A.					
☐ 2122	$10.75 Multicolored	—	—	24.00	14.50
1985. SCHOOL BUS					
☐ 2123	3.4¢ Green	—	—	.12	.08
1985. BUCKBOARD					
☐ 2125	4.9¢ Dark Brown	—	—	.13	.10
1986. STAR ROUTE TRUCK					
☐ 2126	5.5¢ Carmine	.14	.10	—	—

*No hinge pricing from 1941 to date is figured at (N-H ADD 15%)

Scott No.	Mint Sheet	Plate Block	Fine Unused Each	Fine Used Each
1985. TRICYCLE 1880s				
☐2127　6¢ Red	—	—	.15	.06
1985. AMBULANCE				
☐2128　8.3¢ Green	—	—	.18	.10
1985. OIL WAGON 1890s				
☐2129　10.1¢ Black	—	—	.22	.07
1985. STUTZ AUTO				
☐2130　11¢ Green	—	—	.26	.07
1985. STANLEY STEAMER 1909				
☐2131　12¢ Blue	—	—	.27	.08
1985. PUSHCART 1880s				
☐2132　12.5¢ Black	—	—	.28	.08
1985. ICEBOAT 1880s				
☐2134　14¢ Blue	—	—	.32	.08
1986. DOG SLED 1920s				
☐2135　17¢ Blue	.34	.22	—	—
1986. BREAD WAGON 1880s				
☐2136　25¢ Brown	.60	.32	—	—
1985. MARY MCLEOD BETHUNE				
☐2137　22¢ Multicolored	18.75	2.20	.45	.11
1985. DUCKS: BROADBILL				
☐2138　22¢ Multicolored	—	—	.45	.11
1985. DUCKS: MALLARD				
☐2139　22¢ Multicolored	—	—	.45	.11
1985. DUCKS: CANVASBACK				
☐2140　22¢ Multicolored	—	—	.45	.11
1985. DUCKS: REDHEAD				
☐2141　22¢ Multicolored	—	—	.45	.11
1985. WINTER SPECIAL OLYMPICS				
☐2142　22¢ Multicolored	16.00	2.10	.45	.11
1985. LOVE				
☐2143　22¢ Multicolored	18.50	2.15	.45	.11
1985. RURAL ELECTRIFICATION ADMINISTRATION				
☐2144　22¢ Multicolored	18.50	2.15	.45	.11
1985. AMERIPEX SHOW				
☐2145　22¢ Multicolored	18.50	2.15	.45	.11

*No hinge pricing from 1941 to date is figured at (N-H ADD 15%)

Scott No.	Mint Sheet	Plate Block	Fine Unused Each	Fine Used Each
1985. ABIGAIL ADAMS				
☐ 2146 22¢ Multicolored	18.50	2.15	.45	.11
1985. BARTHOLDI, STATUE OF LIBERTY				
☐ 2147 22¢ Multicolored	18.50	2.15	.45	.11
1985. GEORGE WASHINGTON				
☐ 2149 18¢ Multicolored	—	—	.35	.09
1985. ENVELOPES				
☐ 2150 21.1¢ Multicolored	—	—	.42	.10
1985. KOREAN VETERANS				
☐ 2152 22¢ Red & Green	18.20	2.05	.46	.11
1985. SOCIAL SECURITY				
☐ 2153 22¢ Blue	18.20	2.05	.46	.11
1985. WORLD WAR I VETERANS				
☐ 2154 22¢ Red & Green	18.20	2.05	.46	.11
1985. HORSES: QUARTER HORSE				
☐ 2155 22¢ Multicolored	—	—	.46	.11
1985. HORSES: MORGAN				
☐ 2156 22¢ Multicolored	—	—	.46	.11
1985. HORSES: SADDLEBRED				
☐ 2157 22¢ Multicolored	—	—	.46	.11
1985. HORSES: APPALOOSA				
☐ 2158 22¢ Multicolored	—	—	.46	.11
1985. PUBLIC EDUCATION				
☐ 2159 22¢ Multicolored	18.20	2.05	.46	.11
1985. YOUTH YEAR: Y.M.C.A.				
☐ 2160 22¢ Multicolored	—	—	.46	.11
1985. YOUTH YEAR: BOY SCOUTS				
☐ 2161 22¢ Multicolored	—	—	.46	.11
1985. YOUTH YEAR: BIG BROTHERS				
☐ 2162 22¢ Multicolored	—	—	.46	.11
1985. YOUTH YEAR CAMPFIRE				
☐ 2163 22¢ Multicolored			.46	.11
1985. HELP END HUNGER				
☐ 2164 22¢ Multicolored	—	—	.46	.11
1985. MADONNA				
☐ 2165 22¢ Multicolored	—	—	.46	.11

*No hinge pricing from 1941 to date is figured at (N-H ADD 15%)

Scott No.	Mint Sheet	Plate Block	Fine Unused Each	Fine Used Each
1985. POINSETTIA				
☐ 2166 22¢ Multicolored	—	—	.46	.11
1986. ARKANSAS				
☐ 2167 22¢ Multicolored	—	—	.46	.11
1986. MARGARET MITCHELL				
☐ 2168 1¢ Brown	—	—	.05	.03
1987. MARY LYON				
☐ 2169 2¢ Blue	—	—	.05	.02
1986. PAUL DUDLEY WHITE M.D.				
☐ 2170 3¢ Blue	—	—	.06	.03
1986. FATHER FLANAGAN				
☐ 2171 4¢ Blue	—	—	.07	.04
1986. HUGO L. BLACK				
☐ 2172 5¢ Olive Green	—	—	.08	.04
1987. JULIA WARD HOWE				
☐ 2177 14¢ Red	—	—	.17	.07
1986. BELVA ANN LOCKWOOD				
☐ 2179 17¢ Blue Green	—	—	.20	.08
1986. JACK LONDON				
☐ 2183 25¢ Blue	—	—	.48	.12
1986. JOHN HARVARD				
☐ 2191 56¢ Brown	—	—	.63	.17
1986. BERNARD REVEL				
☐ 2194 $1.00 Green	—	—	1.10	.25
1986. WILLIAM JENNINGS BRYAN				
☐ 2195 $2.00 Violet	—	—	2.10	.55
1987. BRET HARTE				
☐ 2196 $5.00 Brown	—	—	5.50	.83
1986. STAMP COLLECTING: AMERICAN PHILATELIC ASSOC.				
☐ 2198 22¢ Multicolored	—	—	.46	.11
1986. STAMP COLLECTING: LITTLE BOY				
☐ 2199 22¢ Multicolored	—	—	.46	.11
1986. STAMP COLLECTING: MAGNIFIER				
☐ 2200 22¢ Multicolored	—	—	.46	.11
1986. STAMP COLLECTING: RUBBER STAMP				
☐ 2201 22¢ Multicolored	—	—	.46	.11

*No hinge pricing from 1941 to date is figured at (N-H ADD 15%)

Scott No.		Mint Sheet	Plate Block	Fine Unused Each	Fine Used Each
1986. LOVE					
☐ 2202	22¢ Multicolored	—	—	.42	.10
1986. SOJOURNER TRUTH					
☐ 2203	22¢ Multicolored	—	—	.42	.10
1986. TEXAS—SAN JACINTO 1836					
☐ 2204	22¢ Multicolored	—	—	.42	.10
1986. FISH: MUSKELLUNGE					
☐ 2205	22¢ Multicolored	—	—	.42	.10
1986. FISH: ATLANTIC COD					
☐ 2206	22¢ Multicolored	—	—	.42	.10
1986. FISH: LARGEMOUTH BASS					
☐ 2207	22¢ Multicolored	—	—	.42	.10
1986. FISH: BLUEFIN TUNA					
☐ 2208	22¢ Multicolored	—	—	.42	.10
1986. FISH: CATFISH					
☐ 2209	22¢ Multicolored	—	—	.42	.10
1986. PUBLIC HOSPITALS					
☐ 2210	22¢ Multicolored	—	—	.42	.10
1986. DUKE ELLINGTON					
☐ 2211	22¢ Multicolored	—	—	.42	.10
1986. AMERIPEX '86-PRESIDENTS I					
☐ 2216	22¢ Brown & Black	2.10	—	—	—
1986. AMERIPEX '86-PRESIDENTS II					
☐ 2217	22¢ Brown & Black	2.10	—	—	—
1986. AMERIPEX '86-PRESIDENTS III					
☐ 2218	22¢ Brown & Black	2.10	—	—	—
1986. AMERIPEX '86-PRESIDENTS IV					
☐ 2219	22¢ Brown & Black	2.10	—	—	—
1986. POLAR EXPLORERS: KANE					
☐ 2220	22¢ Multicolored	—	—	.42	.10
1986. POLAR EXPLORERS: GREELY					
☐ 2221	22¢ Multicolored	—	—	.42	.10
1986. POLAR EXPLORERS: STEFANSSON					
☐ 2222	22¢ Multicolored	—	—	.42	.10
1986. POLAR EXPLORERS: HENSON					
☐ 2223	22¢ Multicolored	—	—	.42	.10

*No hinge pricing from 1941 to date is figured at (N-H ADD 15%)

Scott No.		Mint Sheet	Plate Block	Fine Unused Each	Fine Used Each
1986. LIBERTY					
☐ 2224	22¢ Carmine & Blue	—	—	.42	.10
1986. NAVAJO ART					
☐ 2235	22¢ Multicolored	—	—	.42	.10
1986. NAVAJO ART					
☐ 2236	22¢ Multicolored	—	—	.42	.10
1986. NAVAJO ART					
☐ 2237	22¢ Multicolored	—	—	.42	.10
1986. NAVAJO ART					
☐ 2238	22¢ Multicolored	—	—	.42	.10
1986. T.S. ELIOT					
☐ 2239	22¢ Brown	—	—	.42	.10
1986. FOLK ART: HIGHLANDER					
☐ 2240	22¢ Multicolored	—	—	.42	.10
1986. FOLK ART: SHIP					
☐ 2241	22¢ Multicolored	—	—	.42	.10
1986. FOLK ART: NAUTICAL					
☐ 2242	22¢ Multicolored	—	—	.42	.10
1986. FOLK ART: CIGAR STORE					
☐ 2243	22¢ Multicolored	—	—	.42	.10
1986. CHRISTMAS: PEROGINO GALLERY					
☐ 2244	22¢ Multicolored	—	—	.42	.10
1986. CHRISTMAS: GREETINGS					
☐ 2245	22¢ Multicolored	—	—	.42	.10
1987. MICHIGAN STATEHOOD					
☐ 2246	22¢ Multicolored	—	—	.41	.10
1987. PAN AMERICAN GAMES					
☐ 2247	22¢ Multicolored	—	—	.41	.10
1987. LOVE					
☐ 2248	22¢ Multicolored	—	—	.41	.10
1987. JEAN BAPTISTE POINTE DU SABLE					
☐ 2249	22¢ Multicolored	—	—	.41	.10
1987. ENRICO CARUSO					
☐ 2250	22¢ Multicolored	—	—	.41	.09
1987. GIRL SCOUTS					
☐ 2251	22¢ Multicolored	—	—	.41	.09

*No hinge pricing from 1941 to date is figured at (N-H ADD 15%)

Scott No.		Mint Sheet	Plate Block	Fine Unused Each	Fine Used Each
1987. UNITED WAY UNITING COMMUNITIES					
☐ 2275	22¢ Multicolored	—	—	.41	.09
1987. AMERICAN FLAG					
☐ 2276	22¢ Multicolored	—	—	.41	.09
1987. AMERICAN WILDLIFE					
☐ 2286–2335	22¢ Multicolored	—	—	.41ea.	.09ea.
1987. DELAWARE					
☐ 2336	22¢ Multicolored	—	—	.41	.09
1987. PENNSYLVANIA					
☐ 2337	22¢ Multicolored	—	—	.36	.07
1987. NEW JERSEY					
☐ 2338	22¢ Multicolored	—	—	.36	.07
1987. FRIENDSHIP WITH MOROCCO					
☐ 2349	22¢ Multicolored	—	—	.36	.07
1987. WILLIAM FAULKNER					
☐ 2350	22¢ Green	—	—	.36	.07
1987. LACEMAKING					
☐ 2351–2354	22¢ Blue	—	—	.36ea.	.07ea.
1987. CONSTITUTION (BICENTENNIAL)					
☐ 2355	22¢ Multicolored	—	—	.35	.06
1987. CONSTITUTION (WE THE PEOPLE)					
☐ 2356	22¢ Multicolored	—	—	.35	.06
1987. CONSTITUTION (ESTABLISH JUSTICE)					
☐ 2357	22¢ Multicolored	—	—	.35	.06
1987. CONSTITUTION (AND SECURE)					
☐ 2358	22¢ Multicolored	—	—	.35	.06
1987. CONSTITUTION (DO ORDAIN)					
☐ 2359	22¢ Multicolored	—	—	.35	.06
1987. U.S. CONSTITUTION					
☐ 2360	22¢ Multicolored	—	—	.36ea.	.09ea.
1987. C.P.A. CERTIFIED PUBLIC ACCOUNTANTS					
☐ 2361	22¢ Multicolored	—	—	.36	.07
1987. CHRISTMAS: MARONI, NATIONAL GALLERY					
☐ 2367	22¢ Multicolored	—	—	.36	.07
1987. GREETINGS					
☐ 2368	22¢ Multicolored	—	—	.36	.07

*No hinge pricing from 1941 to date is figured at (N-H ADD 15%)

Scott No.	Mint Sheet	Plate Block	Fine Unused Each	Fine Used Each
1988. OLYMPICS (WINTER)				
☐ 2369 22¢ Multicolored	—	—	.35	.06
1988. AUSTRALIA BICENTENNIAL				
☐ 2370 22¢ Multicolored	—	—	.35	.06
1988. J.W. JOHNSON				
☐ 2371 22¢ Multicolored	—	—	.35	.06
1988. CATS (SHORT HAIR)				
☐ 2372 22¢ Multicolored	—	—	.35	.06
1988. CATS (HIMALAYAN)				
☐ 2373 22¢ Multicolored	—	—	.35	.06
1988. CATS (BURMESE)				
☐ 2374 22¢ Multicolored	—	—	.35	.06
1988. CATS (PERSIAN)				
☐ 2375 22¢ Multicolored	—	—	.35	.06
1988. KNUTE ROCKNE				
☐ 2376 22¢ Multicolored	—	—	.35	.06
1988. FRANCIS OUIMET				
☐ 2377 25¢ Multicolored	—	—	.35	.06
1988. LOVE				
☐ 2378 25¢ Multicolored	—	—	.35	.06
1988. LOVE				
☐ 2379 45¢ Multicolored	—	—	.50	.15
1988. OLYMPICS (SUMMER)				
☐ 2380 25¢ Multicolored	—	—	.35	.06
1988. CARS (LOCOMOBILE)				
☐ 2381 25¢ Multicolored	—	—	.35	.06
1988. CARS (PIERCE-ARROW)				
☐ 2382 25¢ Multicolored	—	—	.35	.06
1988. CARS (CORD)				
☐ 2383 25¢ Multicolored	—	—	.35	.06
1988. CARS (PACKARD)				
☐ 2384 25¢ Multicolored	—	—	.35	.06
1988. CARS (DUESENBERG)				
☐ 2385 25¢ Multicolored	—	—	.35	.06
1988. CHRISTMAS (BOTTICELLI)				
☐ 2399 25¢ Multicolored	—	—	.35	.06
1988. GREETINGS (CHRISTMAS)				
☐ 2400 25¢ Multicolored	—	—	.35	.06

*No hinge pricing from 1941 to date is figured at (N-H ADD 15%)

Scott No.		Mint Sheet	Plate Block	Fine Unused Each	Fine Used Each
1988. MONTANA					
☐2401	25¢ Multicolored	—	—	.35	.06
1988. A. PHILIP RANDOLPH					
☐2402	25¢ Multicolored	—	—	.35	.06
1988. NORTH DAKOTA					
☐2403	25¢ Multicolored	—	—	.35	.06
1988. WASHINGTON					
☐2404	25¢ Multicolored	—	—	.35	.06

Scott No.		Fine Unused Plate Blk	Ave. Unused Plate Blk	Fine Unused Each	Ave. Unused Each	Fine Used Each	Ave. Used Each
AIRMAIL STAMPS							
1918. FIRST ISSUE—(N-H ADD 45%)							
☐C1	6¢ Orange	1200.00	720.00	100.00	71.00	44.00	31.00
☐C2	16¢ Green	2400.00	1600.00	171.00	117.00	54.00	40.00
☐C3	24¢ Carmine & Blue	1350.00	870.00	162.00	113.00	64.00	46.00
1923. SECOND ISSUE—(N-H ADD 35%)							
☐C4	8¢ Dark Green	670.00	420.00	51.00	33.00	25.00	15.00
☐C5	16¢ Dark Blue	3800.00	2500.00	162.00	115.00	55.00	37.00
☐C6	24¢ Carmine	4500.00	3000.00	200.00	140.00	47.00	30.00
1926-1927. LONG MAP (N-H ADD 35%)							
☐C7	10¢ Dark Blue	65.00	46.00	6.00	3.60	.60	.37
☐C8	15¢ Olive Brown	79.00	50.00	6.10	4.10	3.40	2.10
☐C9	20¢ Yellow Green	198.00	133.00	16.50	11.50	2.50	1.70
1927. LINDBERGH TRIBUTE ISSUE (N-H ADD 25%)							
☐C10	10¢ Dark Blue	230.00	150.00	16.00	11.00	3.50	2.10
1928. BEACON (N-H ADD 20%)							
☐C11	5¢ Carmine & Blue	73.00	49.00	8.75	6.10	.82	.57
1930. WINGED GLOBE—FLAT PRESS (N-H ADD 35%)							
☐C12	5¢ Violet	260.00	187.00	18.00	14.00	.60	.39
1930. GRAF ZEPPELIN ISSUE (N-H ADD 20%)							
☐C13	65¢ Green	3700.00	3150.00	400.00	300.00	410.00	290.00
☐C14	$1.30 Brown	8500.00	6400.00	1050.00	700.00	710.00	550.00
☐C15	$2.60 Blue	14100.00	12100.00	1700.00	1200.00	1100.00	750.00
1931-1932. WINGED GLOBE—ROTARY PRESS (N-H ADD 25%)							
☐C16	5¢ Violet	170.00	120.00	7.90	5.20	.57	.37
☐C17	8¢ Olive Bistre	68.00	44.00	3.80	2.50	.35	.35
1933. CENTURY OF PROGRESS ISSUE (N-H ADD 25%)							
☐C18	50¢ Green	1100.00	910.00	160.00	110.00	150.00	.95

*No hinge pricing from 1941 to date is figured at (N-H ADD 15%)

Scott No.		Fine Unused Plate Blk	Ave. Unused Plate Blk	Fine Unused Each	Ave. Unused Each	Fine Used Each	Ave. Used Each
1934. DESIGN OF 1930 (N-H ADD 25%)							
☐ C19	6¢ Orange	42.00	31.00	4.20	3.00	.21	.14
1935-1937. TRANSPACIFIC ISSUE (N-H ADD 10%)							
☐ C20	25¢ Blue	47.00	30.00	2.40	1.80	2.10	1.40
☐ C21	20¢ Green	230.00	142.00	17.00	13.00	2.40	1.50
☐ C22	50¢ Carmine	228.00	142.00	18.00	13.00	6.50	5.10
1938. EAGLE (N-H ADD 20%)							
☐ C23	6¢ Blue & Carmine	15.00	10.00	.57	.41	.12	.10
1939. TRANSATLANTIC (N-H ADD 20%)							
☐ C24	30¢ Dull Blue	230.00	150.00	17.00	12.50	1.80	1.40
1941–1944. TRANSPORT PLANE (N-H ADD 20%)							
☐ C25	6¢ Carmine	1.40	1.00	.23	.16	.12	.10
☐ C26	8¢ Olive Green	2.00	1.50	.25	.18	.12	.10
☐ C27	10¢ Violet	16.00	12.00	2.10	1.50	.24	.19
☐ C28	15¢ Brown Carmine	27.00	15.00	4.50	3.00	.41	.30
☐ C29	20¢ Bright Green	22.00	14.00	3.50	2.00	.37	.31
☐ C30	30¢ Blue	23.00	15.00	3.30	2.00	.40	.32
☐ C31	50¢ Orange	143.00	110.00	13.50	12.00	4.00	3.40

Scott No.		Mint Sheet	Plate Block	Fine Unused Each	Fine Used Each
1946-1947. DC-4 SKYMASTER					
☐ C32	5¢ Carmine	9.75	.65	.17	.12
☐ C33	5¢ Carmine	17.00	.70	.17	.12
1947. REGULAR ISSUE					
☐ C34	10¢ Black	28.00	1.70	.38	.12
☐ C35	15¢ Bright Blue Green	30.00	1.75	.55	.12
☐ C36	25¢ Blue	125.00	6.20	1.80	.14

Scott No.		Fine Unused Line Pair	Ave. Unused Line Pair	Fine Unused Each	Ave. Unused Each	Fine Used Each	Ave. Used Each
1948. DESIGN OF 1947							
☐ C37	5¢ Carmine	12.00	8.00	1.60	1.25	1.50	1.00

Scott No.		Mint Sheet	Plate Block	Fine Unused Each	Fine Used Each
1948. NEW YORK CITY JUBILEE ISSUE					
☐ C38	5¢ Red	37.00	10.00	.18	.19
1949. DESIGN OF 1947					
☐ C39	6¢ Carmine	23.00	.90	.20	.09
1949. ALEXANDRIA BICENTENNIAL					
☐ C40	6¢ Carmine	14.00	.85	.20	.17

*No hinge pricing from 1941 to date is figured at (N-H ADD 15%)

Scott No.	Fine Unused Line Pair	Ave. Unused Line Pair	Fine Unused Each	Ave. Unused Each	Fine Used Each	Ave. Used Each
1949. DESIGN OF 1947						
☐ C41 6¢ Carmine	20.00	13.00	4.50	3.10	.14	.11

Scott No.			Mint Sheet	Plate Block	Fine Unused Each	Fine Used Each
1949. U.P.U—UNIVERSAL POSTAL UNION ISSUE						
☐ C42 10¢ Purple			25.00	2.30	.43	.43
☐ C43 15¢ Ultramarine			35.00	1.80	.54	.58
☐ C44 25¢ Carmine			49.00	11.00	.68	.72
1949. WRIGHT BROTHERS ISSUE						
☐ C45 6¢ Magenta			15.50	1.40	.27	.17
1952. HAWAII—DIAMOND HEAD						
☐ C46 80¢ Bright Red Violet			810.00	64.00	14.00	1.80
1953. 50TH ANNIVERSARY POWERED FLIGHT						
☐ C47 6¢ Carmine			8.00	.75	.24	.20
1954. EAGLE IN FLIGHT						
☐ C48 4¢ Bright Blue			16.00	3.30	.20	.15
1957. 50TH ANNIVERSARY AIR FORCE						
☐ C49 6¢ Blue			11.00	.95	.27	.14
1958. DESIGN OF 1954						
☐ C50 5¢ Red			23.00	2.40	.25	.19
1958. JETLINER SILHOUETTE						
☐ C51 7¢ Blue			25.00	1.20	.28	.11

Scott No.	Fine Unused Line Pair	Ave. Unused Line Pair	Fine Unused Each	Ave. Unused Each	Fine Used Each	Ave. Used Each
☐ C52 7¢ Blue	21.75	13.50	3.30	2.10	.14	.11

Scott No.			Mint Sheet	Plate Block	Fine Unused Each	Fine Used Each
1959. COMMEMORATIVES						
1959. ALASKA STATEHOOD						
☐ C53 7¢ Dark Blue			9.00	1.20	.25	.15
1959. BALLOON JUPITER FLIGHT						
☐ C54 7¢ Dark Blue & Red			9.00	1.20	.25	.15
1959. HAWAII STATEHOOD						
☐ C55 7¢ Rose Red			9.00	1.20	.25	.15
1959. PAN AMERICAN GAMES						
☐ C56 10¢ Red & Blue			17.00	2.50	.42	.45

*No hinge pricing from 1941 to date is figured at (N-H ADD 15%)

Scott No.		Mint Sheet	Plate Block	Fine Unused Each	Fine Used Each
1959–61. REGULAR ISSUE					
☐ C57	10¢ Black & Green	127.00	14.00	2.10	1.25
☐ C58	15¢ Black & Orange	27.00	3.00	.60	.17
☐ C59	25¢ Black & Maroon	32.00	3.00	.76	.12
1960. DESIGN OF 1958					
☐ C60	7¢ Carmine	22.00	1.00	.23	.09

Scott No.		Fine Unused Line Pair	Ave. Unused Line Pair	Fine Unused Each	Ave. Unused Each	Fine Used Each	Ave. Used Each
☐ C61	7¢ Carmine	50.00	41.00	6.00	5.00	.36	.25

Scott No.		Mint Sheet	Plate Block	Fine Unused Each	Fine Used Each
1961. DESIGNS OF 1959–1960					
☐ C62	13¢ Black & Red	28.75	3.50	.65	.18
☐ C63	15¢ Black & Orange	18.00	2.00	.45	.12
1962. JETLINER OVER CAPITOL					
☐ C64	8¢ Carmine	17.75	1.20	.24	.11

Scott No.		Fine Unused Line Pair	Ave. Unused Line Pair	Fine Unused Each	Ave. Unused Each	Fine Used Each	Ave. Used Each
☐ C65	8¢ Carmine	4.30	3.50	.37	.26	.12	.10

Scott No.		Mint Sheet	Plate Block	Fine Unused Each	Fine Used Each
1963. FIRST INTERNATIONAL POSTAL CONFERENCE CENTENARY					
☐ C66	15¢ Dull Red, Dark Brown & Blue	34.00	6.50	1.20	.96
1963. POSTAL CARD RATE					
☐ C67	6¢ Red	21.50	3.50	.33	.19
1963. AMELIA EARHART					
☐ C68	8¢ Carmine & Maroon	13.50	2.10	.38	.25
1964. DR. ROBERT H. GODDARD					
☐ C69	8¢ Blue, Red, Bistre	33.00	4.20	.93	.22
1967–1969.					
1967. ALASKA PURCHASE CENTENARY					
☐ C70	8¢ Dark Brown	20.00	3.50	.53	.25
1967.					
☐ C71	20¢ Blue, Brown, Bistre	62.00	6.50	1.35	.15
1968.					
☐ C72	10¢ Carmine	28.00	1.50	.31	.10

*No hinge pricing from 1941 to date is figured at (N-H ADD 15%)

Scott No.		Fine Unused Line Pair	Ave. Unused Line Pair	Fine Unused Each	Ave. Unused Each	Fine Used Each	Ave. Used Each
☐ C73	10¢ Carmine	3.40	2.60	.45	.36	.14	.08

Scott No.		Mint Sheet	Plate Block	Fine Unused Each	Fine Used Each
1968. 50TH ANNIVERSARY AIR MAIL SERVICE					
☐ C74	10¢ Black, Blue, Red	22.50	6.50	.46	.20
1968.					
☐ C75	20¢ Red, Blue, Black	34.00	4.50	.78	.16
1969. FIRST MAN ON THE MOON					
☐ C76	10¢ Red, Blue, Brown	8.80	2.00	.30	.19
1971–1973.					
☐ C77	9¢ Red	19.75	1.25	.26	.28
☐ C78	11¢ Carmine	25.00	1.60	.29	.09
☐ C79	13¢ Carmine	30.00	1.60	.43	.11
☐ C80	17¢ Green, Blue, Red	26.00	2.30	.56	.15
☐ C81	21¢ Blue, Red, Black	24.00	2.20	.55	.16

Scott No.		Fine Unused Line Pair	Ave. Unused Line Pair	Fine Unused Each	Ave. Unused Each	Fine Used Each	Ave. Used Each
☐ C82	11¢ Carmine	1.20	.95	.35	.26	.12	.08
☐ C83	13¢ Carmine	1.10	.90	.40	.29	.12	.08

Scott No.		Mint Sheet	Plate Block	Fine Unused Each	Fine Used Each
1972. NATIONAL PARKS CENTENNIAL					
☐ C84	11¢ Multicolored	13.20	1.70	.36	.19
1972. OLYMPIC GAMES					
☐ C85	11¢ Multicolored	15.50	3.50	.38	.19
1973. PROGRESS IN ELECTRONICS					
☐ C86	11¢ Multicolored	14.50	2.00	.36	.19
1974.					
☐ C87	18¢ Red, Blue, Black	28.00	2.80	.56	.45
☐ C88	26¢ Red, Blue, Black	32.00	3.50	.78	.15
1976.					
☐ C89	25¢ Red, Blue, Black	33.00	3.60	.75	.16
☐ C90	31¢ Red, Blue, Black	37.00	4.10	.88	.15
1979.					
☐ C91	31¢ Blue, Brown, Red	77.00	5.10	1.05	.22
☐ C92	31¢ Blue, Brown, Red	77.00	5.10	1.05	.22
1979.					
☐ C93	21¢ Blue, Brown, Red	97.00	5.10	1.30	.32
☐ C94	21¢ Blue, Brown, Red	97.00	5.10	1.30	.32

*No hinge pricing from 1941 to date is figured at (N-H ADD 15%)

Scott No.		Mint Sheet	Plate Block	Fine Unused Each	Fine Used Each
1980.					
☐ C95	25¢ Multicolored	117.00	6.10	1.50	.42
☐ C96	25¢ Multicolored	117.00	6.10	1.50	.42
☐ C97	31¢ Multicolored	47.00	17.00	1.25	.43
1981.					
☐ C98	40¢ Multicolored	44.00	13.00	1.00	.19
☐ C99	28¢ Multicolored	35.00	9.50	.75	.23
☐ C100	35¢ Multicolored	40.00	11.00	.82	.23
1983.					
☐ C101	28¢ Multicolored	33.50	2.70	.63	.27
☐ C102	28¢ Multicolored	33.50	2.70	.63	.27
☐ C103	28¢ Multicolored	33.50	2.70	.63	.27
☐ C104	28¢ Multicolored	33.50	2.70	.63	.27
☐ C105	40¢ Multicolored	43.00	4.10	.80	.33
☐ C106	40¢ Multicolored	43.00	3.70	.90	.35
☐ C107	40¢ Multicolored	43.00	3.70	.90	.35
☐ C108	40¢ Multicolored	43.00	3.70	.90	.35
☐ C109	35¢ Multicolored	41.00	3.40	.80	.38
☐ C110	35¢ Multicolored	41.00	3.40	.80	.38
☐ C111	35¢ Multicolored	41.00	3.40	.80	.38
☐ C112	35¢ Multicolored	41.00	3.40	.80	.38
1985.					
☐ C113	33¢ Multicolored	38.00	3.40	.64	.27
☐ C114	39¢ Multicolored	42.00	4.10	.86	.30
☐ C115	44¢ Multicolored	53.00	5.00	1.10	.31
☐ C116	44¢ Multicolored	53.00	5.00	1.10	.31

Scott No.		Fine Unused Plate Blk	Ave. Unused Plate Blk	Fine Unused Each	Ave. Unused Each	Fine Used Each	Ave. Used Each
AIRMAIL SPECIAL DELIVERY							
☐ CE1	16¢ Dark Blue	27.00	20.00	1.20	.75	.91	.66
☐ CE2	16¢ Red & Blue	15.00	11.00	.65	.46	.33	.20
SPECIAL DELIVERY STAMPS							
1885.							
☐ E1	10¢ Blue	—	—	280.00	196.00	37.00	26.00
1888.							
☐ E2	10¢ Blue	—	—	261.00	182.00	10.00	7.10
1893. (N-H ADD 80%)							
☐ E3	10¢ Orange	—	—	192.00	125.00	21.00	13.00
1894. (N-H ADD 80%)							
☐ E4	10¢ Blue	—	—	740.00	535.00	23.00	14.00
1895. (N-H ADD 80%)							
☐ E5	10¢ Blue	—	—	145.00	97.00	3.10	2.00

*No hinge pricing from 1941 to date is figured at (N-H ADD 15%)

Scott No.	Fine Unused Plate Blk	Ave. Unused Plate Blk	Fine Unused Each	Ave. Unused Each	Fine Used Each	Ave. Used Each
1902. (N-H ADD 55%)						
☐E6 10¢ Ultramarine	—	—	106.00	73.00	3.10	1.80
1908. (N-H ADD 55%)						
☐E7 10¢ Green	—	—	88.00	63.00	35.00	23.00
1911. (N-H ADD 40%)						
☐E8 10¢ Ultramarine	—	—	115.00	75.00	4.40	4.00
1914. (N-H ADD 40%)						
☐E9 10¢ Ultramarine	—	—	215.00	118.00	6.50	4.50
1916. (N-H ADD 40%)						
☐E10 10¢ Pale Ultramarine	—	—	350.00	216.00	24.00	16.00
1917. (N-H ADD 40%)						
☐E11 10¢ Ultramarine	—	—	21.00	15.00	.55	.38
1922–1925. (N-H ADD 30%)						
☐E12 10¢ Deep Ultramarine	460.00	305.00	34.00	26.00	.27	.17
☐E13 10¢ Deep Orange	285.00	190.00	29.00	20.00	1.50	.90
☐E14 20¢ Black	56.00	42.00	4.20	3.10	2.30	1.60
1927–1951. (N-H ADD 30%)						
☐E15 10¢ Gray Violet	8.00	5.50	1.30	.96	.12	.50
☐E16 15¢ Orange	7.50	5.50	1.00	.96	.14	.12
☐E17 13¢ Blue	5.00	4.00	1.00	.67	.12	.12
☐E18 17¢ Yellow	35.00	26.00	6.00	4.30	3.30	2.10
☐E19 20¢ Black	15.00	10.00	3.10	2.10	.15	.10

Scott No.	Mint Sheet	Plate Block	Fine Unused Each	Fine Used Each
1954.				
☐E20 20¢ Blue	37.50	4.10	.75	.12
1957.				
☐E21 30¢ Maroon	49.00	4.60	.80	.12
1969.				
☐E22 45¢ Red & Blue	94.00	12.10	1.85	.12
1971.				
☐E23 60¢ Blue & Red	66.00	6.00	1.50	.12

Scott No.	Fine Unused Plate Blk	Ave. Unused Plate Blk	Fine Unused Each	Ave. Unused Each	Fine Used Each	Ave. Used Each
1911. REGISTRATION STAMPS (N-H ADD 30%)						
☐F1 10¢ Ultramarine	1450.00	1050.00	110.00	62.00	5.00	4.20

Scott No.		Mint Sheet	Plate Block	Fine Unused Each	Fine Used Each
☐ FA1	15¢ Postman	55.00	7.60	.62	.52

*No hinge pricing from 1941 to date is figured at (N-H ADD 15%)

Scott No.		Name Block 6	Name Block 4	Plain Block 4	Unused Each	Used Each

UNITED NATIONS
1951.

		Name Block 6	Name Block 4	Plain Block 4	Unused Each	Used Each
☐ 1	1¢ Magenta	.83	.47	.34	.11	.07
☐ 2	1½¢ Blue Green	.92	.62	.38	.11	.07
☐ 2a	1½¢ Precancelled................					14.50
☐ 3	2¢ Purple	1.25	.65	.50	.14	.10
☐ 4	3¢ Magenta & Blue	1.40	.90	.65	.18	.11
☐ 5	5¢ Blue	2.50	1.70	.92	.23	.16
☐ 6	10¢ Chocolate	5.60	3.10	1.50	.30	.21
☐ 7	15¢ Violet & Blue	5.60	3.10	1.50	.30	.21
☐ 8	20¢ Dark Brown	15.00	9.10	7.70	1.50	1.10
☐ 9	25¢ Olive Gray & Blue	14.50	7.75	6.10	1.40	.92
☐ 10	50¢ Indigo	125.00	78.00	64.00	13.00	1.65
☐ 11	$1 Red	32.00	23.00	16.00	3.50	1.60
☐ 1–11	First Postage Set Complete	230.00	121.00	91.00	24.00	15.25

1952.

☐ 12	5¢ War Memorial Bldg.	9.60	7.10	5.50	1.60	.62
☐ 13–14	3¢, 5¢ Fourth H.R. Day	25.00	14.25	9.10	2.60	1.20

1953.

☐ 15–16	3¢, 5¢ Refugees	30.00	18.20	15.00	5.00	2.10
☐ 17–18	3¢, 5¢ U.P.U.	39.00	26.00	23.00	6.10	3.00
☐ 19–20	3¢, 5¢ Technical Assist	26.00	19.00	15.00	5.10	1.60
☐ 21–22	3¢, 5¢ Human Rights	41.00	34.00	28.00	7.10	1.70

1954.

☐ 23–24	3¢, FAO (Agriculture)	40.00	28.00	24.00	6.10	1.70
☐ 25–26	3¢, 8¢ OIT (Labor Org.)	54.00	38.00	31.00	8.50	2.00
☐ 27–28	3¢, 8¢ UN Day	65.00	52.00	44.00	11.00	4.10
☐ 29–30	3¢, 8¢ H.R. Day	160.00	140.00	115.00	24.00	7.20

1955.

☐ 31–32	3¢, 8¢ I.C.A.O.	87.00	63.00	57.00	13.00	4.40
☐ 33–34	3¢, 8¢ UNESCO	30.00	25.00	18.00	6.10	1.20
☐ 35–37	3¢, 4¢, 8¢ UN Day	78.00	62.00	53.00	13.00	2.30
☐ 38	3¢, 4¢, 8¢ UN Day Sheet	—	—	—	250.00	130.00
☐ 39–40	3¢, 8¢ Human Rights	24.00	17.00	15.00	3.20	1.80

1956.

☐ 41–42	3¢, 8¢ Telecommunication	24.00	16.00	14.00	3.00	2.10
☐ 43–44	3¢, 8¢ World Health	24.00	16.00	14.00	3.00	2.10
☐ 45-46	3¢, 8¢ UN Day	5.00	3.00	2.50	.42	.32
☐ 47–48	3¢, 8¢ Human Rights	4.00	2.00	1.50	.26	.20

Scott No.		Name Block 6	Name Block 4	Plain Block 4	Unused Each	Used Each
1957.						
☐ 49–50	3¢, 8¢ W.M.O. Meteorological	2.20	1.40	1.10	.21	.12
☐ 51–52	3¢, 8¢ U.N.E.F. 1st Printing	2.20	1.40	1.10	.21	.12
☐ 53–54	3¢, 8¢ U.N.E.F. 2nd Printing	3.70	2.70	2.00	.40	.30
☐ 55–56	3¢, 8¢ Security Council	2.70	1.60	1.00	.20	.16
☐ 57–58	3¢, 8¢ Human Rights	2.70	1.60	1.00	.20	.16
1958.						
☐ 59–60	3¢, 8¢ Atomic Energy	2.65	1.40	1.15	.25	.20
☐ 61–62	3¢, 8¢ General Assembly	2.65	1.40	1.15	.26	.20
☐ 63–64	4¢, 8¢ Regular Issues	2.65	1.40	1.10	.23	.16
☐ 65–66	4¢, 8¢ Economic Council	2.65	1.40	1.15	.30	.21
☐ 67–68	4¢, 8¢ Human Rights	2.65	1.40	1.15	.30	.21
☐ 69–70	4¢, 8¢ Flushing Meadows	3.00	1.50	1.50	.31	.24
☐ 71–72	4¢, 8¢ E.C.E.	5.00	3.00	3.00	.68	.46
☐ 73–74	4¢, 8¢ Trusteeship	4.00	3.40	2.75	.51	.33
☐ 75–76	4¢, 8¢ World Refugee Year	3.00	2.00	1.70	.42	.31
1960.						
☐ 77–78	4¢, 8¢ Palais de Chaillot	3.00	2.00	1.60	.36	.35
☐ 79–80	4¢, 8¢ Forestry Congress	3.00	2.00	1.60	.36	.35
☐ 83–84	4¢, 8¢ 15th Anniversary	3.00	2.00	1.70	.33	.40
☐ 85	4¢, 8¢ 15th Ann. Souv. Sheet	—	—	—	12.00	9.10
☐ 86–87	4¢, 8¢ International	3.00	2.00	1.70	.39	.37
1961.						
☐ 88–89	4¢, 8¢ Court of Justice	3.00	2.00	1.60	.32	.21
☐ 90–91	4¢, 7¢ Monetary Fund	3.00	2.00	1.60	.32	.21
☐ 92	30¢ Regular Issue	7.10	5.00	4.00	.96	.62
☐ 93–94	4¢, 11¢ E.C. for Latin Am.	8.75	6.00	4.50	1.30	.83
☐ 95–96	4¢, 11¢ E.C. for Africa	5.00	3.00	2.20	.62	.42
☐ 97–99	3¢, 4¢, 13¢ Children's Fund	5.00	3.50	2.50	.65	.44
1962.						
☐ 100–01	4¢, 7¢ Housing	5.00	3.00	3.10	.56	.42
☐ 102–03	4¢, 11¢ Malaria	6.00	4.00	3.00	.78	.52
☐ 104–07	1¢, 3¢, 5¢, 11¢ Reg. Issue	6.00	4.50	3.00	.75	.54
☐ 108–09	5¢, 15¢ Hammarskjold	19.00	13.00	10.00	2.15	1.31
☐ 110–11	4¢, 11¢ U.N. Congo	14.00	10.00	7.00	2.00	1.10
☐ 112–13	4¢, 11¢ Peaceful Space Use	4.50	3.00	3.00	.62	.42
1963.						
☐ 114–15	5¢, 11¢ Econ. Development	5.50	4.60	3.00	.63	.41
☐ 116–17	5¢, 11¢ Freedom—Hunger	5.30	4.60	3.00	.63	.40
☐ 118	25¢ UNTEA W. Irian	10.00	7.00	5.00	1.45	.84
☐ 119–20	5¢, 11¢, 10th Hdqrs. Anniv.	6.00	4.00	3.00	.75	.56
☐ 121–22	5¢, 11¢, 15th Anniv. H. Rights	6.00	4.00	3.00	.69	.61
1964.						
☐ 123–24	5¢, 11¢ Maritime	4.00	3.50	2.50	.68	.50
☐ 125–27	2¢, 7¢, 10¢ Reg. Issue	3.00	2.70	2.00	.65	.41

Scott No.		Name Block 6	Name Block 4	Plain Block 4	Unused Each	Used Each
☐ 128	50¢ New Regular	9.00	6.20	5.20	1.30	.83
☐ 129–30	5¢, 11¢ Trade & Develop	4.40	3.60	2.60	.72	.62
☐ 131–32	5¢, 11¢ Narcotics Control	4.80	3.70	2.90	.70	.52
☐ 133	5¢ Nuclear Tests End	1.60	1.30	.90	.27	.20
☐ 134–36	4¢, 5¢, 11¢ Education	5.20	4.10	3.20	.80	.62

1965.

☐ 137–38	5¢, 11¢ Special Fund	3.10	2.40	1.70	.36	.23
☐ 139–40	5¢, 11¢ U.N. in Cyprus	3.10	2.40	1.70	.36	.23
☐ 141–42	5¢, 11¢ I.T.U. (Satellite)	3.10	2.40	1.70	.36	.23
☐ 143–44	5¢, 15¢ Co-operation	4.70	3.40	2.50	.62	.42
☐ 145	5¢, 15¢ Min. Sheet	—	—	—	1.70	1.25
☐ 146–49	1¢, 15¢, 20¢, 25¢ Regular	34.00	24.00	20.00	3.80	3.10
☐ 150	$1 Regular Issue (1966)	25.00	19.00	14.00	2.50	2.10
☐ 151–53	4¢, 5¢, 11¢ Population Trends	6.00	4.00	2.80	.65	.42

1966.

☐ 154–55	5¢, 15¢ World Federation	5.00	3.70	3.00	.62	.41
☐ 156–57	5¢, 11¢ W.H.O. Building	4.00	3.00	2.00	.60	.41
☐ 158–59	5¢, 11¢ Coffee Agreement	4.00	3.00	2.00	.60	.41
☐ 160	15¢ Peacekeeping	3.50	2.70	2.00	.46	.31
☐ 161–63	4¢, 5¢, 11¢ UNICEF Anniv.	5.00	3.50	2.50	.62	.31

1967.

☐ 164–65	5¢, 11¢ Development	3.80	2.70	2.00	.47	.31
☐ 166–67	1½¢, 5¢ Regular Issue	2.50	1.50	1.00	.26	.19
☐ 168–69	5¢, 11¢ Independence	4.00	3.10	2.00	.52	.42

1967.

☐ 170–74	4¢, 5¢, 8¢, 10¢, 15¢ EXPO	19.00	16.00	12.50	2.70	2.10
☐ 175–76	5¢, 15¢ Intl. Tourist Year	4.60	4.00	2.50	.65	.52
☐ 177–78	6¢, 13¢ Toward Disarm	4.60	4.00	2.50	.65	.52
☐ 179	6¢ Chagall Sheet of Six	—	—	—	1.20	.86
☐ 180	6¢ Chagall Window	1.80	.95	.75	.22	.12

1968.

☐ 181–82	6¢, 13¢ Secretariat	4.40	3.50	2.20	.52	.44
☐ 183–84	6¢, 75¢ Starcke Statue	70.00	53.00	39.00	8.20	5.00
☐ 185–86	6¢, 13¢ ONUDI	4.10	3.00	2.60	.65	.42
☐ 187	6¢ Regular Issue	1.50	1.20	.75	.20	.13
☐ 188–89	6¢, 20¢ Weather Watch	6.10	5.10	3.50	.85	.62
☐ 190–91	6¢, 13¢ Int'l. Year Human Rts.	8.10	6.10	4.60	1.15	.81

1969.

☐ 192–93	6¢, 13¢ UNITAR	4.20	3.00	2.50	.46	.31
☐ 194–95	6¢, 15¢ ECLA Bldg	5.10	4.00	3.00	.65	.42
☐ 196	13¢, Regular Issue	3.00	2.20	1.70	.40	.25
☐ 197–98	6¢, 13¢ Peace thru Law	4.00	3.00	2.50	.55	.32
☐ 199–200	6¢, 20¢ Labor & Devl	6.00	4.00	3.50	.78	.52
☐ 201–02	6¢, 13¢ Art Series	6.00	4.00	3.10	.70	.41
☐ 203–04	6¢, 25¢ Japan Peace Bell	6.00	5.00	4.00	.95	.63
☐ 205–06	6¢, 13¢ Mekong Basin	5.00	3.00	3.00	.62	.51

Scott No.		Name Block 6	Name Block 4	Plain Block 4	Unused Each	Used Each
☐ 207–08	6¢, 13¢ Cancer	4.00	3.40	2.50	.62	.47
☐ 209–11	6¢, 13¢, 25¢ 25th U.V. Anniv.	10.50	8.00	7.10	1.80	1.10
☐ 212	Same, Souvenir Sheet	—	—	—	2.10	1.30
☐ 213–14	6¢, 13¢ Peace, Just. Prog.	4.00	3.00	2.40	.56	.42

1971.

☐ 215	6¢ Sea Bed	1.70	1.40	.95	.21	.16
☐ 216–17	6¢, 13¢ Refugees	4.00	3.30	2.40	.57	.43
☐ 218	13¢ World Food Prog.	3.00	2.50	2.00	.40	.23
☐ 219	20¢ U.P.U. Building	4.60	3.50	2.70	.68	.60
☐ 220–21	8¢, 13¢ Anti-Discrim.	5.00	4.20	2.90	.68	.60
☐ 222–23	8¢, 60¢ Regular Issue	11.75	8.50	6.60	1.50	1.05
☐ 224–25	8¢, 21¢ Intl. Schools	6.70	5.00	4.00	.87	.62

1972.

☐ 226	95¢ Regular Issue	18.75	14.10	11.10	2.50	2.15
☐ 227	8¢ Non-Proliferation	2.00	1.50	.95	.26	.20
☐ 228	15¢ World Health	4.00	3.00	2.00	.52	.32
☐ 229–30	8¢, 15¢ Environment	5.00	4.00	3.00	.62	.44
☐ 231	21¢ E.C. Europe	5.00	4.00	3.00	.62	.44
☐ 232–33	8¢, 15¢ U.N. Art Sert	6.00	4.60	3.20	.67	.44

1973.

☐ 234–35	8¢, 15¢ Disarmament	5.00	4.00	3.40	.68	.56
☐ 236–37	8¢, 15¢ Drug Abuse	6.00	4.50	3.40	.82	.64
☐ 238–39	8¢, 21¢ U.N. Volunteers	6.50	5.00	3.60	.84	.64
☐ 240–41	8¢, 15¢ Namibia	6.00	4.50	3.50	.80	.58
☐ 242–43	8¢, 21¢ Human Rights	6.00	4.50	3.10	.77	.56

1974.

☐ 244–45	10¢, 21¢ ILO Hdqr	12.00	7.70	6.00	1.30	.90
☐ 246	10¢ UPU Centenary	2.70	2.10	1.50	.31	.20
☐ 247–48	10¢, 18¢ Brazil Mural	7.70	5.00	4.70	.92	.63
☐ 249–51	2¢, 10¢, 18¢ Regular	7.50	5.00	4.20	.82	.65
☐ 252–53	10¢, 18¢ Population	6.50	5.00	3.60	.91	.52
☐ 254–55	10¢, 26¢ Law of Sea	8.00	6.70	5.00	1.25	.81

1975.

☐ 256–57	10¢, 26¢ Space Usage	15.00	9.70	8.10	2.15	1.65
☐ 258–59	10¢, 18¢ Women's Year	6.10	5.10	3.60	.80	.61
☐ 260–61	10¢, 26¢ UN 30th Anniv.	6.00	6.10	4.60	1.00	.63
☐ 262	36¢ Same Souv. Sheet	—	—	—	1.30	.72
☐ 263–64	10¢, 18¢ Namibia	6.00	5.20	4.00	.73	.54
☐ 265–66	13¢, 26¢ Peacekeeping	10.00	8.10	6.10	1.20	.82

1976.

☐ 267–71	3¢, 4¢, 9¢, 30¢, 50¢ Regular	23.00	16.70	12.00	2.25	1.72
☐ 272–73	13¢, 26¢ WFUNA	14.00	9.70	7.00	1.45	.95
☐ 274–75	13¢, 31¢ UNCTAD	12.00	7.70	6.00	1.25	.65
☐ 276–77	13¢, 25¢ HABITAT	11.00	7.10	5.50	1.20	.60
☐ 278–79	13¢, 31¢ 25th Postal Anniv.	100.00	78.00	60.00	14.00	8.50
☐ 280	13¢ Food Council	2.70	2.10	1.50	.42	.30

Scott No.	Name Block 6	Name Block 4	Plain Block 4	Unused Each	Used Each

1977.

☐ 281–82 13¢, 31¢ WIPO	12.00	9.00	6.00	1.50	1.05
☐ 283–84 13¢, 25¢ Water Conf.	10.00	8.00	5.00	1.40	.95
☐ 285–86 13¢, 31¢ Security Council	11.00	8.50	6.00	1.40	.95
☐ 287–88 13¢, 25¢ Combat Racism	8.10	6.00	4.00	1.10	.85
☐ 289–90 13¢, 18¢ Atomic Energy	7.00	4.00	3.00	.80	.65

1978.

☐ 291–93 1¢, 25¢, $1 Regular	24.00	19.00	15.00	4.00	3.05
☐ 294–95 13¢, 31¢ Small Pox	9.00	7.10	5.00	1.25	.73
☐ 296–97 13¢, 18¢ Namibia	6.10	4.00	3.50	.80	.53
☐ 298–99 13¢, 25¢ ICAO-Air Safety	7.70	5.00	4.00	.86	.62
☐ 300–01 13¢, 18¢ General Assembly	6.00	4.00	3.00	.76	.56
☐ 302–03 13¢, 31¢ Technical Cooperation	10.00	8.00	6.00	1.35	.85

1979.

☐ 304–07 5¢, 14¢, 15¢, 20¢ Regular Issues	12.00	9.00	7.00	1.60	1.05
☐ 308–09 15¢, 20¢ UNDRO	8.00	6.10	4.50	.75	.52
☐ 310–11 15¢, 31¢ Intl. Year of Child	62.00	39.00	31.00	5.60	4.15
☐ 312–13 15¢, 31¢ Namibia	11.00	7.50	6.00	1.15	.65
☐ 314–15 15¢, 31¢ Court of Justice	11.00	8.00	6.00	1.35	.92

1980.

☐ 316–17 15¢, 31¢ Economic Order	16.00	10.00	7.10	1.25	.91
☐ 318–19 15¢, 20¢, Women's Decade	7.00	6.00	5.00	.90	.68
☐ 320–21 15¢, 31¢ Peacekeeping	8.00	6.10	5.00	.95	.72
☐ 322–23 15¢, 31¢ 35th Anniversary	8.00	6.10	5.00	.95	.72
☐ 324 15¢, Same, Souvenir Sheet	—	—	—	.90	.70
☐ 325–40 15¢ World Flags	—	23.00	—	6.00	5.80
☐ 325–28 15¢ World Flags	—	8.00	—	2.00	1.50
☐ 329–32 15¢ World Flags	—	8.00	—	2.00	1.50
☐ 333–36 15¢ World Flags	—	8.00	—	2.00	1.50
☐ 337–40 15¢ World Flags	—	8.00	—	2.00	1.50
☐ 341–42 15¢, 20¢ Economic and Social Council	8.70	6.00	5.00	2.00	1.40

1981.

☐ 343 15¢ Palestinian People	3.40	3.00	2.00	.46	.32
☐ 344–45 20¢, 35¢ Disabled Persons	10.00	7.00	5.00	1.20	.82
☐ 346–47 20¢, 31¢ Fresco	—	6.00	5.00	.95	.66
☐ 348–49 20¢, 40¢ Sources of Energy	10.00	8.00	6.00	1.25	.90
☐ 350–65 1981 World Flags	—	35.00	—	8.70	7.30
☐ 350–53 20¢ World Flags	—	8.00	—	2.20	1.75
☐ 358–61 20¢ World Flags	—	8.00	—	2.20	1.75
☐ 354–57 15¢, 20¢ World Flags	—	8.00	—	2.20	1.75
☐ 362–65 20¢ World Flags	—	8.00	—	2.20	1.75
☐ 366–67 18¢, 28¢ Volunteers Program	—	6.10	5.00	1.10	1.05

1982.

☐ 368–70 17¢, 28¢, 40¢ Definitives	14.00	11.00	7.00	1.60	.92
☐ 371–72 20¢, 40¢ Human Environment	11.00	9.10	7.00	1.70	.95

Scott No.		Name Block 6	Name Block 4	Plain Block 4	Unused Each	Used Each
☐ 373	20¢ Space Exploration	2.35	1.80	1.50	.30	.21
☐ 374–89	World Flags	37.00	26.00	18.00	4.20	2.30
☐ 390–91	20¢, 28¢ Nature Conservation	5.90	4.50	3.60	.72	.47

1983.

☐ 392–93	20¢, 40¢ Communication	7.20	5.20	4.00	.86	.52
☐ 394–95	20¢, 37¢ Safety at Sea	7.20	5.20	4.00	.82	.53
☐ 396	20¢ World Food	2.40	1.90	1.40	.32	.21
☐ 397–98	20¢, 28¢ Trade	6.00	4.70	3.00	.66	.43
☐ 399–14	World Flags	35.00	23.00	18.00	3.80	2.30
☐ 415–16	20¢, 40¢ Human Rights	7.10	5.50	4.00	.77	.62

1984.

☐ 417–18	20¢, 40¢ Population Conference	7.00	5.20	4.10	.76	.57
☐ 419–20	20¢, 40¢ World Food Day	7.00	5.20	4.10	.76	.57
☐ 421–22	20¢, 50¢ Heritage	7.60	5.80	4.20	.92	.63
☐ 423–24	20¢, 50¢ Refugees	8.10	6.30	4.40	1.10	.72
☐ 425–50	World Flags	35.00	23.00	17.20	3.70	2.50

UNITED NATIONS
1951–1957. AIRMAILS

☐ C1	6¢ Airmail (1951)	2.50	2.10	1.60	.38	.29
☐ C2	10¢ Airmail	5.70	3.70	3.00	.58	.43
☐ C3	15¢ Airmail	27.10	21.00	18.00	4.20	2.50
☐ C4	25¢ Airmail	49.50	35.00	27.00	5.80	4.00
☐ C1–4	First Issue Airmails	73.00	50.00	39.00	7.60	5.80
☐ C5–7	4¢, 5¢, 7¢ Airmail (1957)	3.90	2.70	2.00	.52	.29

1963–1964. AIRMAILS

☐ C8–10	6¢, 8¢, 13¢ Airmail (1963)	4.10	3.20	2.60	.72	.52
☐ C11–12	15¢, 25¢ Airmail (1964)	23.00	18.00	15.00	3.80	1.15

1968–1972. AIRMAILS

☐ C13	20¢ Airmail (1968)	3.50	2.30	2.00	.52	.32
☐ C14	10¢ Airmail (1969)	2.00	1.50	1.50	.42	.26
☐ C15–18	9¢, 11¢, 17¢, 21¢ (1972)	11.20	7.70	5.70	1.30	.92

1974–1977. AIRMAILS

☐ C19–21	13¢, 18¢, 26¢ (1974)	11.50	9.10	7.10	1.60	1.20
☐ C22–23	25¢, 31¢ (1977)	14.50	11.20	7.70	2.10	1.40

					Unused Each	Used Each

UNITED NATIONS SOUVENIR CARDS

		Unused Each	Used Each
☐ 1	WHO, First Printing	4.00	—
☐ 1a	WHO, Second Printing	4.50	—
☐ 2	Art at U.N.	2.30	—
☐ 3	Disarmament	2.40	—
☐ 4	Human Rights	6.70	—
☐ 5	Universal Postal Union	6.10	—
☐ 6	World Population	22.00	—
☐ 7	Outer Space	8.00	—

			Unused Each	Used Each
☐ 8	Peacekeeping		11.00	—
☐ 9	World Federation of U.N.		12.75	—
☐ 10	World Food Council		6.80	—
☐ 11	World Intellectual Property		4.50	—
☐ 12	Combat Racism		3.50	—
☐ 13	Namibia		3.50	—
☐ 14	ICAO-Air Safety		4.00	—
☐ 15	International Year of The Child		2.90	—
☐ 16	Court of Justice		2.90	—
☐ 17	Women's Decade		26.00	—
☐ 18	Economic and Social Council		5.20	—
☐ 19	Disabled Persons		3.50	—
☐ 20	Energy Sources		5.70	—

Scott No.		Name Block 6	Name Block 4	Plain Block 4	Unused Each	Used Each

UNITED NATIONS—GENEVA, SWITZERLAND DENOMINATIONS ARE GIVEN IN SWISS CURRENCY DESIGNS ARE SIMILAR TO U.N. NEW YORK ISSUES

1969–1970.

☐ 1–14	5¢ to 10 franc	206.00	158.00	125.00	30.00	21.00

1971.

☐ 15	30¢ Sea Bed	3.90	3.00	2.15	.47	.33
☐ 16	50¢ Refugees	9.70	7.70	6.20	1.60	1.25
☐ 17	50¢ World Food Prog.	9.70	7.70	6.00	1.30	.92
☐ 18	75¢ U.P.U. Building	21.00	17.00	9.10	2.20	1.65
☐ 19–20	30¢, 50¢ Anti-Discrim.	21.00	17.00	9.00	2.20	1.80
☐ 21	1.10 fr. Intl. Schools	24.00	21.00	15.50	3.20	2.15

1972.

☐ 22	40¢ Regular Issue	3.60	2.70	2.00	.62	.48
☐ 23	40¢ Non-Proliferation	14.00	11.00	8.00	2.10	1.47
☐ 24	80¢ World Health	18.20	14.00	10.00	2.50	1.83
☐ 25–26	40¢, 80¢ Environment	27.50	17.00	12.10	2.60	2.25
☐ 27	1.10 fr. E.C. Europe	27.50	17.00	12.75	2.60	2.25
☐ 28–29	40¢, 80¢ U.N. Art-Sert	27.50	17.00	12.75	2.60	2.25

1973.

☐ 30–31	60¢, 1.10 fr. Disarm	26.00	18.00	13.00	3.30	2.80
☐ 32	60¢ Drug Abuse	10.00	7.00	5.20	1.75	.92
☐ 33	80¢ U.N. Volunteers	18.00	14.00	12.00	2.40	1.90
☐ 34	60¢ Namibia	18.00	14.00	12.00	2.40	1.90
☐ 35–36	40¢, 80¢ Human Rights	14.00	9.70	7.50	1.80	1.10

1974.

☐ 37–38	60¢, 80¢ ILO Hdqrs.	17.00	12.50	11.00	2.10	1.65
☐ 39–40	30¢, 60¢ UPU Centenary	20.00	14.00	6.10	1.60	.95
☐ 41–42	60¢, 1 fr. Brazil Mural	26.00	17.10	12.10	2.60	1.85
☐ 43–44	60¢, 80¢ Population	25.00	16.00	11.20	2.50	1.85
☐ 45	1.30 fr. Law of Sea	25.00	14.00	8.50	2.10	1.10

Scott No.		Name Block 6	Name Block 4	Plain Block 4	Unused Each	Used Each
1975.						
☐46–47	60¢, 80¢ Space Usage	22.00	15.00	9.00	2.30	1.90
☐48–49	60¢, 90¢ Women's Year	27.00	21.00	11.00	3.00	2.20
☐50–51	60¢, 90¢ U.N. Anniv.	14.00	10.00	8.00	2.40	2.00
☐52	1.50 fr. Same, Souv. Sheet	—	—	—	3.00	2.00
☐53–54	50¢ 1.30 fr. Namibia	19.10	16.00	14.00	3.60	2.80
☐55–56	60¢, 70¢ Peacekeeping	15.00	12.00	9.00	2.30	1.80
1976.						
☐57	90¢ WFUNA	9.10	7.00	6.50	1.70	1.20
☐58	1.10 fr. UNCTAD	9.00	7.10	6.00	1.70	1.20
☐59–60	40¢ 1.50 fr. HABITAT	18.50	15.00	12.10	3.70	2.80
☐61–62	80¢, 1.10 fr. U.N. Postal Anniv.	94.00	73.00	57.00	10.00	9.10
☐63	70¢ World Food Council	7.00	6.00	4.20	1.10	.80
1977.						
☐64	80¢ WIPO	7.50	6.20	5.20	2.00	1.30
☐65–66	80¢ 1.10 fr. Water Conf.	22.00	16.10	12.20	2.80	1.92
☐67–68	80¢, 1.10 fr. Security Council	22.00	16.20	12.20	2.80	1.92
☐69–70	40¢ 1.10 fr. Combat Racism	20.00	15.00	12.20	2.50	1.98
☐71–72	80¢, 1.10 fr. Atomic Energy	22.00	17.00	12.20	3.20	2.50
☐73	35¢ Doves	4.00	2.60	1.80	.70	.50
☐74–75	80¢, 1.10 fr. Smallpox	17.20	13.50	12.00	2.60	1.92
☐76	80¢ Namibia	7.70	6.20	4.60	1.20	.83
☐77–78	70¢, 80¢ ICAO–Air Safety	16.00	12.50	9.20	2.15	1.75
☐79–80	70¢, 1.10 Fr. General Assembly	17.50	12.50	9.20	2.60	2.00
☐81	80¢ Technical Cooperation	7.00	4.90	4.00	.98	.83
1979.						
☐82–83	80¢, 1.50 UNDRO	17.50	13.50	11.10	2.60	2.00
☐84–85	80¢, 1.10 Intl. Year of The Child	46.50	33.00	25.00	5.60	1.65
☐86	1.10 fr. Namibia	12.50	9.10	7.00	1.60	1.10
☐87–88	80¢, 1.10 Court of Justice	16.50	13.20	10.50	2.70	1.90
1980.						
☐89	80¢ Economic Order	7.00	6.00	5.20	1.30	.92
☐90–91	40¢, 70¢ Women's Decade	11.00	8.00	6.10	1.40	.96
☐92	1.10 fr. Peacekeeping	11.00	8.00	6.10	1.40	.96
☐93–94	40¢, 70¢, 35th Anniversary	10.00	7.50	6.10	1.40	.92
☐95	40¢, 70¢ Sheet	—	—	—	2.30	1.00
☐96–97	40¢, 70¢ Economic and Social Council	10.00	7.50	5.50	1.30	.83
1981.						
☐98	80¢ Palestinian People	6.80	5.00	4.10	1.25	.83
☐99–100	40¢, 1.50 fr., Disabled Persons	13.00	9.00	7.20	2.15	1.80
☐101	80¢ Bulgarian Mural	6.70	5.70	4.10	1.25	.83
☐102	1.10 fr. Energy Sources	10.10	7.60	7.00	1.72	.92
☐103–04	40¢, 70¢ Volunteers	11.00	7.60	7.00	1.72	.92
1982.						
☐105–06	1 fr., Definitives	13.00	9.75	7.70	1.80	1.15
☐107–08	40¢, 1.20 fr., Human Environment	16.50	13.00	10.00	2.20	1.70

Scott No.		Fine	Ave.

UNUSED BOOKLET PANES

Scott No.		Fine	Ave.
☐319g	2¢ Carmine . . .	136.00	95.00
☐331a	1¢ Green	138.00	98.00
☐332a	2¢ Carmine . . .	143.00	106.00
☐1374a	1¢ Green	116.00	79.00
☐375a	2¢ Carmine . . .	107.00	79.00
☐405a	1¢ Green	62.00	42.00
☐406a	2¢ Carmine . . .	84.00	57.00
☐424d	1¢ Green	7.20	5.00
☐425e	2¢ Carmine . . .	17.50	13.10
☐462a	1¢ Green	12.00	6.70
☐463a	2¢ Carmine . . .	83.00	53.00
☐498e	1¢ Green	4.10	3.00
☐499e	2¢ Rose	4.50	3.20
☐501b	3¢ Violet I	82.00	53.00
☐502b	3¢ Violet II . . .	62.00	45.00
☐552a	1¢ Dark Green .	7.20	6.10
☐554c	2¢ Carmine . . .	7.20	5.10
☐583a	2¢ Carmine . . .	80.00	55.00
☐632a	1¢ Green	5.50	3.20
☐1634d	2¢ Carmine . . .	3.10	2.60
☐720b	3¢ Dark Violet .	40.00	28.00
☐804b	1¢ Green	3.50	2.50
☐806b	2¢ Red Carmine .	5.70	4.60
☐807a	3¢ Dark Violet . .	12.00	7.10
☐1035a	3¢ Dark Violet . .	4.75	3.10
☐1036a	4¢ Red Violet. . .	3.75	2.60
☐1213a	5¢ "ZIP"	3.20	2.60
☐1213x	5¢ Mailman	8.00	6.20
☐1213y	5¢ Zone No. . . .	12.50	9.20
☐1278a	1¢ Jeff. (8)	1.10	.80
☐1278ae	1¢ T. Gum (8) . .	2.60	1.60
☐1278b	1¢ Green (4) . . .	.75	.46
☐1280a	2¢ Blue Gray (5) .	1.20	.82
☐1280c	2¢ Blue Gray (6) . .	.96	.65
☐1284d	6¢ F.D.R. (8) . . .	1.65	1.15
☐1284c	6¢ F.D.R. (5) . . .	1.50	.96
☐1393a	6¢ Ike (8)	1.75	1.25
☐1393ae	6¢ T. Gum	2.20	1.40
☐1393b	6¢ Ike (5)	1.50	1.15
☐1395a	8¢ Ike (8)	2.50	1.85
☐1395b	8¢ Ike (6)	1.90	1.35
☐1395c	8¢ Ike (4)	1.80	1.25
☐1395d	8¢ Ike (7)	2.50	1.70

Scott No.		Fine	Ave.
☐1510b	10¢ Mem'l (5) . .	1.70	1.16
☐1510c	10¢ Mem'l (8) . .	2.50	1.83
☐1510d	10¢ Mem'l (6) . .	3.50	2.40
☐1595a	13¢ Bell (6). . . .	2.70	2.00
☐1595b	13¢ Bell (7). . . .	3.00	2.10
☐1595c	13¢ Bell (8). . . .	3.75	2.60
☐1595d	13¢ Bell (5). . . .	2.50	1.50
☐1623a	13¢ (7), 9¢ (1) . .	3.30	2.15
☐1623c	Same, Perf. 10	43.00	32.00
☐1736a	"A" Eagle (no denomination) .	5.50	4.10
☐1737a	15¢ Multicolored. .	3.20	2.20
☐1742a	15¢ Multicolored. .	3.80	2.80
☐C10a	10¢ Lindbergh . .	125.00	88.00
☐C25a	6¢ Carmine	5.10	3.75
☐C39a	6¢ Small.	18.00	13.00
☐C51a	7¢ Blue	16.00	12.00
☐C60a	7¢ Carmine	28.00	20.00
☐C64c	8¢ Carmine "Zip" .	3.70	2.30
☐C64bx	8¢ Mailman	13.50	9.75
☐C64by	8¢ Zone No. . . .	46.00	33.00
☐C72b	10¢ Carmine (8) . .	4.20	3.20
☐C72c	10¢ Carmine (5) . .	5.30	4.00
☐C78a	11¢ Carmine (4) . .	2.20	1.50
☐C79a	13¢ Letter (5)	2.30	1.70

Scott No.		Fine

SOUVENIR CARDS

		Fine
☐1	Truck w Gum	87.00
☐	Truck w/o gum	13.00
☐2	Barcelona.	330.00
☐3	SIPEX Scenes	175.00
☐3a	SIPEX Miner	11.00
☐4	EFIMEX	5.00
☐5	SANDIPEX	71.00
☐	Ana '69	76.00
☐	FRESNO	415.00
☐6	ASDA '69.	20.00
☐7	INTERPEX '70	51.00
☐8	COMPEX '70	12.00
☐	ANA 1970	120.00
☐9	PHILYMPIA.	3.00
☐10	HAPEX	14.00

Scott No.		Fine		Scott No.		Fine
☐11	INTERPEX '71	3.00		☐	INTERPHIL Program with	
☐12	WESTPEX	3.00			B.E.P. Card	12.00
☐13	NAPEX '71	3.00		☐47	Science BEP	7.80
☐	ANA 1971	3.40		☐48	Science U.S.P.S.	4.60
☐14	TEXANEX	3.50		☐49	Stamp Expo '76	7.70
☐15	EXFILIMA	2.10		☐50	Colorado Statehood	4.00
☐16	ASDA '71	3.00		☐51	HAFNIA '76	3.20
☐17	ANPHILEX	2.00		☐	ANA 1976	8.20
☐18	INTERPEX '72	2.00		☐52	ITALIA '76	3.00
☐19	NOPEX	2.00		☐53	NORDPOSTA '76	3.00
☐20	BELGICA	2.00		☐54	MILCOPEX '77	3.00
☐	ANA 1972	3.10		☐55	ROMPEX '77	4.20
☐21	Olympia Phil. Munchen	2.00		☐56	AMPHILEX '77	3.40
☐22	EXFILBRA	2.00		☐	ANA 1977	4.20
☐23	Postal Forum	2.00		☐57	SAN MARCO	3.70
☐24	SEPAD '72	2.00		☐58	Puripex	3.20
☐25	ASDA '72	1.80		☐59	ASDA '77	4.20
☐26	Stamp Expo '75	2.10		☐60	ROPEX '78	3.50
☐27	INTERPEX '73	2.40		☐	Paper Money Show	5.20
☐28	IBRA	2.40		☐61	NAPOSTA '78	4.10
☐29	COMPEX '73	1.95		☐62	CENTEX '78	4.60
☐30	APEX	1.70		☐63	BRASILIANA '79	5.00
☐	ANA 1973	7.00		☐64	JAPEX '79	6.20
☐31	POLSKA	3.00		☐	ANA '80	48.00
☐32	NAPEX '73	2.50		☐65	LONDON '80	5.00
☐33	ASDA '73	2.50		☐	Money Show '80	9.70
☐34	Stamps Expo '73	2.50		☐66	NORWEX '80	6.10
☐35	Hobby Show Chicago	3.00		☐67	NAPEX '80	11.00
☐36	MILCOPEX '72	3.10		☐	Visitor Center	9.00
☐37	INTERNABA 1974	3.20		☐68	ASDA STAMP	
☐	ANA 1974	14.00			FESTIVAL '80	12.00
☐38	STOCKHOLMIA '74	3.20		☐69	ESSEN '80	1.40
☐39	EXFILMEX '74	3.20		☐70	STAMP EXPO '81	11.00
☐40	ESPANA '75	3.20		☐	Visitor Center	7.80
☐41	NAPEX '75	9.00		☐71	WIPA '81	5.50
☐42	ARPHILA '75	3.00		☐	Paper Money	8.70
☐43	Women's Year	31.00		☐	ANA '81	12.00
☐	ANA 1975	18.00		☐72	STAMP COLLECTORS	
☐44	ASDA '75	47.00			MONTH	4.50
☐45	WERABA '76	4.20		☐73	PHILATOKYO '81	4.70
☐46	INTERPHIL '76	8.00		☐74	NORD POSKTA '81	4.00

Scott No.		Fine Unused Each	Ave. Unused Each	Fine Used Each	Ave. Used Each
POSTAGE DUE STAMPS					
1879 Perforated 12 (N-H ADD 80%)					
☐ J1	1¢ Brown	25.00	15.00	6.10	4.60
☐ J2	2¢ Brown	170.00	107.00	6.00	4.00
☐ J3	3¢ Brown	19.00	12.00	4.00	1.70
☐ J4	5¢ Brown	236.00	138.00	25.00	15.50
☐ J5	10¢ Brown	295.00	175.00	13.00	8.00
☐ J6	30¢ Brown	125.00	80.00	22.00	12.10
☐ J7	50¢ Brown	215.00	160.00	38.00	24.50
1884–1889 SAME DESIGN—PERF. 12 (N-H ADD 80%)					
☐ J15	1¢ Red Brown	32.00	23.00	3.75	2.70
☐ J16	2¢ Red Brown	40.00	29.00	3.75	2.50
☐ J17	3¢ Red Brown	395.00	270.00	110.00	70.00
☐ J18	5¢ Red Brown	198.00	130.00	11.00	7.60
☐ J19	10¢ Red Brown	170.00	110.00	7.10	4.10
☐ J20	30¢ Red Brown	103.00	67.00	26.00	17.50
☐ J21	50¢ Red Brown	985.00	710.00	125.00	76.50
1891–1893 SAME DESIGN—PERF. 12 (N-H ADD 80%)					
☐ J22	1¢ Bright Claret	11.00	7.10	.75	.56
☐ J23	2¢ Bright Claret	12.00	7.60	.70	.60
☐ J24	3¢ Bright Claret	25.00	14.50	4.20	3.20
☐ J25	5¢ Bright Claret	27.00	19.00	4.60	3.20
☐ J26	10¢ Bright Claret	55.00	36.00	12.00	7.10
☐ J27	30¢ Bright Claret	215.00	142.00	87.00	62.00
☐ J28	50¢ Bright Claret	245.00	170.00	94.00	65.00
1894 NEW SMALL DESIGN—NO WTMK.—PERF. 12 (N-H ADD 55%)					
☐ J29	1¢ Vermilion	410.00	261.00	82.00	55.00
☐ J30	2¢ Vermilion	200.00	140.00	40.00	27.00
☐ J31	1¢ Claret	20.00	14.00	6.00	3.60
☐ J32	2¢ Claret	17.00	9.00	5.00	2.60
☐ J33	3¢ Claret	66.00	37.00	22.00	15.00
☐ J34	5¢ Claret	66.00	42.00	25.00	17.00
☐ J35	10¢ Claret	66.00	39.00	16.00	12.00
☐ J36	30¢ Claret (Shades)	195.00	120.00	48.00	32.00
☐ J37	50¢ Claret (Shades)	410.00	260.00	110.00	70.00
1895 SAME NEW SMALL DESIGN—D.L. WTMK.—PERF. 12 (N-H ADD 80%)					
☐ J38	1¢ Claret	6.10	3.60	.46	.33
☐ J39	2¢ Claret	6.10	3.60	.36	.21
☐ J40	3¢ Claret	32.00	18.00	1.45	.79
☐ J41	5¢ Claret	29.00	16.00	1.25	.72
☐ J42	10¢ Claret	33.00	21.00	3.10	1.65
☐ J43	30¢ Claret	240.00	160.00	23.00	13.00
☐ J44	50¢ Claret	160.00	120.00	24.00	13.50

Scott No.		Fine Unused Each	Ave. Unused Each	Fine Used Each	Ave. Used Each

1910–1912 SMALL DESIGN—S.L. WTMK.—PERF. 12 (N-H ADD 80%)

☐ J45	1¢ Claret	21.00	13.00	2.50	1.50
☐ J46	2¢ Claret	21.00	14.00	.31	.19
☐ J47	3¢ Claret	300.00	200.00	15.00	11.00
☐ J48	5¢ Claret	47.00	33.00	5.00	3.50
☐ J49	10¢ Claret	58.00	39.00	12.00	6.10
☐ J50	50¢ Claret	520.00	380.00	74.00	48.00

1914–1916 SAME SMALL DESIGN—S.L. WTMK. PERF. 10 (N-H ADD 80%)

☐ J52	1¢ Carmine	39.00	24.00	9.10	6.20
☐ J53	2¢ Carmine	23.00	13.00	.35	.21
☐ J54	3¢ Carmine	35.00	200.00	12.00	8.50
☐ J55	5¢ Carmine	21.00	14.00	2.20	1.60
☐ J56	10¢ Carmine	33.00	21.00	1.60	.75
☐ J57	30¢ Carmine	125.00	79.00	17.00	12.00
☐ J58	50¢ Carmine	4900.00	3100.00	360.00	212.00
☐ J59	1¢ Rose (No Wtmk.)	850.00	650.00	160.00	140.00
☐ J60	2¢ Rose (No Wtmk.)	74.00	54.00	7.10	4.60

Scott No.		Fine Unused Plate Blk	Ave. Unused Plate Blk	Fine Unused Each	Ave. Unused Each	Fine Used Each	Ave. Used Each

1917–1926 SAME SMALL DESIGN—NO WTMK.—PERF. 11 (N-H ADD 40%)

☐ J61	1¢ Carmine Rose	49.00	34.00	2.10	1.40	.19	.16
☐ J62	2¢ Carmine Rose	47.00	33.00	2.10	1.40	.17	.10
☐ J63	3¢ Carmine Rose	115.00	77.00	7.10	6.00	.19	.15
☐ J64	5¢ Carmine Rose	116.00	78.00	7.60	7.00	.19	.15
☐ J65	10¢ Carmine Rose	180.00	115.00	12.00	7.50	.22	.15
☐ J66	30¢ Carmine Rose	520.00	370.00	52.00	34.00	.63	.42
☐ J67	50¢ Carmine Rose	770.00	570.00	70.00	45.00	.23	.16
☐ J68	½¢ Dull Red	14.00	10.00	.92	.62	.18	.13

1930–1931 NEW DESIGN FLAT PRESS—PERF. 11 x 11 (N-H ADD 30%)

☐ J69	½¢ Carmine	57.00	38.00	3.80	2.70	.93	.62
☐ J70	1¢ Carmine	38.00	26.00	3.00	2.00	.24	.17
☐ J71	2¢ Carmine	51.00	35.00	4.10	2.80	.26	.17
☐ J72	3¢ Carmine	240.00	176.00	17.00	13.00	1.50	.95
☐ J73	5¢ Carmine	260.00	176.00	20.00	17.00	1.90	1.25
☐ J74	10¢ Carmine	450.00	350.00	38.00	26.00	.83	.52
☐ J75	30¢ Carmine	1300.00	930.00	142.00	100.00	1.40	.81
☐ J76	50¢ Carmine	1400.00	1000.00	148.00	105.00	.38	.21
☐ J77	$1 Carmine	335.00	230.00	31.00	21.00	.18	.12
☐ J78	$5 Carmine	385.00	250.00	47.00	30.00	.23	.16

Scott No.		Fine Unused Plate Blk	Ave. Unused Plate Blk	Fine Unused Each	Ave. Unused Each	Fine Used Each	Ave. Used Each
1931–1956 SAME DESIGN—ROTARY PRESS—PERF. 11 x 10½ (N-H ADD 20%)							
☐ J79	½¢ Carmine	23.00	17.00	1.40	.84	.18	.14
☐ J80	1¢ Carmine	2.50	1.70	.20	.14	.10	.08
☐ J81	2¢ Carmine	2.50	1.70	.21	.15	.10	.08
☐ J82	3¢ Carmine	3.40	2.50	.34	.23	.10	.08
☐ J83	5¢ Carmine	4.10	3.00	.42	.32	.10	.08
☐ J84	10¢ Carmine	9.10	5.80	1.40	.95	.14	.11
☐ J85	30¢ Carmine	53.00	39.00	12.00	8.10	.14	.09
☐ J86	50¢ Carmine	64.00	45.00	14.00	9.50	.12	.09
☐ J87	$1 Red (10½x11)	330.00	200.00	47.00	34.00	.22	.18

Scott No.		Mint Sheet	Plate Block	Fine Unused Each	Fine Used Each
1959 NEW SERIES—NEW DESIGN—ROTARY PRESS—PERF. 11 x 10½ (N-H ADD 20%)					
☐ J88	½¢ Red & Black	460.00	193.00	1.85	1.42
☐ J89	1¢ Red & Black	3.40	.62	.10	.09
☐ J90	2¢ Red & Black	4.60	.63	.10	.09
☐ J91	3¢ Red & Black	6.20	.75	.10	.09
☐ J92	4¢ Red & Black	7.70	1.20	.13	.09
☐ J93	5¢ Red & Black	9.20	1.10	.15	.09
☐ J94	6¢ Red & Black	12.00	1.50	.20	.09
☐ J95	7¢ Red & Black	14.00	1.80	.21	.12
☐ J96	8¢ Red & Black	17.00	1.90	.24	.10
☐ J97	10¢ Red & Black	19.00	1.90	.27	.08
☐ J98	30¢ Red & Black	—	5.10	.68	.08
☐ J99	50¢ Red & Black	—	5.00	1.15	.08
☐ J100	$1 Red & Black	—	9.00	2.10	.08
☐ J101	$5 Red & Black	—	40.00	11.00	.17
1978 SAME DESIGN, NEW VALUES					
☐ J102	11¢ Red & Black	25.00	2.50	.32	.28
☐ J103	13¢ Red & Black	31.00	2.90	.42	.28

Scott No.		Fine

U.S. UNUSED ZIP CODE BLOCKS OF FOUR

☐1181	5¢ Battle—Wilderness	1.15
☐1182	5¢ Appomattox	1.21
☐1242	5¢ Sam Houston	.83
☐1243	5¢ Chas. M. Russell	1.35
☐1244	5¢ N.Y. World's Fair	.86
☐1247	5¢ N.J. Tercentenary	.82
☐1248	5¢ Neveda Statehood	.82
☐1249	5¢ Register & Vote	.82
☐1250	5¢ Wm. Shakespeare	.82
☐1251	5¢ Mayo Brothers	.82
☐1252	5¢ American Music	.82
☐1253	5¢ Homemakers	.82
☐1254–57	5¢ Christmas, 1964	2.72
☐1258	5¢ Verr.—Narr. Bridge	.80
☐1259	5¢ Modern Art	.80
☐1260	5¢ Radio Amateurs	.80
☐1261	5¢ Battle—N. Orleans	.80
☐1262	5¢ Physical Fitness	.80
☐1263	5¢ Cancer Crusade	.80
☐1264	5¢ Churchill Mem'l	.80
☐1265	5¢ Magna Carta	.80
☐1266	5¢ Intl. Co-op Year	.80
☐1267	5¢ Salvation Army	.80
☐1268	5¢ Dante Alighieri	.80
☐1269	5¢ Herbert Hoover	.80
☐1270	5¢ Robert Fulton	.87
☐1272	5¢ Traffic Safety	.87
☐1273	5¢ John S. Copley	.93
☐1274	11¢ Intl. Telecom. Un.	5.40
☐1276	5¢ Christmas, 1965	.85
☐1278	1¢ Thomas Jefferson	.35
☐1280	2¢ F. Lloyd Wright	.45
☐1281	3¢ Francis Parkman	.63
☐1284	6¢ F.D. Roosevelt	6.40
☐1285	8¢ Albert Einstein	1.40
☐1286	10¢ Andrew Jackson	1.40
☐1286A	12¢ Henry Ford	1.70
☐1288	15¢ O.W. Holmes	2.70
☐1289	20¢ Geo. C. Marshall	2.30
☐1290	25¢ F. Douglass	2.60
☐1291	30¢ John Dewey	3.50
☐1292	40¢ Thomas Paine	4.70
☐1293	50¢ Lucy Stone	5.20
☐1294	$1 Eugene O'Neill	13.00
☐1306	5¢ Migr. Bird Treaty	.86
☐1307	5¢ Humane to Animals	.82

☐1308	5¢ Indiana Statehood	.78
☐1309	5¢ American Circus	.86
☐1310	5¢ 6th Intl. Phil. Exh.	.79
☐1312	5¢ Bill of rights	.79
☐1313	5¢ Polish Millennium	.79
☐1314	5¢ Natl. Park Service	.79
☐1315	5¢ Marine Reserves	.86
☐1316	5¢ Women's Clubs	.90
☐1317	5¢ Johnny Appleseed	.90
☐1318	5¢ Beautify America	.98
☐1319	5¢ Great River Road	.86
☐1320	5¢ Servicemen-Bonds	.80
☐1321	5¢ Christmas, 1966	.80
☐1322	5¢ Mary Cassatt	1.25
☐1323	5¢ National Grange	.82
☐1324	5¢ Canada Centennial	.90
☐1325	5¢ Erie Canal	.79
☐1326	5¢ Search for Peace	.79
☐1327	5¢ Henry D. Thoreau	.77
☐1328	5¢ Nebraska Statehood	.77
☐1329	5¢ Voice of America	.77
☐1330	5¢ Davy Crockett	.77
☐1331–32	5¢ Twin Space	7.60
☐1333	5¢ Urban Planning	1.20
☐1334	5¢ Finnish Independ.	1.20
☐1336	5¢ Christmas, 1967	.80
☐1337	5¢ Miss. Statehood	1.16
☐1338	6¢ American Flag	.93
☐1339	6¢ Illinois Statehood	.93
☐1341	$1 Airlift	33.00
☐1342	6¢ Support Our Youth	1.20
☐1343	6¢ Law & Order	1.20
☐1344	6¢ Register & Vote	1.20
☐1353–54	6¢ Historic Flags	3.60
☐1355	6¢ Walt Disney	1.40
☐1356	6¢ Fr. Marquette	1.20
☐1357	6¢ Daniel Boone	1.20
☐1358	6¢ Arkansas River	1.20
☐1359	6¢ Leif Erikson	1.20
☐1360	6¢ Cherokee Strip	1.20
☐1361	6¢ Trumbull Painting	1.20
☐1362	6¢ Wildlife Conserv.	1.20
☐1364	6¢ American Indian	1.20
☐1365–68	6¢ Beautify America	6.60
☐1369	6¢ American Legion	.89
☐1370	6¢ Grandma Moses	.89
☐1371	6¢ Apollo 8	1.50
☐1372	6¢ W.C. Handy	.97
☐1373	6¢ California	.97

Scott No.		Fine
☐1374	6¢ J.W. Powell	.97
☐1375	6¢ Alabama	.97
☐1376–79	6¢ Botanical	9.10
☐1380	6¢ Dartmouth Case	.92
☐1381	6¢ Baseball	2.50
☐1382	6¢ Football	1.50
☐1383	6¢ Eisenhower	.92
☐1385	6¢ Rehabilitation	.92
☐1386	6¢ Wm. M. Harnett	.92
☐1387–90	6¢ Natural History	1.40
☐1391	6¢ Maine Statehood	.93
☐1392	6¢ Buffalo	.93
☐1393	6¢ Eisenhower-Reg.	.86
☐1393D	7¢ Franklin	.91
☐1394	8¢ Eisenhower	.93
☐1396	8¢ Postal Service	1.30
☐1397	14¢ F. LaGuardia	1.75
☐1398	8¢ Ernie Pyle	2.45
☐1399	18¢ Dr. E. Blackwell	2.40
☐1400	21¢ A.P. Giannini	2.42
☐1405	6¢ E.L. Masters	.88
☐1406	6¢ Women's Suffrage	.88
☐1407	6¢ So. Carolina	.88
☐1408	6¢ Stone Mountain	.88
☐1409	6¢ Fort Snelling	.88
☐1410–13	6¢ Anti-Pollution	2.50
☐1414	6¢ Nativity	1.00
☐1414a	6¢ Precancelled	1.10
☐1415–18	6¢ Christmas Toys	4.70
☐1415–18a	6¢ Precancelled	10.00
☐1419	6¢ United Nations	.87
☐1420	6¢ Pilgrim Landing	.87
☐1421–22	6¢ D.A.V. & P.O.W.	1.72
☐1423	6¢ Sheep	.90
☐1424	6¢ D. MacArthur	.90
☐1425	6¢ Blood Donors	.90
☐1426	8¢ Mo. Statehood	.90
☐1427–30	8¢ Wildlife Cons.	1.21
☐1431	8¢ Antarctic Traety	.93
☐1432	8¢ Amer. Revolution	1.85
☐1433	8¢ John Sloan	.93
☐1434–35	8¢ Space Achievement	1.15
☐1436	8¢ Emily Dickinson	.93
☐1437	8¢ San Juan	.93
☐1438	8¢ Drug Addiction	.93
☐1439	8¢ CARE	.93
☐1440–43	8¢ Historic Pres.	1.20
☐1444	8¢ Nativity	.93
☐1445	8¢ Partridge	.93

Scott No.		Fine
☐1446	8¢ Sidney Lanier	.93
☐1447	8¢ Peace Corps	.93
☐1448–51	2¢ Cape Hatteras	.90
☐1452	6¢ Wolf Trap Farm	.76
☐1453	8¢ Yellowstone	1.10
☐1454	15¢ Mt. McKinley	1.90
☐1455	8¢ Family Planning	.93
☐1456–59	8¢ Colonial Crafts.	1.15
☐1460	6¢ Olympic Games	1.10
☐1461	8¢ Olympic Games	1.30
☐1462	15¢ Olympic Games	2.50
☐1463	8¢ P.T.A.	1.10
☐1464	8¢ Wildlife	1.30
☐1468	8¢ Mail Order	1.10
☐1469	8¢ Osteopathic	1.10
☐1470	8¢ Tom Sawyer	.97
☐1471	8¢ Xmas-Religious	.97
☐1472	8¢ Xmas-Santa Claus	.97
☐1473	8¢ Pharmacy	.97
☐1474	8¢ Stamp Collectors	.97
☐1475	8¢ Love	.97
☐1476	8¢ Pamphlet Printing	.97
☐1477	8¢ Posting Broadside	.97
☐1478	8¢ Post Rider	.97
☐1479	8¢ Drummer	.97
☐1480–83	8¢ Bost. Tea Party	.97
☐1484	8¢ George Gershwin	.97
☐1485	8¢ Robinson Jeffers	.97
☐1486	8¢ Tanner	.97
☐1487	8¢ Willa Cather	.97
☐1488	8¢ N. Copernicus	.97
☐1500	8¢ Electronics	.97
☐1501	8¢ Electronics	.97
☐1502	15¢ Electronics	1.85
☐1504	8¢ Angus Cattle	.97
☐1505	10¢ Chautauqua	1.22
☐1506	10¢ Winter Wheat	1.22
☐1507	8¢ Xmas-Religious	1.20
☐1508	8¢ Xmas-Tree	1.15
☐1510	10¢ Jefferson Mem'l.	1.30
☐1511	10¢ Zip Code	1.30
☐1525	10¢ V.F.W.	1.17
☐1526	10¢ Robert Frost	1.17
☐1527	10¢ EXPO '74—Envir.	1.17
☐1528	10¢ Horse Racing	1.15
☐1529	10¢ Skylab Project	1.17
☐1538–41	10¢ Minerals	1.25
☐1542	10¢ Fort Harrod	1.17
☐1543–46	10¢ Cont. Congress	1.17

Scott No.		Fine	Scott No.		Fine
☐1547	10¢ Energy Conserv.	1.17	☐1710	13¢ Transatlantic Flight	1.50
☐1548	10¢ Sleepy Hollow	1.17	☐1711	13¢ Colorado	1.50
☐1549	10¢ Retarded Children	1.17	☐1712	13¢ Butterflies	1.50
☐1550	10¢ Xmas-Religious	1.17	☐1716	13¢ Lafayette	1.50
☐1551	10¢ Xmas-Sleigh	1.21	☐1717	20¢, 13¢ Skilled Hands	1.50
☐1553	10¢ B. West	1.21	☐1721	13¢ Peace Bridge	1.50
☐1554	10¢ P. Dunbar	1.21	☐1722	13¢ Herkimer	1.50
☐1555	10¢ D.W. Griffith	1.21	☐1723	24¢, 13¢ Energy	1.50
☐1556	10¢ Pioneer-Jupiter	1.21	☐1725	13¢ Alta	1.50
☐1557	10¢ Mariner 10	1.21	☐1726	13¢ Confederation	1.50
☐1558	10¢ Collective Barg	1.21	☐1727	13¢ Pictures	1.50
☐1559	8¢ Sybil Ludington	1.06	☐1728	13¢ Saratoga	1.50
☐1560	10¢ Salem Poor	1.30	☐1730	13¢ Mailbox	1.50
☐1561	10¢ Haym Solomon	1.30	☐1731	13¢ Sandburg	1.50
☐1562	18¢ Peter Francisco	2.40	☐1732	13¢ Capt. Cook	1.50
☐1563	10¢ Lex.-Concord	1.16	☐1733	13¢ Capt. Cook R&S	1.50
☐1564	10¢ Bunker Hill	1.16	☐1734	13¢ Indian Cent	1.60
☐1565–68	10¢ Uniforms	1.21	☐1735	15¢ No Value "A" Eagle	1.60
☐1569–70	10¢ Apollo-Soyuz	1.21	☐1744	13¢ Harriet Tubman	1.45
☐1571	10¢ Women's Year	1.21	☐1745–48	13¢ Quilts	1.55
☐1572–75	10¢ Postal Service	1.21	☐1749–52	13¢ Dance	1.55
☐1576	10¢ World Peace	1.21	☐1753	13¢ French Alliance	1.55
☐1577–78	10¢ Banking & Com	1.21	☐1754	13¢ Papanicolau	1.55
☐1579	10¢ Xmas-Religious	1.21	☐1755	13¢ Jimmie Rodgers	1.55
☐1580	10¢ Xmas-Post Card	1.21	☐1756	15¢ George M. Cohan	1.60
☐1581a	1¢ Ability to Write	.83	☐1757	13¢ Capex SS	2.85
☐1582	2¢ Freedom to Speak	.83	☐1758	15¢ Photography	1.65
☐1585	4¢ Public that Reads	.83	☐1759	15¢ Viking	1.65
☐1591	9¢ Freedom to Assemble	1.10	☐1760–63	15¢ Owls	1.65
☐1592	10¢ Justice	1.21	☐1764–67	15¢ Trees	1.65
☐1593	11¢ Freedom of Press	1.31	☐1768	15¢ Madonna	1.65
☐1596	13¢ Eagle & Shield	1.45	☐1769	15¢ Xmas Hobby Horse	1.65
☐1603	24¢ Old North Church	2.90	☐1770	15¢ R.F. Kennedy	1.65
☐1729–31	13¢ Spirit of '76	3.70	☐1771	15¢ M.L. King	1.65
☐1732	13¢ Interphil '76	1.50	☐1772	15¢ Intl. Year of Child	1.65
☐1733–82	13¢ State Flags	4.50	☐1773	15¢ Steinbeck	1.65
☐1783	13¢ Telephone	1.42	☐1774	15¢ Einstein	1.65
☐1784	13¢ Aviation	1.42	☐1775–78	15¢ Toleware	1.65
☐1785	13¢ Chemistry	1.42	☐1779–82	15¢ Architecture	1.65
☐1790	13¢ Ben Franklin	1.42	☐1783–86	15¢ Endangered Flora	1.65
☐1791–94	13¢ Dec. of Indep	1.80	☐1788	15¢ Special Olympics	1.65
☐1795–98	13¢ Olympic Games	3.00	☐1789	15¢ John Paul Jones	2.15
☐1799	13¢ Clara Maass	1.45	☐1790	10¢ Olympics	1.45
☐1700	13¢ Adolph Ochs	1.45	☐1791–94	15¢ Summer Olympics	2.30
☐1701	13¢ Nativity	1.45	☐1795–98	15¢ Winter Olympics	3.10
☐1702	13¢ Winter Pastime	1.50	☐1799	15¢ Madonna	1.75
☐1704	13¢ Wash. at Princeton	1.45	☐100	15¢ Xmas Santa	1.75
☐1705	13¢ Sound Recording	1.45	☐1801	15¢ Will Rogers	1.75
☐1706–09	13¢ Pueblo Art (6)	2.50	☐1802	15¢ Vietnam Veterans	1.75

Scott No.		Fine
☐1803	15¢ Fields.	1.72
☐1804	15¢ Banneker.	1.72
☐1805–10	15¢ Letter Writing	1.72
☐1811	15¢ Perkins.	1.72
☐1822	15¢ Madison.	1.72
☐1823	15¢ Bissell	1.72
☐1824	15¢ Keller/Sullivan.	1.72
☐1825	15¢ Vets. Admin.	1.72
☐1826	15¢ De Galvez.	1.70
☐1827–30	15¢ Coral Reefs	1.70
☐1831	15¢ Org. Labor.	1.70
☐1832	15¢ Wharton.	1.70
☐1833	15¢ Education	1.70
☐1834–37	15¢ Indian Masks.	2.85
☐1838–41	15¢ Architecture	2.40
☐1842	15¢ Christmas Madonna	1.75
☐1849	17¢ Rachel Carson	1.75
☐1850	18¢ Geo. Mason.	1.75
☐1851	19¢ Sequoyah	1.75
☐1859	35¢ Dr. Charles Drew.	2.40
☐1874	15¢ Everett Dirksen.	1.75
☐1875	15¢ Whitney Young.	1.75
☐1876–79	18¢ Flowers.	2.15
☐1910	18¢ Red Cross.	2.15
☐1911	18¢ Savings & Loan.	2.15
☐1912–19	18¢ Space Achievement	2.15
☐1920	18¢ Management.	2.15
☐1921–24	18¢ Habitats	2.15
☐1925	18¢ Disabled	2.15
☐1926	18¢ Edna St. Vincent Millay	2.15
☐1928–31	18¢ Architecture	2.15
☐1932	18¢ Babe Zaharias.	2.15
☐1933	18¢ Bobby Jones.	2.15
☐1934	18¢ Remington.	2.15
☐1935	18¢ James Hoban.	2.15
☐1936	20¢ James Hoban.	2.15
☐1937–38	18¢ Yorktown, Virginia.	2.15
☐1939	20¢ Christmas Madonna	2.15
☐1940	20¢ Christmas Child Art.	2.15
☐1941	20¢ John Hanson.	2.15
☐1942–45	20¢ Desert Plants.	2.15
☐C69	8¢ Robert H. Goddard.	4.20
☐C70	8¢ Alaska Purchase.	2.30
☐C71	20¢ Columbia Jays.	7.20
☐C72	10¢ Stars.	5.60
☐C74	10¢ 50 Years Airmail	2.70
☐C75	20¢ U.S.A. & Jet.	3.90
☐C76	10¢ Moon Landing.	1.50
☐C77	9¢ Delta Plane	1.30

Scott No.		Fine
☐C78	11¢ Plane Silhouette.	1.40
☐C79	13¢ Letter.	1.50
☐C80	17¢ Liberty Head.	1.45
☐C81	21¢ "USA".	2.15
☐C84	11¢ City of Refuge.	1.40
☐C85	11¢ Olympic Games.	1.50
☐C86	11¢ Electronics.	1.40
☐C87	18¢ Statue of Liberty	2.15
☐C88	26¢ Mount Rushmore.	2.90
☐C89	5¢ Plane & Globes.	2.90
☐C90	31¢ Plane, Flag & Globes.	3.30
☐C91–2	31¢ Wright Bros.	4.10
☐C93–4	21¢ Chanute.	4.60
☐C95–6	25¢ Wiley Post.	6.20
☐C97	31¢ Olympics.	4.40
☐C98	40¢ Mazzel.	5.10
☐C99	28¢ Scott.	3.30
☐C100	35¢ Curtiss.	4.50
☐E22	45¢ Special Delivery.	9.10
☐E23	60¢ Special Delivery.	6.20

U.S. UNUSED MAIL EARLY INSCRIPTION BLOCKS

Scott No.		Fine
☐1278	1¢ T. Jefferson	.52
☐1280	2¢ F.L. Wright.	.52
☐1281	3¢ Parkman.	.83
☐1284	6¢ F.D. Roosevelt	7.70
☐1285	8¢ A. Einstein.	1.85
☐1286	10¢ A. Jackson.	1.85
☐1286A	12¢ Henry Ford.	2.10
☐1288	15¢ O.W. Holmes.	3.70
☐1289	20¢ G.C. Marshall	3.30
☐1290	25¢ F. Douglass.	3.70
☐1291	30¢ John Dewey.	5.50
☐1292	40¢ T. Paine.	5.90
☐1293	50¢ Lucy Stone.	7.20
☐1294	$1 E. O'Neill.	18.00
☐1338	6¢ American Flag.	1.30
☐1340	6¢ Hemis Fair '68.	1.50
☐1341	$1 Airlift	40.00
☐1342	6¢ Support Our Youth	1.35
☐1343	6¢ Law & Order.	1.35
☐1344	6¢ Register & Vote.	1.35
☐1347–49	6¢ Historic Flags	3.60
☐1355	6¢ Walt Disney	1.70
☐1356	6¢ Fr. Marquette.	1.25
☐1357	6¢ Daniel Boone	1.25
☐1358	6¢ Arkansas River	1.25
☐1359	6¢ Leif Erickson.	1.25

Scott No.		Fine
☐1360	6¢ Cherokee Strip	1.45
☐1361	6¢ Trumbull Painting	1.80
☐1362	6¢ Wildlife Conserv.	2.10
☐1364	6¢ American Indian.	2.40
☐1365–68	6¢ Beautify America	6.70
☐1369	6¢ American Legion	1.30
☐1370	6¢ Grandma Moses	1.30
☐1371	6¢ Apollo 8	1.85
☐1372	6¢ W.C. Handy	1.15
☐1373	6¢ California.	1.15
☐1374	6¢ J.W. Powell	1.15
☐1375	6¢ Alabama	1.15
☐1376–79	6¢ Botanical	13.70
☐1380	6¢ Dartmouth Case.	1.15
☐1381	6¢ Baseball	2.90
☐1382	6¢ Football	1.70
☐1383	6¢ Eisenhower	1.21
☐1385	6¢ Rehabilitation	1.21
☐1386	6¢ W.M. Harnett	1.21
☐1387–90	6¢ Nat. History	1.71
☐1391	6¢ Maine.	1.15
☐1392	6¢ Buffalo	1.15
☐1393	6¢ Eisenhower	1.06
☐1393D	7¢ B. Franklin	1.21
☐1394	8¢ Eisenhower	1.30
☐1396	8¢ Postal Service	1.10
☐1397	14¢ F. LaGuardia.	2.35
☐1398	16¢ Ernie Pyle	2.70
☐1399	18¢ Dr. E. Blackwell	3.10
☐1400	21¢ A.P. Giannini.	3.20
☐1405	6¢ E.L. Masters.	1.25
☐1406	6¢ Women's Suffrage	1.25
☐1407	6¢ South Carolina	1.25
☐1408	6¢ Stone Mountain	1.25
☐1409	6¢ Fort Snelling.	1.25
☐1410–13	6¢ Anti-Pollution	3.40
☐1414	6¢ Nativity	1.30
☐1414a	6¢ Precancelled.	1.35
☐1415–18	6¢ Christmas Toys	6.20
☐1415a–18a	6¢ Precancelled.	15.00
☐1419	6¢ United Nations	1.15
☐1420	6¢ Pilgrim Landing	1.15
☐1421–22	6¢ D.A. & P.O.W.	2.35
☐1423	6¢ Sheep	1.25
☐1424	6¢ Gen. MacArthur	1.25
☐1425	6¢ Blood Donors	1.25
☐1426	8¢ Missouri (4)	1.10
☐1427–30	8¢ Wildlife	1.70
☐1431	8¢ Antarctic	1.50

Scott No.		Fine
☐1432	8¢ Bicentennial	2.40
☐1433	8¢ J. Sloan Painting	1.50
☐1434–35	8¢ Space Accomp	1.50
☐1436	8¢ Emily Dickinson	1.40
☐1437	8¢ San Juan	1.40
☐1438	8¢ Drug Addiction.	1.40
☐1439	8¢ CARE.	1.40
☐1440–43	8¢ Historic Press	1.72
☐1444	8¢ Nativity (4)	1.15
☐1445	8¢ Partridge (4)	1.15
☐1446	8¢ Sidney Lanier	1.45
☐1447	8¢ Peace Corps.	1.45
☐1448–51	2¢ Hatteras (8)	1.10
☐1452	6¢ Wolf Trap Farm	1.25
☐1453	8¢ Yellowstone	1.40
☐1454	15¢ Mt. McKinley.	2.80
☐1455	8¢ Family Planning	1.45
☐1456–59	8¢ Craftman	2.00
☐1460	6¢ Olympic Games	1.60
☐1461	8¢ Olympic Games	1.72
☐1462	15¢ Olympic Games	3.20
☐1463	8¢ P.T.A.	1.34
☐1464–67	8¢ Wildlife	1.60
☐1468	8¢ Mail Order (4)	1.15
☐1469	8¢ Osteopathic	1.65
☐1470	8¢ Tom Sawyer	1.55
☐1471	8¢ Religious	1.10
☐1472	8¢ Santa Claus	1.10
☐1473	8¢ Pharmacy	1.30
☐1474	8¢ Stamp Collector	1.30
☐1475	8¢ Love	1.21
☐1476	8¢ Pamphlet Printing	1.36
☐1477	8¢ Posting Broadside	1.36
☐1478	8¢ Post Rider	1.36
☐1479	8¢ Drummer.	1.36
☐1480–83	8¢ Bost. Tea Party	1.36
☐1488	8¢ Copernicus	1.36
☐1500	6¢ Electronics	1.21
☐1501	8¢ Electronics	1.40
☐1502	15¢ Electronics	2.40
☐1504	8¢ Angus Cattle.	1.35
☐1505	10¢ Chautauqua	2.15
☐1506	10¢ Winter Wheat	2.05
☐1507	8¢ Religious (4)	1.10
☐1508	8¢ Xmas Tree (4)	1.10
☐1510	10¢ Jefferson Mem'l.	1.74
☐1511	10¢ Zip Code	1.74
☐1525	10¢ V.F.W.	1.74
☐1526	10¢ Robert Frost.	1.74

Scott No.		Fine
☐1528	10¢ Horse Racing (4)	1.30
☐1529	10¢ Skylab Project	1.65
☐1538–41	10¢ Minerals	1.70
☐1542	10¢ Fort Harrod	1.70
☐1543–46	10¢ Cont. Cong.	1.70
☐1547	10¢ Energy Cons.	1.70
☐1548	10¢ Sleepy Hollow	1.70
☐1549	10¢ Retarded Children	1.70
☐1550	10¢ Xmas-Religious	1.85
☐1551	10¢ Xmas-Sleigh (4)	1.35
☐1553	10¢ Benjamin West	1.70
☐1554	10¢ Paul Dunbar	1.70
☐1555	10¢ D.W. Griffith	1.70
☐1556	10¢ Pioneer-Jupiter	1.70
☐1557	10¢ Mariner 10	1.70
☐1558	10¢ Coll. Bargaining	1.70
☐1559	8¢ Sybil Ludington	1.45
☐1560	10¢ Salem Poor	1.70
☐1561	10¢ Haym Salomon	1.70
☐1562	18¢ Peter Francisco	3.70
☐1565–68	10¢ Uniforms (4)	1.35
☐1571	10¢ Women's Year	1.30
☐1572–75	10¢ Postal Service (4)	1.30
☐1576	10¢ World Peace	1.50
☐1577–78	10¢ Banking & Comm.	1.50
☐1579	10¢ Xmas-Religious	1.30
☐1580	10¢ Xmas Post Card(4)	1.30
☐1581	1¢ Ability Write	.62
☐1582	2¢ Freedom to Speak	.65
☐1584	3¢ Cast A Ballot	.75
☐1585	4¢ Public that Reads	.85
☐1591	9¢ Freedom to Assemble	1.45
☐1593	11¢ Freedom of Press.	1.75
☐1596	13¢ Eagle & Shield	1.50
☐1603	24¢ Old North Church	3.90
☐1632	13¢ Interphil '76	2.20
☐1633–82	13¢ State Flags	4.20
☐1683	13¢ Telephone	2.15
☐1684	13¢ Aviation	2.15
☐1685	13¢ Chemistry	1.50
☐1690	13¢ Ben. Franklin	2.15
☐1691–94	13¢ Independence	2.50
☐1695–98	13¢ Olympic Games	3.00
☐1700	13¢ Adolph Ochs	2.10
☐1701	13¢ "Nativity" (4)	1.60
☐1702	13¢ "Winter Pastime"	2.15
☐1705	13¢ Sound Recording	2.15
☐1710	13¢ Transatlic	2.15
☐1711	13¢ Colorado	1.60

Scott No.		Fine
☐1712–15	13¢ Butterflies	1.60
☐1716	13¢ Lafayette	2.00
☐1717–20	13¢ Skilled Hands (4)	1.70
☐1721	13¢ Peace Bridge	2.10
☐1725	13¢ California	2.10
☐1726	13¢ Articles of Conf.	2.10
☐1727	13¢ Talking Pictures	2.10
☐1730	13¢ Mailbox	2.10
☐1735	15¢ Eagle Issue "A"	2.80
☐1818	18¢ Eagle Issue "B"	3.00
☐C72	10¢ Stars	6.60
☐C74	10¢ Airmail 50th Ann.	3.70
☐C75	20¢ U.S.A. Airmail	5.20
☐C76	10¢ Moon Landing	1.80
☐C77	9¢ Delta Plane	1.50
☐C78	1¢ Silhouette	2.05
☐C79	13¢ Letter	2.05
☐C80	17¢ Liberty Head	3.30
☐C81	21¢ U.S.A. Airmail	3.15
☐C84	11¢ City of Refuge	2.15
☐C85	11¢ Olympic Games	2.15
☐C86	11¢ Electronics	2.15
☐C87	18¢ Liberty	2.90
☐C88	26¢ Mt. Rushmore	4.60
☐C89	25¢ Plane & Globes	4.70
☐C90	31¢ Plane/Flag/Globes	4.90
☐E22	45¢ Arrows	13.00
☐E23	60¢ Arrows	10.00

Scott No.		Fine Ctr Line Blk of 4	Fine Arrow Blk of 4
U.S. UNUSED CENTER LINE AND ARROW BLOCKS			
☐314	1¢ Imperforate	280.00	162.00
☐320	2¢ Imperforate	270.00	167.00
☐343	1¢ Imperforate	61.00	41.00
☐344	2¢ Imperforate	71.00	49.00
☐345	3¢ Imperforate	142.00	97.00
☐346	4¢ Imperforate	280.00	190.00
☐347	5¢ Imperforate	370.00	270.00
☐368	2¢ Lincoln, Imp.	240.00	185.00
☐371	2¢ Alaska-Yukon, Imperf.	330.00	245.00
☐373	2¢ Hudson-Fulton, Imperf	410.00	280.00
☐383	1¢ Imperforate	38.00	22.00
☐384	2¢ Imperforate	72.00	41.00
☐408	1¢ Imperforate	15.00	7.60

Scott No.		Fine Ctr Line Blk of 4	Fine Arrow Blk of 4
☐409	2¢ Imperforate . .	19.00	11.00
☐481	1¢ Imperforate . .	12.00	6.10
☐482	2¢ Imperforate . .	10.00	7.70
☐484	3¢ Imperforate Type II.	75.00	57.00
☐524	5¢ Green & Blk	2700.00	2500.00
☐531	1¢ Offset, Imperf.	90.00	56.00
☐532	2¢ Offset, Imperf. type IV	240.00	190.00
☐534	2¢ Offset, Imperf. Type Va . . .	100.00	70.00
☐534A	2¢ Offset, Imp. Type VI . . .	205.00	195.00
☐535	3¢ Offset, Imperf.	70.00	48.00
☐547	$2 Carm. & Blk.	2600.00	2200.00
☐573	$5 Carm. & Blk.	2450.00	1800.00
☐575	1¢ Imperforate . .	65.00	71.00
☐576	1½¢ Imperf.	21.00	14.00
☐577	2¢ Imperforate . .	22.00	16.00
☐611	2¢ Harding Imperf	90.00	62.00
☐620	2¢ Norse-Amer'n.	43.00	33.00
☐621	5¢ Norse-Ameri'n	140.00	110.00
☐631	1½¢ Harding, Rotary/ Imperf	31.00	18.00
☐703	2¢ Yorktown . . .	3.00	2.10
☐832	$1 Purple & Blk .	47.00	47.00
☐833	$2 Yel./Gm./Blk	130.00	120.00
☐834	$5 Red & Blk. .	600.00	510.00
☐C1	6¢ Airmail	550.00	450.00
☐C2	16¢ Airmail	770.00	730.00
☐C3	24¢ Airmail	750.00	710.00
☐C23	36¢ Airmail	3.75	3.10
☐CE2	16¢ Spec. Del. Airmail	3.10	2.60

Scott No.		Fine

1927–1940 MINT SHEETS

☐643	2¢ Vermont	315.00
☐644	2¢ Burgoyne.	430.00
☐645	2¢ Valley Forge.	200.00
☐646	2¢ Molly Pitcher	225.00
☐647	2¢ Hawaii	830.00
☐648	5¢ Hawaii	2800.00
☐649	2¢ Aeronautics	121.00
☐650	5¢ Aeronautics	780.00
☐651	2¢ George R. Clark. . . .	73.00
☐654	2¢ Edison-Flat.	210.00

Scott No.		Fine
☐655	2¢ Edison-Rotary	186.00
☐657	2¢ Sullivan.	182.00
☐680	2¢ Fallen Timbers	210.00
☐681	2¢ Ohio River Canal . . .	150.00
☐682	2¢ Mass. Bay	151.00
☐683	2¢ Carolina-Charleston. .	260.00
☐688	2¢ Braddock.	220.00
☐689	2¢ Von Steuben.	121.00
☐690	2¢ Pulaski	67.00
☐702	2¢ Red Cross	29.00
☐703	2¢ Yorktown.	30.00
☐704	½¢ Wash. Bicent'l	21.00
☐705	1¢ Wash. Bicent'l	30.00
☐706	1½¢ Wash. Bicent'l	96.00
☐707	2¢ Wash. Bicent'l	18.00
☐708	3¢ Wash. Bicent'l	121.00
☐709	4¢ Wash. Bicent'l	53.00
☐710	5¢ Wash. Bicent'l	340.00
☐711	6¢ Wash. Bicent'l	865.00
☐712	7¢ Wash. Bicent'l	69.00
☐713	8¢ Wash. Bicent'l	910.00
☐714	9¢ Wash. Bicent'l	670.00
☐715	10¢ Wash. Bicent'l	2600.00
☐716	2¢ Lake Placid	89.00
☐717	2¢ Arbor Day	39.00
☐718	3¢ Olympics	290.00
☐719	5¢ Olympics	430.00
☐724	3¢ Penn	69.00
☐725	3¢ Webster	121.00
☐726	3¢ Oglethorpe.	85.00
☐727	3¢ Newburgh	30.00
☐728	1¢ Chicago	21.00
☐729	3¢ Chicago	31.00
☐732	3¢ N.R.A.	22.00
☐733	3¢ Byrd.	76.00
☐734	5¢ Kosciuszko.	150.00
☐736	3¢ Maryland	44.00
☐737	3¢ Mother's Day (R) . . .	13.00
☐738	3¢ Mother's Day (F) . . .	23.00
☐739	3¢ Wisconsin	23.00
☐740	1¢ Natl. Parks.	9.50
☐741	2¢ Natl. Parks.	12.10
☐742	3¢ Natl. Parks.	17.00
☐743	4¢ Natl. Parks.	46.00
☐744	5¢ Natl. Parks.	83.00
☐745	6¢ Natl. Parks.	135.00
☐746	7¢ Natl. Parks.	74.00
☐747	8¢ Natl. Parks.	172.00

Scott No.		Fine
☐748	9¢ Natl. Parks	162.00
☐749	10¢ Natl. Parks	319.00
☐772	3¢ Connecticut	13.00
☐773	3¢ San Diego	12.00
☐774	3¢ Boulder Dam	12.00
☐775	3¢ Michigan	11.00
☐776	3¢ Texas	11.00
☐777	3¢ Rhode Island	12.00
☐782	3¢ Arkansas	10.00
☐783	3¢ Oregon	10.00
☐784	3¢ Susan B. Anthony	16.00
☐785	1¢ Army	7.00
☐786	2¢ Army	8.00
☐787	3¢ Army	16.00
☐788	4¢ Army	47.00
☐789	5¢ Army	64.00
☐790	1¢ Navy	7.50
☐791	2¢ Navy	8.00
☐792	3¢ Navy	13.00
☐793	4¢ Navy	45.00
☐794	5¢ Navy	61.00
☐795	3¢ N.W. Territory	9.00
☐796	5¢ Virginia Dare	25.00
☐798	3¢ Constitution	9.10
☐799	3¢ Hawaii	12.00
☐800	3¢ Alaska	12.00
☐801	3¢ Puerto Rico	12.00
☐802	3¢ Virgin Islands	12.00
☐835	3¢ Ratification	16.00
☐836	3¢ Swede-Finn	13.00
☐837	3¢ N.W. Territory	33.00
☐838	3¢ Iowa	17.50
☐852	3¢ Golden Gate	10.00
☐853	3¢ N.Y. Fair	10.00
☐854	3¢ Inauguration	29.00
☐855	3¢ Baseball	33.00
☐856	3¢ Canal Zone	20.00
☐857	3¢ Printing	9.60
☐858	3¢ Four States	9.60
☐859	1¢ Irving	7.10
☐860	2¢ Cooper	9.00

Scott No.		Fine
☐861	3¢ Emerson	13.00
☐862	5¢ Alcott	43.00
☐863	10¢ Clemens	215.00
☐864	1¢ Longfellow	13.00
☐865	2¢ Whittier	12.00
☐866	3¢ Lowell	17.00
☐867	5¢ Whitman	48.00
☐868	10¢ Riley	250.00
☐869	1¢ Mann	11.00
☐870	2¢ Hopkins	9.50
☐871	3¢ Elliot	24.00
☐872	5¢ Willard	55.00
☐873	10¢ B.T. Washington	170.00
☐874	1¢ Audubon	7.60
☐875	2¢ Long	9.10
☐876	3¢ Burbank	9.70
☐877	5¢ Reed	35.00
☐878	10¢ Addams	160.00
☐879	1¢ Fosters	7.70
☐880	2¢ Sousa	13.00
☐881	3¢ Herbert	14.00
☐882	5¢ MacDowell	63.00
☐883	10¢ Nevin	440.00
☐884	1¢ Sturat	7.00
☐885	2¢ Whistler	9.20
☐886	3¢ St. Gaudens	9.40
☐887	5¢ French	50.00
☐888	10¢ Remington	250.00
☐889	1¢ Whitney	14.00
☐890	2¢ Morse	13.00
☐891	3¢ McCormick	21.00
☐892	5¢ Howe	144.00
☐893	10¢ Bell	1300.00
☐894	3¢ Pony Express	26.00
☐895	3¢ Pan American	25.00
☐896	3¢ Idaho	16.00
☐897	3¢ Wyoming	15.00
☐898	3¢ Coronado	15.00
☐899	1¢ Defense	9.00
☐900	2¢ Defense	11.00
☐901	3¢ Defense	16.00
☐902	3¢ Emancipation	21.00

NOTE: Mint Sheets from 1941 to date are included with individual listing.

Scott No.		Fine Unused Each	Ave. Unused Each	Fine Used Each	Ave. Used Each

OFFICIAL STAMPS 1873 CONTINENTAL PRINTING (N-H ADD 70%)

Scott No.		Fine Unused Each	Ave. Unused Each	Fine Used Each	Ave. Used Each
☐ O1	1¢ Agricultural Department	62.00	42.00	34.00	22.00
☐ O2	2¢	41.00	27.00	16.00	10.00
☐ O3	3¢	34.00	23.00	5.00	4.00
☐ O4	4¢	42.00	27.00	14.00	12.00
☐ O5	10¢	90.00	60.00	53.00	41.00
☐ O6	12¢	136.00	89.00	72.00	48.00
☐ O7	15¢	90.00	55.00	50.00	33.00
☐ O8	24¢	112.00	75.00	62.00	42.00
☐ O9	30¢	145.00	100.00	89.00	61.00
☐ O10	1¢ Executive Department	225.00	160.00	110.00	74.00
☐ O11	2¢	140.00	94.00	75.00	52.00
☐ O12	3¢	175.00	120.00	67.00	40.00
☐ O13	6¢	280.00	195.00	160.00	105.00
☐ O14	10¢	246.00	165.00	160.00	106.00
☐ O15	1¢ Interior Department	16.00	11.00	3.10	2.10
☐ O16	2¢	14.00	9.00	2.30	1.80
☐ O17	3¢	22.00	15.00	2.30	1.80
☐ O18	6¢	17.00	9.60	2.30	1.80
☐ O19	10¢	13.00	8.00	4.30	3.20
☐ O20	12¢	20.00	15.00	3.15	2.20
☐ O21	15¢	36.00	24.00	9.00	6.70
☐ O22	24¢	31.00	18.00	7.00	5.00
☐ O23	30¢	42.00	26.00	7.00	5.00
☐ O24	90¢	82.00	51.00	15.00	9.10
☐ O25	1¢ Justice Department	38.00	21.00	21.00	14.00
☐ O26	2¢	55.00	36.00	23.00	16.00
☐ O27	3¢	62.00	40.00	9.10	7.10
☐ O28	6¢	52.00	32.00	13.00	9.10
☐ O29	10¢	60.00	39.00	25.00	18.00
☐ O30	12¢	45.00	28.00	15.00	12.00
☐ O31	15¢	92.00	66.00	51.00	37.00
☐ O32	24¢	273.00	160.00	120.00	80.00
☐ O33	30¢	250.00	150.00	94.00	64.00
☐ O34	90¢	370.00	220.00	183.00	125.00
☐ O35	1¢ Navy Department	31.00	21.00	13.00	9.00
☐ O36	2¢	22.00	15.00	10.00	8.00
☐ O37	3¢	25.00	17.00	4.00	2.50
☐ O38	6¢	24.00	15.00	5.00	5.00
☐ O39	7¢	150.00	100.00	65.00	42.00
☐ O40	10¢	31.00	19.00	12.00	11.00
☐ O41	12¢	41.00	23.00	11.00	8.00
☐ O42	15¢	72.00	46.00	29.00	18.00
☐ O43	24¢	75.00	50.00	32.00	21.00
☐ O44	30¢	57.00	30.00	16.00	12.00
☐ O45	90¢	280.00	171.00	100.00	63.00
☐ O47	1¢ Post Office Department	9.00	6.50	4.60	3.00

Scott No.			Fine Unused Each	Ave. Unused Each	Fine Used Each	Ave. Used Each
☐ 048	2¢	....	9.00	6.10	5.00	2.50
☐ 049	3¢	....	2.70	1.60	1.15	.75
☐ 050	6¢	....	8.00	5.40	2.40	1.25
☐ 051	10¢	....	35.00	24.00	20.00	12.00
☐ 052	12¢	....	18.00	13.00	6.00	3.40
☐ 053	15¢	....	21.00	14.00	9.00	5.50
☐ 054	24¢	....	28.00	18.00	11.00	6.60
☐ 055	30¢	....	27.00	17.00	9.00	6.60
☐ 056	90¢	....	42.00	26.00	14.00	8.75
☐ 057	1¢ State Department	....	47.00	24.00	13.00	8.75
☐ 058	2¢	....	85.00	59.00	30.00	20.00
☐ 059	3¢	....	30.00	18.00	9.10	6.70
☐ 060	6¢	....	29.00	18.00	9.60	6.70
☐ 061	7¢	....	60.00	35.00	19.00	12.00
☐ 062	10¢	....	37.00	22.00	15.00	9.00
☐ 063	12¢	....	74.00	47.00	31.00	19.00
☐ 064	15¢	....	58.00	39.00	20.00	13.00
☐ 065	24¢	....	150.00	92.00	92.00	58.00
☐ 066	30¢	....	140.00	88.00	62.00	41.00
☐ 067	90¢	....	300.00	185.00	125.00	83.00
☐ 068	$2	....	500.00	350.00	250.00	170.00
☐ 072	1¢ Treasury Department	....	12.00	9.00	2.50	1.90
☐ 073	2¢	....	18.00	13.00	2.40	1.50
☐ 074	3¢	....	12.00	7.00	1.70	1.00
☐ 075	6¢	....	19.00	15.00	1.60	1.00
☐ 076	7¢	....	39.00	21.00	13.00	6.70
☐ 077	10¢	....	38.00	21.00	6.00	3.50
☐ 078	12¢	....	39.00	21.00	4.00	1.60
☐ 079	15¢	....	40.00	23.00	5.00	2.80
☐ 080	24¢	....	160.00	100.00	59.00	37.00
☐ 081	30¢	....	50.00	40.00	5.00	3.20
☐ 082	90¢	....	61.00	41.00	4.50	3.10
☐ 083	1¢ War Department	....	54.00	36.00	5.00	3.30
☐ 084	2¢	....	57.00	36.00	6.00	4.10
☐ 085	3¢	....	49.00	32.00	2.00	.95
☐ 086	6¢	....	220.00	150.00	4.50	2.80
☐ 087	7¢	....	50.00	34.00	31.00	17.00
☐ 088	10¢	....	17.00	10.00	4.10	2.60
☐ 089	12¢	....	58.00	39.00	2.90	1.60
☐ 090	15¢	....	15.00	10.00	2.10	1.20
☐ 091	24¢	....	15.00	11.00	2.50	1.30
☐ 092	30¢	....	15.00	11.00	2.50	1.25
☐ 093	90¢	....	39.00	25.00	13.00	8.00

1879. AMERICAN PRINTING—SOFT POROUS PAPER (N-H ADD 80%)

☐ 094	1¢ Agricultural Department	....	1300.00	830.00	—	—
☐ 095	3¢	....	175.00	120.00	26.00	18.00

Scott No.			Fine Unused Each	Ave. Unused Each	Fine Used Each	Ave. Used Each
☐ O96	1¢	Interior Department	121.00	80.00	64.00	42.00
☐ O97	2¢		3.50	2.10	1.50	.88
☐ O98	3¢		2.30	1.50	1.20	.66
☐ O99	6¢		3.10	2.00	1.50	.92
☐ O100	10¢		33.00	23.00	20.00	13.00
☐ O101	12¢		60.00	37.00	33.00	21.00
☐ O102	15¢		128.00	83.00	65.00	40.00
☐ O103	24¢		1200.00	880.00	—	—
☐ O106	3¢	Justice Department	47.00	31.00	19.00	12.00
☐ O107	6¢		97.00	64.00	67.00	41.00
☐ O108	3¢	Post Office Department	12.00	7.00	2.40	1.60
☐ O109	3¢	Treasury Department	25.00	16.00	4.00	2.45
☐ O110	6¢		56.00	36.00	26.00	12.00
☐ O111	10¢		67.00	44.00	18.00	12.00
☐ O112	30¢		730.00	470.00	165.00	105.00
☐ O113	90¢		730.00	470.00	165.00	105.00
☐ O114	1¢	War Department	2.10	1.50	1.30	.92
☐ O115	2¢		3.10	2.10	1.50	1.05
☐ O116	3¢		3.10	1.75	1.20	.65
☐ O117	6¢		3.10	1.75	1.25	.70
☐ O118	10¢		16.00	12.00	8.75	5.60
☐ O119	12¢		13.00	8.00	2.15	1.60
☐ O120	30¢		43.00	29.00	30.00	16.00

1910–1911. POSTAL SAVINGS (N-H ADD 70%)

Scott No.			Fine Unused Each	Ave. Unused Each	Fine Used Each	Ave. Used Each
☐ O121	2¢	Black, D.L. Wmk	16.00	10.00	1.50	.96
☐ O122	50¢	Dark Green, D.L. Wmk	112.00	80.00	35.00	23.00
☐ O123	$1	Ultramarine, D.L. Wmk	112.00	80.00	13.00	8.00
☐ O124	1¢	Dark Violet, S.L. Wmk	4.20	3.00	1.75	.92
☐ O125	2¢	Black, S.L. Wmk	34.00	23.00	4.50	3.00
☐ O126	10¢	Carmine, S.L. Wmk	9.10	6.10	1.50	.86

Scott No.			Fine Unused Block	Ave. Unused Block	Fine Unused Each	Ave. Unused Each	Fine Used Each	Ave. Used Each
1912. PARCEL POST DUE (N-H ADD 45%)								
☐ JQ1	1¢	Dark Green	110.00	60.00	13.00	7.50	3.60	2.30
☐ JQ2	2¢	Dark Green	640.00	430.00	87.00	65.00	20.00	13.00
☐ JQ3	5¢	Dark Green	135.00	90.00	16.00	10.00	4.70	3.20
☐ JQ4	10¢	Dark Green	1500.00	1210.00	175.00	120.00	43.00	27.50
☐ JQ5	25¢	Dark Green	670.00	500.00	94.00	63.00	5.00	3.30
1912–1913. PARCEL POST STAMPS (N-H ADD 45%)								
☐ Q1	1¢	P.O. Clerk	44.00	30.00	5.60	3.40	1.30	.92
☐ Q2	2¢	City Carrier	63.00	45.00	5.60	4.00	.95	.62
☐ Q3	3¢	Railway Clerk	122.00	89.00	13.00	8.00	9.10	6.10
☐ Q4	4¢	Rural Carrier	166.00	115.00	33.00	21.00	2.70	1.80
☐ Q5	5¢	Mail Train	212.00	143.00	34.00	21.00	2.00	1.30
☐ Q6	10¢	Steamship	280.00	182.00	50.00	33.00	3.00	1.90

Scott No.		Fine Unused Block	Ave. Unused Block	Fine Unused Each	Ave. Unused Each	Fine Used Each	Ave. Used Each
☐ Q7	15¢ Mail Truck	420.00	250.00	76.00	50.00	10.00	6.10
☐ Q8	20¢ Airplane	740.00	530.00	150.00	100.00	21.00	12.50
☐ Q9	25¢ Manufacturing	410.00	270.00	80.00	54.00	6.00	4.50
☐ Q10	50¢ Dairying	1600.00	1300.00	200.00	161.00	42.00	27.00
☐ Q11	75¢ Harvesting	470.00	410.00	87.00	63.00	29.00	18.00
☐ Q12	$1 Fruit Growing	2200.00	1600.00	400.00	280.00	23.00	16.00

1925–1929. SPECIAL HANDLING STAMPS (N-H ADD 35%)

☐ QE1	10¢ Yellow Green	20.00	13.00	2.20	1.60	1.20	.73
☐ QE2	15¢ Yellow Green	23.00	17.00	2.60	1.70	1.20	.75
☐ QE3	20¢ Yellow Green	36.00	25.00	5.10	3.00	2.00	1.30
☐ QE4	25¢ Yellow Green	240.00	160.00	28.00	16.00	8.60	6.00
☐ QE4A	25¢ Deep Green	280.00	180.00	30.00	23.00	6.70	5.00

1919–1922. U.S. OFFICES IN CHINA (N-H ADD 60%)
SHANGHAI 2¢ CHINA

☐ K1	2¢ on 1¢	106.00	75.00	21.00	14.00	25.00	18.00
☐ K2	4¢ on 2¢	106.00	75.00	21.00	14.00	25.00	18.00
☐ K3	6¢ on 3¢	260.00	170.00	40.00	26.00	47.00	33.00
☐ K4	8¢ on 4¢	290.00	196.00	43.00	31.00	49.00	34.00
☐ K5	10¢ on 2¢	310.00	241.00	60.00	40.00	60.00	44.00
☐ K6	12¢ on 6¢	310.00	240.00	60.00	40.00	60.00	44.00
☐ K7	14¢ on 7¢	320.00	250.00	63.00	40.00	70.00	53.00
☐ K8	16¢ on 8¢ Olive Bistre	295.00	210.00	53.00	37.00	63.00	42.00
☐ K8a	16¢ on 8¢ Olive Green	300.00	210.00	53.00	36.00	63.00	43.00
☐ K9	18¢ on 9¢	295.00	200.00	56.00	37.00	63.00	43.00
☐ K10	20¢ on 10¢	295.00	200.00	56.00	37.00	63.00	43.00
☐ K11	24¢ on 12¢ Br. Car.	295.00	200.00	56.00	37.00	65.00	43.00
☐ K11a	24¢ on 12¢ Cl. Br.	380.00	290.00	82.00	61.00	80.00	60.00
☐ K12	30¢ on 15¢	330.00	230.00	70.00	40.00	77.00	55.00
☐ K13	40¢ on 20¢	520.00	410.00	115.00	70.00	112.00	78.00
☐ K14	60¢ on 30¢	500.00	370.00	98.00	60.00	112.00	79.00
☐ K15	$1 on 50¢	3400.00	2200.00	650.00	421.00	500.00	330.00
☐ K16	$2 on $1	2300.00	1500.00	480.00	311.00	435.00	260.00
☐ K17	2¢ on 1¢ Loc. Sur.	400.00	300.00	85.00	60.00	77.00	47.00
☐ K18	4¢ on 2¢ Loc. Sur.	370.00	240.00	80.00	55.00	75.00	47.00

Scott No.		Imperforated (a)		Part Perforated (b)		Perforated (c)	
		Fine	Ave.	Fine	Ave.	Fine	Ave.

1862–1971. UNITED STATES REVENUES

☐ R1	1¢ Express	50.00	34.00	42.00	27.00	1.30	.69
☐ R2	1¢ Play Cards	780.00	500.00	370.00	230.00	95.00	63.00
☐ R3	1¢ Proprietary	560.00	330.00	100.00	72.00	.96	.63
☐ R4	1¢ Telegraph	210.00	120.00	—	—	9.30	6.10
☐ R5	2¢ Bank Ck., Blue	1.30	.65	1.35	.80	.19	.12
☐ R6	2¢ Bank Ck., Orange	—	—	92.00	60.00	.13	.09
☐ R7	2¢ Certif., Blue	12.00	6.70	—	—	32.00	20.00
☐ R8	2¢ Certif., Orange	—	—	—	—	26.00	16.00

*No hinge pricing from 1941 to date is figured at (N-H ADD 15%)

Scott No.		Imperforated (a) Fine	Imperforated (a) Ave.	Part Perforated (b) Fine	Part Perforated (b) Ave.	Perforated (c) Fine	Perforated (c) Ave.
☐R9	2¢ Express, Blue	12.50	7.70	16.00	12.00	.45	.25
☐R10	2¢ Express, Orange	—	—	—	—	6.50	5.50
☐R11	2¢ Ply. Cds., Blue	—	—	120.00	73.00	3.10	1.80
☐R12	2¢ Ply. Cds., Orange	—	—	—	—	29.00	18.00
☐R13	2¢ Proprietary, Blue	—	—	97.00	60.00	.46	.30
☐R14	2¢ Proprietary, Orange ...	—	—	—	—	34.00	22.00
☐R15	2¢ U.S.I.R.	—	—	—	—	.12	.10
☐R16	3¢ Foreign Ex.	—	—	131.00	75.00	2.00	1.15
☐R17	3¢ Playing Cds.	—	—	—	—	97.00	60.00
☐R18	3¢ Proprietary	—	—	140.00	82.00	1.70	.97
☐R19	3¢ Telegraph	42.00	27.00	17.00	12.00	2.15	1.45
☐R20	4¢ Inland Exch.	—	—	—	—	2.10	1.40
☐R21	4¢ Playing Cards	—	—	—	—	300.00	178.00
☐R22	4¢ Proprietary	—	—	140.00	91.00	2.16	1.21
☐R23	5¢ Agreement	—	—	—	—	.65	.37
☐R24	5¢ Certificate	1.65	.92	12.00	5.50	.22	.13
☐R26	5¢ Foreign Ex.	—	—	—	—	.93	.62
☐R27	5¢ Inland Exch.	3.00	1.75	3.00	1.75	.24	.13
☐R28	5¢ Playing Cds.	—	—	—	—	5.50	3.40
☐R29	5¢ Proprietary	—	—	—	—	13.00	8.10
☐R30	6¢ Inland Exch.	—	—	—	—	1.50	.86
☐R32	10¢ Bill of Ldg.	48.00	32.00	213.00	74.00	.95	.62
☐R33	10¢ Certificate	80.00	59.00	77.00	55.00	.66	.46
☐R34	10¢ Contract Bill	—	—	80.00	62.00	.66	.46
☐R35	10¢ For Ex. Bill	—	—	—	—	3.20	2.30
☐R36	10¢ Inland Exch.	106.00	64.00	3.20	1.96	.43	.26
☐R37	10¢ Power of Aty.	311.00	191.00	20.00	13.00	.74	.49
☐R38	10¢ Proprietary	—	—	—	—	15.00	11.60
☐R39	15¢ Foreign Exch.	—	—	—	—	11.00	8.10
☐R40	15¢ Inland Exch.	25.00	17.00	14.00	7.50	1.60	1.00
☐R41	20¢ Foreign Exch.	50.00	40.00	—	—	29.00	19.10
☐R42	20¢ Inland Exch.	15.00	12.00	19.00	13.00	.86	.60
☐R43	25¢ Bond	67.00	50.00	6.00	3.20	1.95	1.10
☐R44	25¢ Certificate	8.00	6.50	6.20	3.60	.26	.14
☐R45	25¢ Entry of Gds.	20.00	13.00	33.00	22.00	1.10	.72
☐R46	25¢ Insurance	10.00	6.50	11.00	6.50	.76	.50
☐R47	25¢ Life Insur.	32.00	24.00	80.00	57.00	4.80	2.20
☐R48	25¢ Power of Atty.........	6.00	3.10	18.00	10.00	.55	.35
☐R49	25¢ Protest	22.00	13.00	132.00	100.00	5.30	3.10
☐R50	25¢ Warehouse Rct.	39.00	26.00	133.00	100.00	22.00	15.00
☐R51	30¢ Foreign Exch.	60.00	39.00	202.00	130.00	50.00	33.00
☐R52	30¢ Inland Exch.	47.00	33.00	28.00	18.00	3.10	1.60
☐R53	40¢ Inland Exch.	433.00	275.00	4.70	3.00	3.10	1.80
☐R54	50¢ Convey, Blue	12.00	8.10	1.50	.92	.48	.34
☐R55	50¢ Entry of Gds.	—	—	14.00	7.00	.65	.40
☐R56	50¢ Foreign Exch.	39.00	25.00	36.00	20.00	3.70	2.15
☐R57	50¢ Lease	23.00	13.00	43.00	28.00	5.00	3.00
☐R58	50¢ Life Insur.	30.00	16.00	50.00	33.00	1.30	.75

*No hinge pricing from 1941 to date is figured at (N-H ADD 15%)

Scott No.		Imperforated (a) Fine	Ave.	Part Perforated (b) Fine	Ave.	Perforated (c) Fine	Ave.
☐ R59	50¢ Mortgage	17.00	11.00	3.40	2.10	1.30	.56
☐ R60	50¢ Orig. Process	2.60	1.70	—	—	.92	.56
☐ R61	50¢ Passage Tkt.	69.00	40.00	100.00	71.00	1.30	.75
☐ R62	50¢ Prob. of Will	36.00	21.00	41.00	26.00	25.00	15.00
☐ R63	50¢ Sty. Bond, Bl.	123.00	82.00	4.00	2.30	.52	.28
☐ R64	60¢ Inland Exch.	87.00	57.00	43.00	30.00	5.60	3.40
☐ R65	70¢ Foreign Exch.	270.00	160.00	90.00	63.00	6.00	3.40
☐ R66	$1 Conveyance	13.00	8.60	272.00	151.00	2.50	1.60
☐ R67	$1 Entry of Gds.	26.00	16.00	—	—	2.10	1.20
☐ R68	$1 Foreign Exch.	57.00	34.00	—	—	1.30	.75
☐ R69	$1 Inland Exch.	16.00	11.00	222.00	127.00	.95	.60
☐ R70	$1 Lease	34.00	21.00	—	—	1.55	.86
☐ R71	$1 Life Insur.	115.00	64.00	—	—	4.00	2.50
☐ R72	$1 Manifest	60.00	42.00	—	—	25.00	16.00
☐ R73	$1 Mortgage	26.00	17.00	—	—	127.00	81.00
☐ R74	$1 Passage Tkt.	135.00	92.00	—	—	127.00	80.00
☐ R75	$1 Power of Atty.	62.00	39.00	—	—	2.00	.96
☐ R76	$1 Prob. of Will	46.00	26.00	—	—	30.00	16.00
☐ R77	$1.30 Foreign Exch.	1650.00	1200.00	—	—	39.00	23.00
☐ R78	$1.50 Inland Exch.	30.00	18.00	—	—	3.40	1.90
☐ R79	$1.60 Foreign Exch.	520.00	315.00	—	—	95.00	53.00
☐ R80	$1.90 Foreign Exch.	1600.00	1100.00	—	—	48.00	30.00
☐ R81	$2 Conveyance	120.00	55.00	580.00	340.00	2.20	1.60
☐ R82	$2 Mortgage	64.00	40.00	—	—	2.20	1.60
☐ R83	$2 Prob. of Will	1800.00	1250.00	—	—	30.00	14.50
☐ R84	$2.50 Inland Exch.	861.00	610.00	—	—	3.80	2.20
☐ R85	$3 Chart. Pty.	105.00	60.00	—	—	4.00	2.50
☐ R86	$3 Manifest	77.00	42.00	—	—	15.00	7.60
☐ R87	$3.50 Inland Exch.	782.00	520.00	—	—	29.00	17.00
☐ R88	$5 Chtr. Party	120.00	63.00	—	—	8.50	5.50
☐ R89	$5 Conveyance	45.00	28.00	—	—	6.00	3.10
☐ R90	$5 Manifest	90.00	65.00	—	—	89.00	63.00
☐ R91	$5 Mortgage	90.00	65.00	—	—	21.00	12.10
☐ R92	$5 Prob. of Will	340.00	200.00	—	—	22.00	15.50
☐ R93	$10 Chrt. Party	360.00	220.00	—	—	22.00	15.50
☐ R94	$10 Conveyance	80.00	48.00	—	—	85.00	47.00
☐ R95	$10 Mortgage	266.00	140.00	—	—	28.00	19.00
☐ R96	$10 Prob. of Will	670.00	430.00	—	—	28.00	17.00
☐ R97	$15 Mortgage	790.00	440.00	—	—	110.00	67.00
☐ R98	$20 Conveyance	55.00	36.00	—	—	36.00	20.00
☐ R99	$20 Prob. of Will	800.00	470.00	—	—	760.00	460.00
☐ R100	$25 Mortgage	600.00	350.00	—	—	94.00	58.00
☐ R101	$50 U.S.I.R.	150.00	103.00	—	—	121.00	90.00
☐ R102	$200 U.S.I.R.	1000.00	780.00	—	—	590.00	340.00

*No hinge pricing from 1941 to date is figured at (N-H ADD 15%)

Scott No.		Fine Used Each	Ave. Used Each
1871. SECOND ISSUE R103 THROUGH R131 HAVE BLUE FRAMES AND A BLACK CENTER			
☐R103	1¢	31.00	18.00
☐R104	2¢	1.70	.96
☐R105	3¢	15.00	9.20
☐R106	4¢	48.00	33.00
☐R107	5¢	1.70	.92
☐R108	6¢	55.00	34.00
☐R109	10¢	.95	.67
☐R110	15¢	26.00	17.00
☐R111	20¢	7.00	5.00
☐R112	25¢	.96	.67
☐R113	30¢	59.00	44.00
☐R114	40¢	31.00	23.00
☐R115	50¢	1.70	.75
☐R116	60¢	64.00	42.00
☐R117	70¢	29.00	18.00
☐R118	$1	5.00	3.00
☐R119	$1.30	233.00	151.00
☐R120	$1.50	14.00	9.10
☐R121	$1.60	300.00	202.00
☐R122	$1.90	135.00	80.00
☐R123	$2	14.00	10.00
☐R124	$2.50	25.00	18.00
☐R125	$3	32.00	22.00
☐R126	$3.50	123.00	88.00
☐R127	$5	16.00	10.00
☐R128	$10	115.00	65.00
☐R129	$20	350.00	222.00
☐R130	$25	315.00	198.00
☐R131	$50	360.00	215.00

Scott No.		Fine Used Each	Ave. Used Each
1871–1872. THIRD ISSUE SAME DESIGNS AS SECOND ISSUE			
☐R134	1¢ Claret & Blk. .	22.00	13.00
☐R135	2¢ Org. & Blk.	.16	.12
☐R136	4¢ Brn. & Blk . . .	32.00	20.00
☐R137	5¢ Org. & Blk.	.83	.49
☐R138	6¢ Rog. & Blk. . . .	26.00	16.00
☐R139	15¢ Brn. & Blk. . . .	9.20	5.00
☐R140	30¢ Org. & Blk. . . .	14.00	8.10
☐R141	40¢ Brn. & Blk. . . .	18.00	13.00
☐R142	60¢ Org. & Blk. . . .	43.00	27.00
☐R143	70¢ Grn. & Blk. . . .	33.00	22.00
☐R144	$1 Grn. & Blk. . . .	1.70	1.00
☐R145	$2 Verm'n & Blk. .	25.00	17.00
☐R146	$2.50 Claret & Blk. .	31.00	19.00
☐			
☐R147	$3 Grn. & Blk. . .	32.00	20.00
☐R148	$5 Verm'n & Blk..	22.00	13.00
☐R149	$10 Grn. & Blk. . .	98.00	60.00
☐R150	$20 Org. & Blk. . .	372.00	252.00
1874. FOURTH ISSUE			
☐R151	2¢ Org. & Blk, Grn. Paper	.13	.09
1875. ISSUE			
☐R152a	2¢ Blue, Silk Paper .	.13	.09
☐R152b	2¢ Blue, Watermarked .	.13	.09
☐R152c	2¢ Blue, Rouletted	27.50	18.20

Scott No.		Fine Un-cancelled Each	Ave. Un-cancelled Each	Fine Used Each	Ave. Used Each
1898. POSTAGE AND NEWSPAPER STAMPS SURCHARGED I.R.					
☐R153	1¢ Green, Small I.R.	1.50	.86	1.16	.68
☐R154	1¢ Green, Large I.R.	.36	.23	.32	.18
☐R154a	1¢ Green Inverted Surch	8.00	4.70	6.10	3.90
☐R155	2¢ Carmine, Large I.R.	.36	.18	.17	.10
☐R155a	2¢ Carmine, Inverted Surch	1.30	.76	.99	.67
☐R159	$5 Blue, Surch. down	179.00	110.00	142.00	108.00
☐R160	$5 Blue, Surch. up	83.00	52.00	57.00	39.00
1898. DOCUMENTARY "BATTLESHIP" DESIGN					
☐R161	½¢ Orange	1.95	1.35	7.10	5.10
☐R162	½¢ Dark Gray	.23	.14	.17	.12
☐R163	1¢ Pale Blue	.12	.09	.13	.10
☐R164	2¢ Carmine	.12	.08	.13	.10
☐R165	3¢ Dark Blue	.66	.46	.20	.14
☐R166	4¢ Pale Rose	.62	.35	.20	.14
☐R167	5¢ Lilac	.52	.28	.13	.12
☐R168	10¢ Dark Brown	.55	.31	.13	.12
☐R169	25¢ Purple Brown	.55	.31	.17	.16
☐R170	40¢ Blue Lilac (cut .25)	32.00	20.00	1.45	1.10
☐R171	50¢ Slate Violet	1.70	1.06	.23	.16
☐R172	80¢ Bistre (cut .15)	13.00	7.10	.52	.27
1898–1899. DOCUMENTARY STAMPS					
☐R173	$1 Dark Green	3.60	1.80	.62	.31
☐R174	$3 Dark Brown (cut .18)	4.70	2.90	.41	.27
☐R175	$5 Orange (cut .25)	—	—	1.40	.85
☐R176	$10 Black (cut .75)	—	—	3.20	2.20
☐R177	$30 Red (cut 25.00)	—	—	74.00	46.00
☐R178	$50 Gray Brown (cut 1.50)	—	—	4.60	2.60
☐R179	$100 Brown & Black (cut 12.00)	—	—	33.00	20.00
☐R180	$500 Lake & Black (cut 180.00)	—	—	470.00	340.00
☐R181	$100 Green & Black (cut 100.00)	—	—	360.00	260.00
1900. DOCUMENTARY STAMPS					
☐R182	$1 Carmine (cut .15)	4.60	2.90	.63	.43
☐R183	$3 Lake (cut 8.00)	58.00	37.00	42.00	26.00
1900-1902. SURCHARGED LARGE BLACK NUMERALS					
☐R184	$1 Gray (cut .09)	2.15	1.35	.27	.19
☐R185	$2 Gray (cut .09)	2.50	1.70	.27	.19
☐R186	$3 Gray (cut 1.15)	22.00	14.00	12.00	7.10
☐R187	$5 Gray (cut .40)	11.00	8.00	4.10	2.70
☐R188	$10 Gray (cut 3.25)	45.00	30.00	11.00	6.10
☐R189	$50 Gray (cut 80.00)	500.00	350.00	340.00	215.00
☐R190	$1 Green (cut .35)	4.20	2.70	2.20	1.15
☐R191	$2 Green (cut .30)	4.20	2.40	1.50	.87
☐R192	$5 Green (cut 1.60)	26.00	16.00	13.00	8.15
☐R193	$10 Green (cut 27.50)	220.00	145.00	160.00	92.00
☐R194	$50 Green (cut 220.00)	900.00	620.00	670.00	425.00

Scott No.		Fine Un-cancelled Each	Ave. Un-cancelled Each	Fine Used Each	Ave. Used Each

1914. DOCUMENTARY SINGLE LINE WATERMARK

☐R195	½¢ Rose	3.90	2.50	1.90	1.30
☐R196	1¢ Rose	1.30	.68	.23	.16
☐R197	2¢ Rose	1.30	.68	.23	.16
☐R198	3¢ Rose	24.00	16.00	19.00	12.10
☐R199	4¢ Rose	6.00	4.00	.90	.66
☐R200	5¢ Rose	1.80	1.30	.36	.19
☐R201	10¢ Rose	1.70	1.10	.26	.13
☐R202	25¢ Rose	9.30	6.70	.66	.40
☐R203	40¢ Rose	8.00	5.10	.84	.54
☐R204	50¢ Rose	2.70	1.50	.52	.34
☐R205	80¢ Rose	33.00	23.00	6.40	4.10

1914. DOCUMENTARY DOUBLE LINE WATERMARK

☐R206	½¢ Rose	1.30	.84	.72	.49
☐R207	1¢ Rose	.17	.14	.13	.10
☐R208	2¢ Rose	.22	.13	.12	.06
☐R209	3¢ Rose	.87	.47	.33	.18
☐R210	4¢ Rose	1.85	1.20	.55	.29
☐R211	5¢ Rose	.86	.52	.20	.13
☐R212	10¢ Rose	.65	.46	.13	.09
☐R213	25¢ Rose	3.15	1.86	.90	.47
☐R214	40¢ Rose (cut .60)	27.00	17.10	6.00	3.20
☐R215	50¢ Rose	7.10	4.00	.30	.17
☐R216	80¢ Rose (cut 1.10)	34.00	23.00	7.40	5.10
☐R217	$1 Green (cut .06)	5.10	2.10	.27	.17
☐R218	$2 Carmine (cut .10)	13.00	7.60	.56	.30
☐R219	$2 Carmine (cut .25)	24.00	17.00	1.75	.95
☐R220	$5 Blue (cut .65)	23.00	14.00	2.15	1.40
☐R221	$10 Orange (cut 1.10)	40.00	27.00	5.60	3.60
☐R222	$30 Vermilion (cut 2.35)	105.00	78.00	13.00	8.00
☐R223	$50 Violet (cut 200.00)	840.00	565.00	610.00	415.00
☐R224	$60 Brown (cut 47.50)	—	—	112.00	70.00
☐R225	$100 Green (cut 14.50)	—	—	45.00	30.00

1917–1933. TENTH ISSUE DOCUMENTARY STAMPS—PERF. 11

☐R228	1¢ Rose	.25	.14	.16	.10
☐R229	2¢ Rose	.12	.08	.12	.08
☐R230	3¢ Rose	.56	.32	.32	.18
☐R231	4¢ Rose	.27	.17	.15	.08
☐R232	5¢ Rose	.28	.17	.15	.09
☐R233	8¢ Rose	1.82	1.25	.22	.13
☐R234	10¢ Rose	.52	.22	.14	.09
☐R235	20¢ Rose	.73	.40	.15	.10
☐R236	25¢ Rose	1.15	.62	.14	.10
☐R237	40¢ Rose	.98	.52	.16	.10
☐R238	50¢ Rose	1.30	.70	.15	.10
☐R239	80¢ Rose	3.15	2.20	.15	.10

Scott No.		Fine Un-cancelled Each	Ave. Un-cancelled Each	Fine Used Each	Ave. Used Each
☐ R240	$1 Green	2.70	1.70	.13	.08
☐ R241	$2 Rose	8.00	5.20	.16	.10
☐ R242	$3 Violet (cut .15)	19.50	12.30	.76	.46
☐ R243	$4 Brown (cut .20)	12.10	6.60	1.60	.95
☐ R244	$5 Blue (cut .13)	8.60	6.10	.30	.18
☐ R245	$10 Orange (cut .20)	13.60	11.00	.75	.47

1917 DOCUMENTARY STAMPS—PERF. 12

☐ R246	$30 Vermilion (cut .80)	30.00	19.00	2.70	1.70
☐ R247	$60 Brown (cut 1.00)	40.00	26.00	7.80	5.00
☐ R248	$100 Green (cut .45)	24.00	19.00	1.60	.78
☐ R249	$500 Blue (cut 9.50)	—	—	35.00	24.00
☐ R250	$1000 Orange (cut 3.50)	92.00	63.00	12.00	7.60

1928–1929 DOCUMENTARY STAMPS—PERF. 10

☐ R251	1¢ Carmine Rose	1.50	1.05	.55	.35
☐ R252	2¢ Carmine Rose	.36	.17	.18	.15
☐ R253	4¢ Carmine Rose	4.60	3.15	2.90	1.71
☐ R254	5¢ Carmine Rose	.93	.60	.28	.18
☐ R255	10¢ Carmine Rose	1.15	.60	.70	.49
☐ R256	20¢ Carmine Rose	3.15	2.15	1.95	1.22
☐ R257	$1 Green (cut 1.90)	47.00	33.00	29.00	16.50
☐ R258	$2 Rose	8.75	6.00	.86	.57
☐ R259	$10 Orange (cut 8.00)	44.00	32.00	15.00	9.90

1929–1930 DOCUMENTARY STAMPS—PERF. 11 x 10

☐ R260	2¢ Carmine Rose	1.90	1.21	1.15	.67
☐ R261	5¢ Carmine Rose	1.70	1.05	.96	.62
☐ R262	10¢ Carmine Rose	6.60	4.10	3.70	2.95
☐ R263	20¢ Carmine Rose	12.10	7.60	5.60	4.50

Scott No.		Fine Used Each Violet Paper (a)	Ave. Used Each	Fine Used Each Green Paper (b)	Ave. Used Each

1871–1874 PROPRIETARY (ALL USED)

☐ RB1	1¢ Green & Black	3.50	2.70	5.70	4.10
☐ RB2	2¢ Green & Black	5.60	3.70	9.20	7.20
☐ RB3	3¢ Green & Black	9.00	6.10	33.00	19.00
☐ RB4	4¢ Green & Black	7.00	4.50	13.00	9.00
☐ RB5	4¢ Green & Black	115.00	75.00	105.00	72.00
☐ RB6	6¢ Green & Black	34.00	21.00	87.00	63.00
☐ RB7	10¢ Green & Black	160.00	105.00	37.00	25.00
☐ RB8	50¢ Green & Black	700.00	515.00	888.00	670.00

Scott No.		Silk Paper (a) Fine	Ave.	Watermarked (b) Fine	Ave.	Rouletted (c) Fine	Ave.

1875–1881 PROPRIETARY STAMPS (ALL USED)

☐ RB11	1¢ Green	1.90	1.10	.52	.35	34.00	23.00
☐ RB12	2¢ Brown	2.10	1.35	2.10	1.25	42.00	31.00

Scott No.		Silk Paper (a) Fine	Ave.	Watermarked (b) Fine	Ave.	Rouletted (c) Fine	Ave.
☐ RB13	3¢ Orange	13.00	11.00	3.00	1.75	54.00	36.00
☐ RB14	4¢ Red Brown	5.00	3.10	4.00	2.80	—	—
☐ RB15	4¢ Red	—	—	4.50	3.20	56.00	40.00
☐ RB16	5¢ Black	89.00	59.00	77.00	53.00	630.00	424.00
☐ RB17	6¢ Violet Blue	22.00	14.00	15.00	10.00	143.00	98.00
☐ RB18	6¢ Violet	—	—	23.00	14.00	175.00	120.00
☐ RB19	10¢ Blue	—	—	180.00	112.00	—	—

Scott No.		Fine Un-cancelled Each	Ave. Un-cancelled Each	Fine Used Each	Ave. Used Each
1898 PROPRIETARY STAMPS (BATTLESHIP)					
☐ RB20	⅛¢ Yellow Green	.14	.11	.12	.09
☐ RB21	¼¢ Pale Green	.15	.11	.12	.09
☐ RB22	⅜¢ Deep Orange	.26	.18	.29	.17
☐ RB23	⅝¢ Deep Ultramarine	.25	.16	.22	.15
☐ RB24	1¢ Dark Green	.38	.21	.43	.15
☐ RB25	1¼¢ Violet	.22	.11	.22	.12
☐ RB26	1⅞¢ Dull Blue	1.50	.76	1.35	.72
☐ RB27	2¢ Violet Brown	.62	.36	.66	.36
☐ RB28	2½¢ Lake	.45	.29	.28	.16
☐ RB29	3¾¢ Olive Gray	4.00	2.60	2.65	1.80
☐ RB30	4¢ Purple	1.50	.92	1.50	.76
☐ RB31	5¢ Brown Orange	1.80	1.01	1.15	.75
1914 BLACK PROPRIETARY STAMPS—S.L. WTMK.					
☐ RB32	⅛¢ Black	.38	.24	.32	.20
☐ RB33	¼¢ Black	1.25	.74	.85	.63
☐ RB34	⅜¢ Black	.38	.24	.40	.23
☐ RB35	⅝¢ Black	2.65	1.65	2.50	1.25
☐ RB36	1¼¢ Black	1.40	.67	1.25	.66
☐ RB37	1⅞¢ Black	19.00	14.00	14.00	8.60
☐ RB38	2¼¢ Black	2.70	1.60	3.60	1.30
☐ RB39	3⅛¢ Black	52.00	34.00	34.00	23.00
☐ RB40	3¾¢ Black	15.00	9.00	10.00	6.10
☐ RB41	4¢ Black	34.00	22.00	20.00	13.50
☐ RB42	4⅜¢ Black	740.00	510.00	—	—
☐ RB43	5¢ Black	88.00	53.00	43.00	32.00
1914 BLACK PROPRIETARY STAMPS—D.L. WTMK.					
☐ RB44	⅛¢ Black	.19	.14	.15	.10
☐ RB45	¼¢ Black	.19	.14	.15	.11
☐ RB46	⅜¢ Black	.80	.62	.78	.44
☐ RB47	½¢ Black	2.75	1.70	2.15	1.30
☐ RB48	⅝¢ Black	.16	.10	.16	.11
☐ RB49	1¢ Black	4.10	2.50	2.00	1.35
☐ RB50	1¼¢ Black	.35	.22	.47	.25
☐ RB51	1½¢ Black	2.60	1.70	2.15	1.50
☐ RB52	1⅞¢ Black	.85	.55	.54	.35
☐ RB53	2¢ Black	5.20	3.50	4.30	2.85

Scott No.		Fine Un-cancelled Each	Ave. Un-cancelled Each	Fine Used Each	Ave. Used Each
☐ RB54	2½¢ Black	1.25	.77	1.00	.66
☐ RB55	3¢ Black	2.85	2.00	3.15	1.92
☐ RB56	3⅛¢ Black	3.70	2.30	2.90	2.00
☐ RB57	3¾¢ Black	9.10	6.10	6.20	4.15
☐ RB58	4¢ Black	.35	.19	.26	.16
☐ RB59	4⅜¢ Black	8.10	6.00	6.20	4.30
☐ RB60	5¢ Black	2.00	1.30	1.70	.93
☐ RB61	6¢ Black	44.00	27.00	27.00	18.50
☐ RB62	8¢ Black	14.00	9.70	8.60	6.50
☐ RB63	10¢ Black	9.00	6.00	6.00	4.10
☐ RB64	20¢ Black	18.00	12.00	12.00	8.00

1919 PROPRIETARY STAMPS

☐ RB65	1¢ Dark Blue	.12	.10	.13	.09
☐ RB66	2¢ Dark Blue	.15	.11	.13	.09
☐ RB67	3¢ Dark Blue	1.10	.65	.75	.38
☐ RB68	4¢ Dark Blue	1.25	.70	.75	.38
☐ RB69	5¢ Dark Blue	1.25	.70	.75	.38
☐ RB70	8¢ Dark Blue	12.00	8.00	6.60	4.70
☐ RB71	10¢ Dark Blue	2.10	1.25	2.60	1.25
☐ RB72	20¢ Dark Blue	5.15	3.15	3.40	2.10
☐ RB73	40¢ Dark Blue	21.00	12.00	6.10	4.00

1918–1934 FUTURE DELIVERY STAMPS

☐ RC1	2¢ Carmine Rose	.16	.12	.13	.09
☐ RC2	3¢ Carmine Rose (cut 7.50)	33.00	21.00	17.00	13.00
☐ RC3	4¢ Carmine Rose	.43	.42	.13	.09
☐ RC3A	5¢ Carmine Rose	—	—	2.40	1.40
☐ RC4	10¢ Carmine Rose	.58	.40	.11	.09
☐ RC5	20¢ Carmine Rose	.80	.53	.12	.09
☐ RC6	25¢ Carmine Rose (cut .10)	3.40	2.20	.55	.34
☐ RC7	40¢ Carmine Rose (cut .10)	4.00	2.70	.55	.33
☐ RC8	50¢ Carmine Rose	1.30	.75	.34	.18
☐ RC9	80¢ Carmine Rose (cut .75)	9.80	6.70	3.70	2.25
☐ RC10	$1 Green (cut .10)	—	—	.23	.12
☐ RC11	$2 Rose (cut .08)	—	—	.26	.18
☐ RC12	$3 Violet (cut .12)	—	—	.78	.54
☐ RC13	$5 Dark Blue (cut .09)	—	—	.36	.21
☐ RC14	$10 Orange (cut .20)	—	—	.87	.56
☐ RC15	$20 Olive Bistre (cut .50)	—	—	3.90	2.60
☐ RC16	$30 Vermilion (cut .95)	—	—	5.00	3.70
☐ RC17	$50 Olive Green (cut .30)	—	—	.67	.50
☐ RC18	$60 Brown (cut .55)	—	—	2.50	1.25
☐ RC19	$100 Yellow Green (cut 5.00)	—	—	22.00	15.00
☐ RC20	$500 Blue (cut 3.00)	—	—	13.00	9.00
☐ RC21	$1000 Orange (cut 1.60)	—	7.60	8.00	5.00
☐ RC22	1¢ Carmine Rose Narrow Overprint	.15	.09	.14	.10
☐ RC23	80¢ Narrow Overprint (cut .20)	—	—	1.25	1.00

Scott No.		Fine Un-cancelled Each	Ave. Un-cancelled Each	Fine Used Each	Ave. Used Each
☐ RC25	$1 Serif Overprint (cut .08)	2.00	1.36	.33	.21
☐ RC26	$10 Serif Overprint (cut 4.50)	—	—	4.90	3.90

1918–1929 STOCK TRANSFER STAMPS—PERF. 11 or 12

☐ RD1	1¢ Carmine Rose, Perf. 11	.43	.29	.22	.15
☐ RD2	2¢ Carmine Rose, Perf. 11	.44	.26	.14	.09
☐ RD3	4¢ Carmine Rose, Perf. 11	.20	.16	.15	.10
☐ RD4	5¢ Carmine Rose, Perf. 11	.36	.21	.14	.09
☐ RD5	10¢ Carmine Rose, Perf. 11	.19	.16	.15	.09
☐ RD6	20¢ Carmine Rose, Perf. 11	.29	.17	.14	.09
☐ RD7	25¢ Carmine Rose, Perf. 12 (cut .07)	.98	.54	.22	.14
☐ RD8	40¢ Carmine Rose, Perf. 11	1.07	.52	.15	.10
☐ RD9	50¢ Carmine Rose, Perf. 11	.33	.21	.15	.10
☐ RD10	80¢ Carmine Rose, Perf. 11 (cut .07)	1.40	.63	.27	.26
☐ RD11	$1 Green, perf. 11, Red Ovpt. (cut .40)	17.00	11.00	9.60	7.00
☐ RD12	$1 Green, Perf. 11, Black Ovpt	1.10	.56	.12	.10
☐ RD13	$2 Rose, Perf. 11	1.00	.41	.14	.08
☐ RD14	$3 Violet, Perf. 11 (cut .17)	4.70	2.75	1.25	.70
☐ RD15	$4 Y. Brown, Perf. 11 (cut .07)	1.90	1.20	.14	.08
☐ RD16	$5 Blue, Perf. 11 (cut .07)	1.90	1.20	.15	.09
☐ RD17	$10 Orange, Perf. 11 (cut .07)	3.50	2.10	.37	.22
☐ RD18	$20 Bistre, Perf. 11 (cut 4.25)	19.20	13.10	.17	9.60
☐ RD19	$30 Vermilion (cut 1.05)	18.30	12.10	6.10	3.20
☐ RD20	$50 Olive Green (cut 9.75)	68.10	50.00	55.00	40.00
☐ RD21	$60 Brown (cut 4.60)	53.00	35.00	24.00	19.00
☐ RD22	$100 Green (cut 1.10)	18.50	11.50	5.10	3.00
☐ RD23	$500 Blue (cut 38.00)	—	—	116.00	64.00
☐ RD24	$1000 Orange (cut 10.00)	—	—	78.00	55.00
☐ RD25	2¢ Carmine Rose, Perf. 10	.30	.21	.12	.10
☐ RD26	4¢ Carmine Rose, Perf. 10	.30	.21	.12	.10
☐ RD27	10¢ Carmine Rose, Perf. 10	.39	.25	.11	.10
☐ RD28	20¢ Carmine Rose, Perf. 10	.39	.26	.11	.10
☐ RD29	50¢ Carmine Rose, Perf. 10	.63	.44	.20	.14
☐ RD30	$1 Green, Perf. 10	.30	.22	.12	.10
☐ RD31	$2 Carmine Rose, Perf. 10	.32	.22	.11	.10
☐ RD32	$10 Orange, Perf. 10 (cut .07)	2.65	1.65	.30	.18

1919–1928
STOCK TRANSFER STAMPS, SERIF OVERPRINT

☐ RD33	2¢ Carmine Rose, Perf. 11	1.70	.90	.77	.53
☐ RD34	10¢ Carmine Rose, Perf. 11	.46	.23	.11	.08
☐ RD35	20¢ Carmine Rose, Perf. 11	.41	.23	.12	.09
☐ RD36	50¢ Carmine Rose, Perf. 11	.95	.74	.36	.27
☐ RD37	$1 Green, Perf. 11 (cut. 11)	4.90	2.80	3.70	3.30
☐ RD38	$2 Rose, Perf. 11 (cut .12)	3.10	1.96	2.11	1.40
☐ RD39	2¢ Carmine Rose, Perf. 10	.41	.18	.15	.11
☐ RD40	10¢ Carmine Rose, Perf. 10	.36	.18	.15	.08
☐ RD41	20¢ Carmine Rose, Perf. 10	.63	.34	.11	.08

Scott No.		Fine Unused Block	Ave. Unused Block	Fine Unused Each	Ave. Unused Each	Fine Used Each	Ave. Used Each
CONFEDERATE STATES OF AMERICA (N.H. ADD 80%)							
☐ 1	5¢ J. Davis, Green	—	1070.00	230.00	140.00	122.00	75.00
☐ 2	10¢ Jefferson, Blue	—	1780.00	310.00	215.00	210.00	150.00
☐ 3	2¢ Jackson, Green	—	—	610.00	420.00	750.00	575.00
☐ 4	5¢ J. Davis, Blue	790.00	560.00	125.00	75.00	120.00	72.00
☐ 5	10¢ Jefferson, Rose	—	—	970.00	610.00	670.00	430.00
☐ 6	5¢ Davis, Lon. Print	88.00	63.00	16.00	10.00	21.00	14.50
☐ 7	5¢ Davis, Local Print	140.00	94.00	20.00	14.00	25.00	17.00
1863							
☐ 8	2¢ Jackson, Br. Red	615.00	420.00	73.00	53.00	360.00	260.00
☐ 9	10¢ Davis (len)	—	—	820.00	612.00	640.00	410.00
☐ 10	10¢ Davis (w fr. lin.)	—	—	3300.00	1970.00	1760.00	1170.00
☐ 11	10¢ Davis (no fr.)	86.00	65.00	15.00	9.00	20.00	12.00
☐ 12	10¢ Davis (fill. com)	130.00	105.00	18.00	11.00	22.00	17.00
☐ 13	20¢ Washington	490.00	360.00	62.00	42.00	320.00	230.00
1862							
☐ 14	1¢ J.C. Calhoun	1210.00	780.00	155.00	115.00	—	—

Scott No.		Fine Plate Block	Block	Fine Unused Each	Fine Used Each
1935. "FARLEY SPECIAL PRINTINGS"					
☐ 752	3¢ Newburgh	20.00	1.10	.22	.24
☐ 753	3¢ Byrd, Perf	29.00	3.30	.65	.70
☐ 754	3¢ Mother's Day	29.00	5.20	.92	.85
☐ 755	3¢ Wisconsin	28.00	5.20	.83	.85
☐ 756	1¢ Park	9.00	1.60	.33	.27
☐ 757	2¢ Park	13.00	3.10	.42	.37
☐ 758	3¢ Park	27.00	6.40	.75	.73
☐ 759	4¢ Park	36.00	12.00	1.80	1.90
☐ 760	5¢ Park	36.00	20.00	3.20	2.20
☐ 761	6¢ Park	70.00	23.00	3.40	2.15
☐ 762	7¢ Park	72.00	21.00	3.00	2.15
☐ 763	8¢ Park	72.00	21.00	3.00	2.10
☐ 764	9¢ Park	70.00	24.00	3.00	2.00
☐ 765	10¢ Park	77.00	36.00	5.00	4.65
☐ 766a	1¢ Chicago	—	5.20	.90	.75
☐ 767a	3¢ Chicago	—	6.50	.85	.68
☐ 768a	3¢ Byrd	—	30.00	4.00	2.25
☐ 769a	1¢ Park	—	17.00	2.00	1.75
☐ 770a	3¢ Park	—	44.00	3.00	3.65
☐ 771	16¢ Air Spec. Del	130.00	35.00	3.10	3.50

Scott No.		Center Line Block	Fine Arrow Block	Block W/Vert. Line	Pair W/Vert. Line	Block W/Horiz. Line	Fair W/Horiz. Line
1935. FARLEY POSITION BLOCKS AND PAIRS							
☐752	3¢ Newburgh	50.00	82.00	21.00	9.10	14.00	4.70
☐753	3¢ Byrd	115.00	172.00	97.00	46.00	4.50	2.00
☐754	3¢ Mother's Day	13.00	17.00	5.00	3.00	5.00	2.25
☐755	3¢ Wisconsin	13.00	17.00	5.00	3.00	5.00	2.25
☐756	1¢ Park	5.00	9.00	2.00	.90	1.50	.86
☐757	2¢ Park	7.10	12.00	2.00	1.35	2.60	1.20
☐758	3¢ Park	9.00	16.00	4.00	1.70	4.50	1.65
☐759	4¢ Park	14.50	45.00	9.00	3.70	8.20	4.00
☐760	5¢ Park	21.50	55.00	15.00	6.20	13.10	5.20
☐761	6¢ Park	29.00	88.00	21.00	8.20	17.10	7.20
☐762	7¢ Park	25.00	62.00	18.00	6.10	14.00	5.25
☐763	8¢ Park	27.00	66.00	19.00	6.20	15.00	5.10
☐764	9¢ Park	28.00	71.00	21.00	7.50	18.00	6.50
☐765	10¢ Park	45.00	212.00	32.00	16.10	31.00	13.50
☐766a	1¢ Chicago	22.00	—	24.00	9.50	14.00	7.70
☐767a	3¢ Chicago	20.00	—	18.00	8.00	11.00	7.60
☐768a	3¢ Byrd	23.00	—	18.00	13.50	15.00	9.00
☐769a	1¢ Park	15.00	—	17.00	7.00	11.00	5.50
☐770a	3¢ Park	33.00	—	20.00	14.20	22.00	15.00
☐771	16¢ Air Spec. Del	90.00	138.00	26.00	9.50	22.00	9.10

Scott No.		Fine Plate Block	Ave. Plate Block	Fine Unused Each	Ave. Unused Each	Fine Used Each	Ave. Used Each
HUNTING PERMIT STAMPS							
☐RW1 (1934)	$1 Blue	3100.00	2400.00	220.00	140.00	53.00	37.00
☐RW2 (1935)	$1 Rose Lake	4400.00	3800.00	285.00	190.00	110.00	63.00
☐RW3 (1936)	$1 Brown Blk...........	1950.00	1320.00	155.00	95.00	50.00	33.00
☐RW4 (1937)	$1 Lt. Green	1200.00	1000.00	110.00	72.00	22.00	15.00
☐RW5 (1938)	$1 Lt. Violet	1250.00	970.00	125.00	72.00	25.00	15.00
☐RW6 (1939)	$1 Chocolate	830.00	640.00	84.00	55.00	23.00	16.00
☐RW7 (1940)	$1 Sepia	850.00	670.00	75.00	50.00	16.00	10.00
☐RW8 (1941)	$1 Brn. Carmine	780.00	640.00	73.00	47.00	16.00	12.00
☐RW9 (1942)	$1 Violet Brn.	780.00	640.00	73.00	47.00	16.00	12.00
☐RW10 (1943)	$1 Deep Rose	320.00	210.00	41.00	28.00	14.00	10.00
☐RW11 (1944)	$1 Red Org.	310.00	195.00	38.00	26.00	9.50	7.50

Scott No.		Fine Plate Block	Ave. Plate Block	Fine Unused Each	Ave. Unused Each	Fine Used Each	Ave. Used Each
☐ RW12 (1945)	$1 Black	207.00	135.00	25.00	17.00	8.50	7.00
☐ RW13 (1946)	$1 Red Brn	223.00	147.00	24.00	18.00	8.00	6.00
☐ RW14 (1947)	$1 Black	223.00	147.00	24.00	18.00	8.00	6.00
☐ RW15 (1948)	$1 Brt. Blue	223.00	147.00	24.00	18.00	8.00	6.00
☐ RW16 (1949)	$2 Brt. Green	290.00	197.00	45.00	31.00	8.00	5.00
☐ RW17 (1950)	$2 Violet	290.00	197.00	45.00	31.00	8.00	5.00
☐ RW18 (1951)	$2 Gray Blk	290.00	197.00	45.00	31.00	8.00	5.00
☐ RW19 (1952)	$2 Ultramarine	290.00	197.00	45.00	31.00	8.00	5.00
☐ RW20 (1953)	$2 Dk. Rose Brn........	306.00	208.00	52.00	36.00	8.00	5.00
☐ RW21 (1954)	$2 Black	306.00	208.00	52.00	36.00	7.50	5.00
☐ RW22 (1955)	$2 Dk. Blue	306.00	208.00	52.00	36.00	7.50	5.00
☐ RW23 (1956)	$2 Black	306.00	208.00	52.00	36.00	7.50	5.00
☐ RW24 (1957)	$2 Emerald	306.00	208.00	52.00	36.00	7.50	5.00
☐ RW25 (1958)	$2 Black	306.00	208.00	52.00	36.00	5.40	4.10
☐ RW26 (1959)	$3 Bl./Ochre/Blk.	306.00	208.00	65.00	47.00	5.40	4.10
☐ RW27 (1960)	$3 Red Brn./Bl./Bist	306.00	208.00	65.00	47.00	5.40	4.10
☐ RW28 (1961)	$3 Bl./Bist./Brn.	335.00	222.00	82.00	53.00	5.40	4.10
☐ RW29 (1962)	$3 Bl./Brn./Blk	365.00	245.00	92.00	65.00	5.40	4.10
☐ RW30 (1963)	$3 Blk./Bl. Yel./Grn	365.00	245.00	92.00	65.00	5.40	4.10
☐ RW31 (1964)	$3 Bl./Blk./Bist	2300.00	1760.00	87.00	62.00	4.50	3.50
☐ RW32 (1965)	$3 Grn./Blk./Brn	370.00	245.00	86.00	57.00	4.50	3.50
☐ RW33 (1966)	$3 Bl./Grn./Blk.	350.00	230.00	80.00	57.00	4.50	3.50
☐ RW34 (1967)	$3 Multicolored	330.00	230.00	82.00	52.00	4.50	3.50
☐ RW35 (1968)	$3 Grn./Blk./Brn.	165.00	115.00	45.00	32.00	4.50	3.50

Scott No.			Fine Plate Block	Ave. Plate Block	Fine Unused Each	Ave. Unused Each	Fine Used Each	Ave. Used Each
☐ RW36 (1969)	$3	Multicolored	163.00	112.00	45.00	32.00	4.60	3.50
☐ RW37 (1970)	$3	Multicolored	163.00	112.00	33.00	20.00	4.60	3.50
☐ RW38 (1971)	$3	Multicolored	163.00	112.00	29.00	22.00	4.60	3.50
☐ RW39 (1972)	$5	Multicolored	122.00	82.00	22.00	14.00	4.60	3.50
☐ RW40 (1973)	$5	Multicolored	82.00	62.00	20.00	13.00	4.60	3.50
☐ RW41 (1974)	$5	Multicolored	82.00	50.00	14.50	12.00	4.60	3.50
☐ RW42 (1975)	$5	Multicolored	78.00	52.00	13.50	12.00	4.60	3.50
☐ RW43 (1976)	$5	Emerald & Blk.	72.00	47.00	13.50	12.00	450.00	4.25
☐ RW44 (1977)	$5	Multicolored	72.00	47.00	13.50	12.00	450.00	4.25
☐ RW45 (1978)	$5	Multicolored	67.00	44.00	13.50	12.00	450.00	4.25
☐ RW46 (1979)	$7.50	Multicolored	67.00	44.00	12.50	9.00	450.00	4.25
☐ RW47 (1980)	$7.50	Multicolored	63.00	42.00	12.50	7.75	4.20	3.10
☐ RW48 (1981)	$7.50	Multicolored	63.00	42.00	12.00	7.50	4.20	3.10

Scott No.			Fine Unused Each	Ave. Unused Each	Fine Used Each	Ave. Used Each

HAWAII
1851–1952. "MISSIONARIES"

			Fine Unused Each	Ave. Unused Each	Fine Used Each	Ave. Used Each
☐ 1	2¢	Blue	—	280,000.00	—	205,000.00
☐		On Cover				252,000
☐ 2	5¢	Blue	—	33,000.00		17,000.00
☐		On Cover				25,000.00
☐ 3	13¢	Blue	—	19,000.00		11,000.00
☐		On Cover				16,000.00
☐ 4	13¢	Blue	—	46,000.00	—	21,000.00
☐		On Cover				27,000.00

NOTE: Prices on the above classic stamps of Hawaii vary greatly depending on the individual specimen and circumstances of sale.

NOTE: Beware of fake cancels on Hawaiian stamps, when the value is higher used than unused.

Scott No.		Fine Unused Each	Ave. Unused Each	Fine Used Each	Ave. Used Each
1853. KING KAMEHAMEHA III					
☐5	5¢ Blue	—	505.00	—	315.00
☐6	13¢ Dark Red	—	315.00	—	290.00
☐7	5¢ on 13¢ Dark Red	—	3200.00	—	3700.00
1857.					
☐8	5¢ Blue	—	185.00	—	185.00
1861.					
☐9	5¢ Blue	—	82.00	—	82.00
1868. RE-ISSUE					
☐10	5¢ Blue	—	19.00	—	—
☐11	13¢ Rose	—	160.00	—	—
1859–1862.					
☐12	1¢ Light Blue	—	2510.00	—	2600.00
☐13	2¢ Light Blue	—	1920.00	—	1100.00
☐14	2¢ Black	—	2520.00	—	990.00
1863.					
☐15	1¢ Black	—	165.00	—	190.00
☐16	2¢ Black	—	375.00	—	325.00
☐17	2¢ Dark Blue	—	3000.00	—	1500.00
☐18	2¢ Black	—	650.00	—	1100.00
1864–1865.					
☐19	1¢ Black	—	250.00	—	396.00
☐20	2¢ Black	—	250.00	—	385.00
☐21	5¢ Blue	—	185.00	—	190.00
☐22	5¢ Blue	—	155.00	—	165.00
1864. LAID PAPER					
☐23	1¢ Black	160.00	116.00	520.00	330.00
☐24	2¢ Black	160.00	116.00	520.00	350.00
1865. WOVE PAPER					
☐25	1¢ Blue	175.00	108.00	140.00	100.00
☐26	2¢ Blue	150.00	105.00	140.00	100.00
☐27	2¢ Rose	185.00	117.00	115.00	85.00
☐28	2¢ Rose Vert	185.00	117.00	115.00	85.00
1869. ENGRAVED					
☐29	2¢ Red	57.00	38.00	—	—

Scott No.		Fine Unused Each	Ave. Unused Each	Fine Used Each	Ave. Used Each
1864–1871.					
☐ 30	1¢ Purple	9.00	7.50	7.00	6.10
☐ 31	2¢ Vermilion	12.00	8.50	7.00	5.10
☐ 32	5¢ Blue	53.00	34.00	20.00	12.20
☐ 33	6¢ Green	21.00	15.00	7.50	5.75
☐ 34	18¢ Rose	92.00	59.00	18.50	11.20
1875.					
☐ 35	2¢ Brown	8.10	5.00	3.00	2.00
☐ 36	12¢ Black	45.00	29.00	23.00	15.00
☐ 37	1¢ Blue	6.00	4.50	6.50	3.80
☐ 38	2¢ Lilac Rose	92.00	55.00	34.00	20.00
☐ 39	5¢ Ultramarine	15.00	8.50	3.10	1.80
☐ 40	10¢ Black	23.20	16.00	17.20	12.00
☐ 41	15¢ Red Brown	42.50	27.00	25.10	17.00
1883–1886.					
☐ 42	1¢ Green	2.70	1.70	1.86	1.25
☐ 43	2¢ Rose	4.10	2.60	1.25	.75
☐ 44	10¢ Red Brown	20.00	14.00	12.00	6.70
☐ 45	10¢ Vermilion	21.00	14.00	16.00	9.70
☐ 46	12¢ Red Lilac	65.00	42.00	32.00	22.00
☐ 47	25¢ Dark Violet	87.00	56.00	46.00	29.00
☐ 48	50¢ Red	145.00	88.00	78.00	53.00
☐ 49	$1 Rose Red	210.00	132.00	89.00	58.00
☐ 50	2¢ Orange	165.00	102.00	—	—
☐ 51	2¢ Carmine	27.00	19.00	—	—
1890–1891.					
☐ 52	2¢ Dull Violet	4.75	3.00	1.75	1.00
☐ 52C	5¢ Dark Blue	110.00	75.00	84.00	55.00
1893. PROVISIONAL GOVT. RED OVERPRINT					
☐ 53	1¢ Purple	4.70	3.30	4.30	3.10
☐ 54	1¢ Blue	4.70	3.30	4.30	3.10
☐ 55	1¢ Green	2.00	1.30	2.00	1.60
☐ 56	2¢ Brown	5.00	3.40	7.10	5.50
☐ 57	2¢ Dull Violet	1.75	1.20	2.00	1.10
☐ 58	5¢ Dark Blue	12.00	5.80	13.00	7.10
☐ 59	5¢ Ultramarine	6.00	4.20	4.50	3.10
☐ 60	6¢ Green	12.00	7.20	14.00	8.10
☐ 61	10¢ Black	9.00	6.00	8.00	6.20
☐ 62	12¢ Black	10.00	6.00	12.00	6.75
☐ 63	12¢ Red Lilac	125.00	78.00	142.00	86.00
☐ 64	25¢ Dark Violet	23.00	14.00	22.00	13.50

Scott No.		Fine Unused Each	Ave. Unused Each	Fine Used Each	Ave. Used Each
BLACK OVERPRINT					
☐65	2¢ Vermilion	56.00	34.00	44.00	29.00
☐66	2¢ Rose	1.80	.98	2.00	1.40
☐67	10¢ Vermilion	11.10	8.10	16.00	9.60
☐68	10¢ Red Brown	7.00	6.20	7.10	4.60
☐69	12¢ Red Lilac	215.00	140.00	260.00	175.00
☐70	15¢ Red Brown	18.00	13.00	24.00	16.00
☐71	18¢ Dull Rose	23.00	15.00	27.00	17.00
☐72	50¢ Red	54.00	33.00	55.00	34.00
☐73	$1 Rose Red	110.00	70.00	110.00	69.00
☐74	1¢ Yellow	2.50	1.70	1.80	1.21
☐75	2¢ Brown	2.50	1.70	1.20	.72
☐76	5¢ Rose Lake	4.20	2.50	2.10	1.65
☐77	10¢ Yellow Green	5.50	3.80	6.10	4.60
☐78	12¢ Blue	13.00	6.70	9.20	7.70
☐79	25¢ Deep Blue	13.00	7.00	12.00	9.00
1899.					
☐80	1¢ Dark Green	2.20	1.00	1.75	.97
☐81	2¢ Rose	1.90	.90	1.75	.97
☐82	5¢ Blue	5.10	3.30	3.50	2.15
1896. OFFICIAL STAMPS					
☐O1	2¢ Green	31.00	19.00	22.00	14.00
☐O2	5¢ Dark Brown	31.00	19.00	22.00	14.00
☐O3	6¢ Deep Ultramarine	31.00	19.00	22.00	14.00
☐O4	10¢ Rose	31.00	19.00	22.00	14.00
☐O5	12¢ Orange	31.00	19.00	22.00	14.00
☐O6	25¢ Gray Violet	31.00	19.00	22.00	14.00

Scott No.		Single	Block Of 4

UNITED STATES
FIRST DAY COVERS
UNCACHETED

Scott No.		Single	Block Of 4
☐ 551	½¢ Hale	28.00	42.00
☐ 552	1¢ Franklin	39.00	95.00
☐ 553	1½¢ Harding	35.00	50.00
☐ 554	2¢ Washington	50.00	73.00
☐ 555	3¢ Lincoln	50.00	73.00
☐ 556	4¢ Martha Washington	50.00	73.00
☐ 557	5¢ Roosevelt	120.00	150.00
☐ 558	6¢ Garfield	170.00	230.00
☐ 559	7¢ McKinley	108.00	530.00
☐ 560	8¢ Grant	108.00	530.00
☐ 561	9¢ Jefferson	108.00	530.00
☐ 562	10¢ Monroe	120.00	550.00
☐ 563	11¢ Hayes	410.00	530.00
☐ 564	12¢ Cleveland	130.00	700.00
☐ 565	14¢ Indian	300.00	1100.00
☐ 566	15¢ Statue of Liberty	345.00	—
☐ 568	25¢ Niagara Falls	425.00	1200.00
☐ 569	30¢ Bison	520.00	1200.00
☐ 570	50¢ Arlington	615.00	1300.00
☐ 571	$1 Lincoln Memorial	2800.00	5000.00
☐ 572	$2 U.S. Capitol	5600.00	—
☐ 573	$5 America	8600.00	—
☐ 576	1½¢ Harding	35.00	55.00
☐ 581	1¢ Franklin	1600.00	—
☐ 582	1½¢ Harding	43.00	60.00
☐ 583a	2¢ Washington	460.00	—
☐ 584	3¢ Lincoln	45.00	68.00
☐ 585	4¢ Martha Washington	45.00	68.00
☐ 586	5¢ Roosevelt	45.00	68.00
☐ 587	6¢ Garfield	54.00	80.00
☐ 588	7¢ McKinley	54.00	84.00
☐ 589	8¢ Grant	60.00	85.00
☐ 590	9¢ Jefferson	60.00	93.00
☐ 591	10¢ Monroe	70.00	110.00
☐ 597	1¢ Franklin	310.00	465.00
☐ 598	1½¢ Harding	40.00	64.00
☐ 599	2¢ Washington	520.00	—
☐ 600	3¢ Lincoln	55.00	84.00
☐ 602	5¢ Roosevelt	65.00	91.00
☐ 603	10¢ Monroe	79.00	110.00
☐ 604	1¢ Franklin	75.00	81.00
☐ 605	1½¢ Harding	50.00	72.00
☐ 606	2¢ Washington	63.00	92.00
☐ 610	2¢ Harding	20.00	37.00
☐ 611	2¢ Harding	70.00	105.00
☐ 612	2¢ Harding	100.00	120.00
☐ 614	1¢ Huguenot-Walloon	48.00	68.00
☐ 615	2¢ Huguenot-Walloon	65.00	86.00
☐ 616	5¢ Huguenot-Walloon	110.00	160.00
☐ 617	1¢ Lexington-Concord	44.00	65.00
☐ 618	2¢ Lexington Concord	65.00	86.00
☐ 619	5¢ Lexington-Concord	100.00	140.00
☐ 620	2¢ Norse-American	40.00	63.00
☐ 621	5¢ Norse-American	59.00	116.00
☐ 622	13¢ Harrison	33.00	53.00
☐ 623	17¢ Wilson	30.00	53.00
☐ 627	2¢ Sesquicenten-nial	20.00	34.00
☐ 628	5¢ Ericsson	27.00	44.00
☐ 629	2¢ White Plains	14.00	20.00
☐ 630	2¢ White Plains Sheet	1170.00	—
☐ 631	1½ Harding	28.00	48.00
☐ 632	1¢ Franklin	42.00	65.00
☐ 633	1½¢ Harding	42.00	65.00
☐ 634	2¢ Washington	42.00	65.00
☐ 635	3¢ Lincoln	42.00	65.00
☐ 635a	3¢ Bright Violet	22.00	34.00
☐ 636	4¢ Martha Washington	42.00	62.00
☐ 637	5¢ Roosevelt	42.00	62.00
☐ 638	6¢ Garfield	47.00	71.00
☐ 639	7¢ McKinley	52.00	76.00
☐ 6640	8¢ Grant	52.00	77.00
☐ 641	9¢ Jefferson	56.00	84.00
☐ 642	10¢ Monroe	60.00	88.00
☐ 643	2¢ Vermont	7.00	14.00
☐ 644	2¢ Burgoyne	19.00	27.00
☐ 645	2¢ Valley Forge	9.00	15.00
☐ 646	2¢ Molly Pitcher	14.00	26.00
☐ 647	2¢ Hawaii	15.00	33.00
☐ 648	5¢ Hawaii	32.00	74.00
☐ 649	2¢ Aero Conf.	12.00	17.00

Scott No.		Single	Block Of 4
☐650	5¢ Aero Conf. . .	15.00	27.00
☐651	2¢ Clark	6.50	10.00
☐653	½¢ Hale	18.00	28.00
☐654	2¢ Electric Light .	12.00	17.00
☐655	2¢ Electric Light .	45.00	69.00
☐656	2¢ Electric Light .	60.00	—
☐657	2¢ Sullivan	6.00	12.00
☐658	1¢ Kansas	19.00	34.00
☐659	1½¢ Kansas	19.00	34.00
☐660	2¢ Kansas	19.00	34.00
☐661	3¢ Kansas	34.00	63.00
☐662	4¢ Kansas	25.00	47.00
☐663	5¢ Kansas	27.00	50.00
☐664	6¢ Kansas	42.00	75.00
☐665	7¢ Kansas	46.00	85.00
☐666	8¢ Kansas	86.00	206.00
☐667	9¢ Kansas	43.00	65.00
☐668	10¢ Kansas	46.00	69.00
☐669	1¢ Nebraska . . .	19.00	30.00
☐670	1½¢ Nebraska . . .	17.50	—
☐671	2¢ Nebraska . . .	22.00	37.00
☐672	3¢ Nebraska . . .	30.00	72.00
☐673	4¢ Nebraska . . .	34.00	77.00
☐674	5¢ Nebraska . . .	42.00	78.00
☐675	6¢ Nebraska . . .	51.00	100.00
☐676	7¢ Nebraska . . .	42.00	98.00
☐677	8¢ Nebraska . . .	54.00	110.00
☐678	9¢ Nebraska . . .	54.00	110.00
☐679	10¢ Nebraska . . .	62.00	116.00
☐6680	2¢ Fallen Timbers .	4.10	9.10
☐681	2¢ Ohio River. . . .	4.10	9.10
☐682	2¢ Massachusetts Bay Colony. . . .	4.10	9.10
☐683	2¢ Carolina-Charleston . . .	4.10	9.00
☐684	1½¢ Harding	4.00	8.00
☐685	4¢ Taft.	6.00	8.00
☐686	1½¢ Harding	5.00	7.00
☐687	4¢ Taft.	18.00	—
☐688	2¢ Braddock . . .	6.00	17.00
☐689	2¢ Von Steuben . .	5.50	11.00
☐690	2¢ Pulaski.	5.00	6.00
☐692	11¢ Hayes	55.00	77.00
☐693	12¢ Cleveland . . .	58.00	81.00
☐694	13¢ Harrison . . .	56.00	75.00
☐695	14¢ Indian	51.00	75.00
☐696	15¢ Liberty	65.00	90.00
☐697	17¢ Wilson	220.00	—
☐698	20¢ Golden Gate	105.00	143.00

Scott No.		Single	Block Of 4
☐699	25¢ Niagara Falls	230.00	330.00
☐700	30¢ Bison.	160.00	240.00
☐701	50¢ Arlington. . .	246.00	360.00
☐702	2¢ Red Cross. . .	2.40	3.25
☐703	2¢ Yorktown	3.00	4.60
☐704	½¢ Olive Brown. . .	4.80	7.10
☐705	1¢ Green	6.50	8.00
☐706	1½¢ Brown	6.50	8.00
☐707	2¢ Carmine Rose .	6.50	8.00
☐708	3¢ Deep Violet . .	6.50	11.00
☐709	4¢ Light Brown. . .	6.50	12.00
☐710	5¢ Blue	6.70	12.00
☐711	6¢ Red Orange. . .	8.20	15.00
☐712	7¢ Black.	8.20	15.00
☐713	8¢ Olive Bistre . .	8.50	15.00
☐714	9¢ Pale Red . . .	11.00	16.00
☐715	10¢ Orange Yellow	15.00	17.00
☐716	2¢ Olympic Winter Games.	8.00	14.00
☐717	2¢ Arbor Day	5.00	7.10
☐718	3¢ Olympic Summer Games.	6.10	9.70
☐719	5¢ Olympic Summer Games.	6.00	11.50
☐720	3¢ Washington . . .	6.00	10.50
☐721	3¢ Washington (coil)	13.10	19.00
☐722	3¢ Washington (coil)	13.50	18.50
☐723	6¢ Garfield (coil) . .	14.00	18.50
☐724	3¢ William Penn . .	2.20	3.50
☐725	3¢ Daniel Webster .	2.20	3.50
☐726	3¢ Gen. Oglethorpe	2.20	3.50
☐727	3¢ Peace Proclamation.	2.20	3.50
☐728	1¢ Century of Progress.	2.20	3.50
☐729	3¢ Century of Progress.	2.20	3.50
☐730	1¢ American Philatelic Society, full sheet on cover.	112.00	12.00
☐730a	1¢ American Philatelic Society	3.10	4.60
☐731	3¢ American Philatelic Society . . .	115.00	—
☐731a	3¢ American Philatelic Society	2.25	3.50

Scott No.		Single	Block Of 4
☐732	3¢ National Recovery Administration	2.30	3.60
☐733	3¢ Byrd Antarctic	5.70	9.10
☐734	5¢ Kosciuszko	5.70	9.10
☐735	3¢ National Exhibition	41.00	—
☐735a	3¢ National Exhibition	4.65	8.10
☐736	3¢ Maryland Tercentenary	2.60	4.10
☐737	3¢ Mothers of America	2.60	4.10
☐738	3¢ Mothers of America	2.20	3.50
☐739	3¢ Wisconsin	2.25	3.75
☐740	1¢ Parks, Yosemite	3.60	4.50
☐741	2¢ Parks, Grand Canyon	3.20	4.70
☐742	3¢ Parks, Mt. Ranier	3.20	4.70
☐743	4¢ Parks, Mesa Verde	3.25	4.80
☐744	5¢ Parks, Yellowstone	3.25	4.80
☐745	6¢ Parks, Crater Lake	4.00	6.70
☐746	7¢ Parks, Acadia	4.20	9.10
☐747	8¢ Parks, Zion	4.50	18.00
☐748	9¢ Parks, Glacier Park	4.50	9.10
☐749	10¢ Parks, Smoky Mountains	9.10	16.10
☐750	3¢ American Philatelic Society, full sheet on cover	49.00	—
☐750a	3¢ American Philatelic Society	7.60	13.10
☐751	1¢ Trans-Mississippi Philatelic Expo, full sheet on cover	37.00	—
☐751a	1¢ Trans-Mississippi Philadelic Expo.	6.10	8.20
☐752	3¢ Peace Commemoration	9.20	19.40
☐753	34¢ Byrd	12.50	21.75
☐754	3¢ Mothers of America	12.50	21.75
☐755	3¢ Wisconsin	12.50	21.75
☐756	1¢ Parks, Yosemite	12.50	21.75

Scott No.		Single	Block Of 4
☐757	2¢ Parks, Grand Canyon	12.50	21.75
☐758	3¢ Parks, Mount Ranier	12.50	24.00
☐759	4¢ Parks, Mesa Verde	12.50	24.00
☐760	5¢ Parks, Yellowstone	12.50	24.00
☐761	6¢ Parks, Carter Lake	16.00	28.00
☐762	7¢ Parks, Acadia	16.00	28.00
☐763	8¢ Parks, Zion	15.00	31.00
☐764	9¢ Parks, Glacier Park	15.00	30.00
☐765	10¢ Parks, Smoky Mountains	16.50	34.00
☐766a	1¢ Century of Progress	15.00	21.00
☐767a	3¢ Century of Progress	15.00	21.00
☐768a	3¢ Byrd	15.00	21.00
☐769	1¢ Parks, Yosemite	12.00	18.00
☐770a	3¢ Parks, Mount Ranier	12.00	18.00
☐771	16¢ Air Mail, special delivery	28.00	42.00

UNITED STATES FIRST DAY COVERS CACHETED

Scott No.		Single	Block Of 4
☐610	2¢ Harding	310.00	—
☐617	1¢ Lexington-Concord	125.00	—
☐618	2¢ Lexington-Concord	125.00	—
☐619	5¢ Lexington-Concord	160.00	—
☐623	17¢ Wilson	250.00	—
☐627	2¢ Sesquicentennial	65.00	—
☐628	5¢ Ericsson	180.00	—
☐629	2¢ White Plains	56.00	—
☐630	2¢ White Plains Sheet	1650.00	—
☐635a	3¢ Bright Violet	45.00	—
☐643	2¢ Vermont	53.00	130.00
☐644	2¢ Burgoyne	59.00	129.00
☐645	2¢ Valley Forge	52.00	128.00

Scott No.		Single	Block Of 4
☐646	2¢ Molly Pitcher	93.00	—
☐647	2¢ Hawaii	69.00	121.00
☐648	5¢ Hawaii	92.00	134.00
☐649	2¢ Aero Conf.	26.00	66.00
☐650	5¢ Aero Conf.	43.00	84.00
☐651	2¢ Clark	34.00	74.00
☐654	2¢ Electric Light	48.00	100.00
☐655	2¢ Electric Light	122.00	272.00
☐656	2¢ Electric Light	120.00	—
☐657	2¢ Sullivan, Auburn, N.Y.	35.00	79.00
☐680	2¢ Fallen Timbers	35.00	79.00
☐681	2¢ Ohio River	33.00	70.00
☐682	2¢ Massachusetts Bay Colony	36.00	78.00
☐683	2¢ California-Charleston	36.00	78.00
☐684	1½¢ Harding	29.50	56.00
☐685	4¢ Taft	29.50	56.00
☐686	1½¢ Harding	29.50	56.00
☐687	4¢ Taft	29.50	56.00
☐688	2¢ Braddock	29.50	62.00
☐689	2¢ Von Steuben	29.50	56.00
☐690	2¢ Pulaski	34.00	55.00
☐702	2¢ Red Cross	28.00	43.00
☐703	2¢ Yorktown	33.00	52.00
☐704	1½¢ Olive Brown	21.00	30.00
☐705	1¢ Green	21.00	30.00
☐706	1½¢ Brown	21.00	30.00
☐707	2¢ Carmine Rose	21.00	30.00
☐708	3¢ Deep Violet	21.00	30.00
☐709	4¢ Light Brown	21.00	30.00
☐710	5¢ Blue	21.00	30.00
☐711	6¢ Red Orange	21.00	30.00
☐712	7¢ Black	21.00	30.00
☐713	8¢ Olive Bistre	24.00	37.00
☐714	9¢ Pale Red	24.00	37.00
☐715	10¢ Orange Yellow	24.00	37.00
☐716	2¢ Olympic Winter Games	27.00	42.00
☐717	2¢ Arbor Day	18.00	31.00
☐718	3¢ Olympic Summer Games	31.00	49.00
☐719	5¢ Olympic Summer Games	31.00	49.00
☐720	3¢ Washington	31.00	49.00
☐720b	3¢ Booklet pane	142.00	—
☐721	3¢ Washington (coil)	40.00	—

Scott No.		Single	Block Of 4
☐722	3¢ Washington (coil)	40.00	—
☐723	6¢ Garfield (coil)	30.00	—
☐724	3¢ William Penn	20.00	32.00
☐725	3¢ Daniel Webster	20.00	32.00
☐726	3¢ Gen. Oglethorpe	20.00	32.00
☐727	3¢ Peace Proclamation	22.00	38.00
☐728	1¢ Century of Progress	14.00	24.00
☐729	3¢ Century of Progress	17.00	27.00
☐730	1¢ American Philatelic Society, full sheet on cover	133.00	—
☐730a	1¢ American Philatelic Society	16.00	26.00
☐731	3¢ American Philatelic Society	137.00	—
☐731a	3¢ American Philatelic Society	19.50	31.00
☐732	3¢ National Recovery Administration	19.50	31.00
☐733	3¢ Byrd Antarctic	26.00	40.00
☐734	5¢ Kosciuszko	22.00	33.00
☐735	3¢ National Exhibition	55.00	—
☐735a	3¢ National Exhibition	19.00	27.50
☐736	3¢ Maryland Tercentenary	14.50	22.00
☐737	3¢ Mothers of America	14.50	22.00
☐738	3¢ Mothers of America	16.50	24.50
☐739	2¢ Wisconsin	12.00	18.50
☐740	1¢ Parks, Yosemite	12.00	18.50
☐741	2¢ Parks, Grand Canyon	12.00	18.50
☐742	35¢ Parks, Mt. Rainier	12.00	18.50
☐743	4¢ Parks, Mesa Verde	12.00	18.50
☐744	5¢ Parks, Yellowstone	15.00	21.50
☐745	6¢ Parks, Crater Lake	15.00	21.50
☐746	7¢ Parks, Acadia	15.00	21.50
☐747	8¢ Parks, Zion	15.00	21.50

Scott No.		Single	Block Of 4
☐748	9¢ Parks, Glacier Park	18.00	27.00
☐749	10¢ Parks, Smoky Mountains	18.00	27.00
☐750	3¢ American Philatelic Society, full sheet on cover	59.00	—
☐750a	3¢ American Philatelic Society	17.00	23.50
☐751	1¢ Trans-Mississippi Philatelic Expo., full sheet on cover	50.00	—
☐751a	1¢ Trans-Mississippi Philatelic Expo.	12.00	17.00
☐752	3¢ Peace Commemoration	23.00	32.00
☐753	3¢ Byrd	23.00	34.00
☐754	3¢ Mothers of America	25.00	36.00
☐755	3¢ Wisconsin Tercentenary	25.00	36.00
☐756	1¢ Parks, Yosemite	25.00	36.00
☐757	2¢ Parks, Grand Canyon	25.00	36.00

Scott No.		Single	Block Of 4
☐758	3¢ Parks, Mount Rainier	25.00	36.00
☐759	4¢ Parks, Mesa Verde	27.00	42.00
☐760	5¢ Parks, Yellowstone	27.00	42.00
☐761	6¢ Parks, Crater Lake	27.00	42.00
☐762	7¢ Parks, Acadia	27.00	42.00
☐763	8¢ Parks, Zion	27.00	42.00
☐764	9¢ Parks, Glacier Park	27.00	42.00
☐765	10¢ Parks, Smoky Mountains	27.00	42.00
☐766a	1¢ Century of Progress	27.00	42.00
☐767a	3¢ Century of Progress	27.00	42.00
☐768a	3¢ Byrd	27.00	42.00
☐769a	1¢ Parks, Yosemite	27.00	42.00
☐770a	3¢ Parks, Mount Rainier	27.00	42.00
☐771	16¢ Air Mail, special delivery	35.00	49.00

Scott No.		Single	Block	Plate Block
☐772	3¢ Connecticut Tercentenary	6.20	8.10	11.20
☐773	3¢ California Exposition	6.20	8.10	11.20
☐774	3¢ Boulder Dam	9.60	14.00	16.00
☐775	3¢ Michigan Centenary	6.00	8.00	11.00
☐776	3¢ Texas Centennial	6.20	9.00	12.00
☐777	3¢ Rhode Island Tercentenary	6.20	9.00	12.00
☐778	3¢ TIPEX	21.00	—	—
☐782	3¢ Arkansas Centennial	7.10	9.00	14.00
☐783	3¢ Oregon Territory	6.60	8.00	11.00
☐784	3¢ Susan B. Anthony	10.70	15.00	18.00
☐785	1¢ Army	5.00	6.70	9.00
☐786	2¢ Army	5.00	6.70	9.00
☐787	3¢ Army	5.00	6.70	9.00
☐788	5¢ Army	5.00	6.70	9.00
☐790	1¢ Navy	5.00	6.70	9.00
☐791	2¢ Navy	5.00	6.70	9.00
☐792	3¢ Navy	5.00	6.70	9.00
☐793	4¢ Navy	5.00	6.70	9.00
☐794	5¢ Navy	5.00	6.70	9.00
☐795	3¢ Ordinance of 1787	5.70	7.80	10.50
☐796	5¢ Virginia Dare	5.80	8.00	11.50
☐797	10¢ Souvenir Sheet	5.80	—	—

Scott No.		Single	Block	Plate Block
☐ 798	3¢ Constitution	5.70	8.00	11.00
☐ 799	3¢ Hawaii	5.70	8.00	11.00
☐ 800	3¢ Alaska	5.70	8.00	11.00
☐ 801	3¢ Puerto Rico	5.70	8.00	11.00
☐ 802	3¢ Virgin Islands	5.70	8.00	11.00
☐ 803	½¢ Franklin	2.25	3.10	4.30
☐ 804	1¢ Washington	2.25	3.10	4.30
☐ 805	1½¢ Martha Washington	2.25	3.10	4.30
☐ 806	2¢ Adams	2.25	3.10	4.30
☐ 807	3¢ Jefferson	2.25	3.10	4.30
☐ 808	4¢ Madison	2.25	3.10	4.30
☐ 809	4½¢ White House	3.40	5.00	7.00
☐ 810	5¢ Monroe	3.40	5.00	7.00
☐ 811	6¢ Adams	3.40	5.00	7.00
☐ 812	7¢ Jackson	3.40	5.00	7.00
☐ 813	8¢ VanBuren	3.40	5.00	7.00
☐ 814	9¢ Harrison	3.40	5.00	7.00
☐ 815	10¢ Tyler	4.10	6.10	8.00
☐ 816	11¢ Polk	4.10	6.10	8.00
☐ 817	12¢ Taylor	4.10	6.10	8.00
☐ 818	13¢ Fillmore	4.10	6.10	8.00
☐ 819	14¢ Pierce	4.10	6.10	8.00
☐ 820	15¢ Buchanan	4.10	6.10	8.00
☐ 821	16¢ Lincoln	4.10	6.10	8.00
☐ 822	17¢ Johnson	4.10	6.10	8.00
☐ 823	18¢ Grant	4.10	6.10	8.00
☐ 824	19¢ Hayes	4.10	6.10	8.00
☐ 825	20¢ Garfield	4.10	6.10	8.00
☐ 826	21¢ Arthur	6.30	8.80	13.20
☐ 827	22¢ Cleveland	6.30	8.80	13.20
☐ 828	24¢ Harrison	6.30	8.80	13.20
☐ 829	25¢ McKinley	7.00	9.60	13.20
☐ 830	30¢ Roosevelt	7.00	12.00	16.10
☐ 831	50¢ Taft	13.00	15.00	24.00
☐ 832	$1 Wilson	42.00	61.00	83.00
☐ 832c	$1 Wilson	23.00	32.00	42.00
☐ 833	$2 Harding	77.00	117.00	162.00
☐ 834	$5 Coolidge	125.00	202.00	306.00
☐ 835	3¢ Constitution	6.10	8.30	11.00
☐ 836	3¢ Swedes and Finns	6.10	8.30	11.00
☐ 837	3¢ Northwest Sesquicentennial	6.10	8.30	11.00
☐ 838	3¢ Iowa	6.10	8.30	11.00
☐ 852	3¢ Golden Gate Expo	6.10	8.30	11.00
☐ 853	3¢ N.Y. World's Fair	6.10	8.30	11.00
☐ 854	3¢ Washington Inauguration	6.10	8.30	11.00
☐ 855	3¢ Baseball Centennial	9.30	16.00	19.00
☐ 856	3¢ Panama Canal	5.40	7.70	10.00
☐ 857	3¢ Printing Tercentenary	5.40	7.70	10.00

Scott No.			Single	Block	Plate Block
☐858	3¢	50th Statehood Anniversary	5.40	7.20	9.60
☐859	1¢	Washington Irving	2.10	3.10	4.40
☐860	2¢	James Fenimore Cooper	2.10	3.10	4.40
☐861	3¢	Ralph Waldo Emerson	2.10	3.10	4.40
☐862	5¢	Louisa May Alcott	3.50	4.80	6.20
☐863	10¢	Samuel L. Clemens	6.20	8.70	13.60
☐864	1¢	Henry W. Longfellow	2.10	3.10	4.30
☐865	2¢	John Greenleaf Whittier	2.10	3.10	4.30
☐866	3¢	James Russell Lowell	2.10	3.10	4.30
☐867	5¢	Walt Whitman	3.10	4.35	6.10
☐868	10¢	James Whitcomb Riley	5.75	8.20	13.10
☐869	1¢	Horace Mann	2.05	3.05	4.40
☐870	2¢	Mark Hopkins	2.05	3.05	4.40
☐871	3¢	Charles W. Eliot	2.05	3.05	4.40
☐872	5¢	Frances E. Willard	2.85	4.25	5.75
☐873	10¢	Booker T. Washington	5.70	8.10	13.00
☐874	1¢	John James Audubon	2.10	3.10	4.60
☐875	2¢	Dr. Crawford W. Long	2.10	3.10	4.60
☐876	3¢	Luther Burbank	2.10	3.10	4.60
☐877	5¢	Dr. Walter Reed	2.95	4.60	6.10
☐878	10¢	Jane Addams	5.75	8.60	13.10
☐879	1¢	Stephen Collins Foster	2.20	3.25	5.10
☐880	2¢	John Philip Sousa	2.20	3.25	5.10
☐881	3¢	Victor Herbert	2.20	3.25	5.10
☐882	5¢	Edward A MacDowell	3.00	4.15	6.10
☐883	10¢	Ethelbert Nevin	6.70	9.35	16.25
☐884	1¢	Gilbert Charles Stuart	2.30	3.35	5.60
☐885	2¢	James A. McNeill Whistler	2.30	3.35	5.60
☐886	3¢	Augustus Saint-Gaudens	2.30	3.35	5.60
☐887	5¢	Daniel Chester French	2.85	4.20	5.60
☐888	10¢	Frederic Remington	6.70	9.20	15.20
☐889	1¢	Eli Whitney	2.35	3.40	5.60
☐890	2¢	Samuel F.B. Morse	2.35	3.40	5.60
☐891	3¢	Cyrus Hall McCormick	2.35	3.40	5.60
☐892	5¢	Elias Howe	3.10	4.30	6.50
☐893	10¢	Alexander Graham Bell	9.90	17.00	27.00
☐894	3¢	Pony Express	3.65	4.95	7.10
☐895	3¢	Pan American Union	3.65	4.95	7.10
☐896	3¢	Idaho Statehood	3.65	4.95	7.10
☐897	3¢	Wyoming Statehood	3.65	4.95	7.10
☐898	3¢	Coronado Expedition	3.65	4.95	7.10
☐899	1¢	Defense	3.65	4.95	7.10
☐900	2¢	Defense	3.65	4.95	7.10
☐901	3¢	Defense	3.65	4.95	7.10
☐902	3¢	Thirteenth Amendment	3.65	4.95	7.10
☐903	3¢	Vermont Statehood	3.65	4.95	7.10
☐904	3¢	Kentucky Statehood	3.65	4.95	7.10
☐905	3¢	"Win the War"	3.65	4.95	7.10

Scott No.		Single	Block	Plate Block
☐ 906	5¢ Chinese Commemorative	4.80	7.00	11.00
☐ 907	2¢ United Nations	3.30	4.70	6.70
☐ 908	1¢ Four Freedoms	3.40	4.90	7.10
☐ 909	5¢ Poland	4.00	5.70	8.10
☐ 910	5¢ Czechoslovakia	3.80	5.70	8.35
☐ 911	5¢ Norway	3.80	5.70	8.35
☐ 912	5¢ Luxembourg	3.80	5.70	8.35
☐ 913	5¢ Netherlands	3.80	5.70	8.35
☐ 914	5¢ Belgium	3.80	5.70	8.35
☐ 915	5¢ France	3.80	5.70	8.35
☐ 916	5¢ Greece	3.80	5.70	8.35
☐ 917	5¢ Yugoslavia	3.80	5.70	8.35
☐ 918	5¢ Albany	3.80	5.70	8.35
☐ 919	5¢ Austria	3.80	5.70	8.35
☐ 920	5¢ Denmark	3.80	5.70	8.35
☐ 921	5¢ Korea	3.80	5.70	8.35
☐ 922	3¢ Railroad	5.50	7.60	12.00
☐ 923	3¢ Steamship	3.40	5.15	7.80
☐ 924	3¢ Telegraph	3.40	5.15	7.80
☐ 925	3¢ Philippines	3.40	5.15	7.80
☐ 926	3¢ Motion Picture	3.40	5.15	7.80
☐ 927	3¢ Florida	3.40	5.15	7.80
☐ 928	5¢ United Nations Conference	3.40	5.15	7.80
☐ 929	3¢ Iwo Jima	3.40	5.15	7.80
☐ 930	1¢ Roosevelt	2.90	4.10	5.40
☐ 931	2¢ Roosevelt	2.90	4.10	5.40
☐ 932	3¢ Roosevelt	2.90	4.10	5.40
☐ 933	3¢ Roosevelt	2.90	4.10	5.40
☐ 934	3¢ Army	2.90	4.10	5.40
☐ 935	3¢ Navy	2.90	4.10	5.40
☐ 936	3¢ Coast Guard	2.90	4.10	5.40
☐ 937	3¢ Alfred E. Smith	2.90	4.10	5.40
☐ 938	3¢ Texas	2.90	4.10	5.40
☐ 939	3¢ Merchant Marine	2.90	3.95	5.40
☐ 940	3¢ Honorable Discharge	2.90	3.95	5.15
☐ 941	3¢ Tennessee	2.90	3.95	5.15
☐ 942	3¢ Iowa	2.90	3.95	5.15
☐ 943	3¢ Smithsonian	2.90	3.95	5.15
☐ 944	3¢ Santa Fe	2.90	3.95	5.15
☐ 945	3¢ Thomas A. Edison	2.90	3.95	5.15
☐ 946	3¢ Joseph Pulitzer	2.90	3.95	5.15
☐ 947	3¢ Stamp Centenary	2.90	3.95	5.15
☐ 948	5¢ and 10¢ Centenary Exhibition Sheet	4.60	—	—
☐ 949	3¢ Doctors	2.65	3.65	4.60
☐ 950	3¢ Utah	2.70	3.65	4.60
☐ 951	3¢ "Constitution"	2.70	3.65	4.60
☐ 952	3¢ Everglades Park	2.70	3.65	4.60
☐ 953	3¢ Carver	2.70	3.65	4.60

Scott No.			Single	Block	Plate Block
☐ 954	3¢	California Gold	2.70	3.70	4.70
☐ 955	3¢	Mississippi Territory	2.70	3.70	4.70
☐ 956	3¢	Four Chaplains	2.70	3.70	4.70
☐ 957	3¢	Wisconsin Centennial	2.70	3.70	4.70
☐ 958	5¢	Swedish Pioneers	2.70	3.70	4.70
☐ 959	3¢	Women's Progress	2.70	3.70	4.70
☐ 960	3¢	William Allen White	2.70	3.70	4.70
☐ 961	3¢	U.S.-Canada Friendship	2.70	3.70	4.70
☐ 962	3¢	Francis Scott Key	2.70	3.70	4.70
☐ 963	3¢	Salute to Youth	2.70	3.70	4.70
☐ 964	3¢	Oregon Territory	2.70	3.70	4.70
☐ 965	3¢	Harlan Fiske Stone	2.70	3.70	4.70
☐ 966	3¢	Palomar Observatory	2.70	3.70	4.70
☐ 967	3¢	Clara Barton	2.70	3.70	4.70
☐ 968	3¢	Poultry Industry	2.70	3.70	4.70
☐ 969	3¢	Gold Star Mothers	2.70	3.70	4.70
☐ 970	3¢	Volunteer Fireman	2.70	3.70	4.70
☐ 972	3¢	Indian Centennial	2.70	3.70	4.70
☐ 973	3¢	Rough Riders	2.50	3.50	4.30
☐ 974	3¢	Juliette Low	2.50	3.50	4.30
☐ 975	3¢	Will Rogers	2.50	3.50	4.30
☐ 976	3¢	Fort Bliss	2.50	3.50	4.30
☐ 977	3¢	Moina Michael	2.50	3.50	4.30
☐ 978	3¢	Gettysburg Address	2.50	3.50	4.30
☐ 979	3¢	American Turners Society	2.50	3.50	4.30
☐ 980	3¢	Joel Chandler Harris	2.50	3.50	4.30
☐ 981	3¢	Minnesota Territory	2.50	3.50	4.30
☐ 982	3¢	Washington and Lee University	2.50	3.50	4.30
☐ 983	3¢	Puerto Rico Election	2.50	3.50	4.30
☐ 984	3¢	Annapolis, Md.	2.50	3.50	4.30
☐ 985	3¢	G.A.R.	2.50	3.50	4.30
☐ 986	3¢	Edgar Allan Poe	2.50	3.50	4.30
☐ 987	3¢	American Bankers Association	2.50	3.50	4.30
☐ 988	3¢	Samuel Gompers	2.50	3.50	4.30
☐ 990	3¢	Nat. Capital Sesqui. (Executive)	2.50	3.50	4.30
☐ 991	3¢	Nat. Capital Sesqui. (Judicial)	2.50	3.50	4.30
☐ 992	3¢	Nat. Capital Sesqui. (Legislative)	2.50	3.50	4.30
☐ 993	3¢	Railroad Engineers	2.50	3.50	4.30
☐ 994	3¢	Kansas City Centenary	2.40	3.15	4.20
☐ 995	3¢	Boy Scout	2.40	3.15	4.20
☐ 996	3¢	Indiana Ter. Sesquicentennial	2.40	3.15	4.20
☐ 997	3¢	California Statehood	2.40	3.15	4.20
☐ 998	3¢	United Confederate Veterans	2.40	3.15	4.20
☐ 999	3¢	Nevada Centennial	2.40	3.15	4.20
☐ 1000	3¢	Landing of Cadillac	2.40	3.15	4.20
☐ 1001	3¢	Colorado Statehood	2.40	3.15	4.20
☐ 1002	3¢	American Chemical Society	2.40	3.15	4.20
☐ 1003	3¢	Battle of Brooklyn	2.40	3.15	4.20

Scott No.		Single	Block	Plate Block
☐ 1004	3¢ Betsy Ross	2.45	3.15	4.20
☐ 1005	3¢ 4-H Clubs	2.45	3.15	4.20
☐ 1006	3¢ B & O Railroad	2.45	3.15	4.20
☐ 1007	3¢ American Automobile Assoc.	2.45	3.15	4.20
☐ 1008	3¢ NATO	2.45	3.15	4.20
☐ 1009	3¢ Grand Coulee Dam	2.45	3.15	4.20
☐ 1010	3¢ Lafayette	2.45	3.15	4.20
☐ 1011	3¢ Mt. Rushmore Memorial	2.45	3.15	4.20
☐ 1012	3¢ Civil Engineers	2.45	3.15	4.20
☐ 1013	3¢ Service Women	2.45	3.15	4.20
☐ 1014	3¢ Gutenberg Bible	2.45	3.15	4.20
☐ 1015	3¢ Newspaper boys	2.45	3.15	4.20
☐ 1016	3¢ Red Cross	2.45	3.15	4.20
☐ 1017	3¢ National Guard	2.45	3.15	4.20
☐ 1018	3¢ Ohio Sesquicentennial	2.45	3.15	4.20
☐ 1019	3¢ Washington Territory	2.45	3.15	4.20
☐ 1020	3¢ Louisiana Purchase	2.45	3.15	4.20
☐ 1021	5¢ Opening of Japan	2.45	3.15	4.20
☐ 1022	3¢ American Bar Association	2.45	3.15	4.20
☐ 1023	3¢ Sagamore Hill	2.45	3.15	4.20
☐ 1024	3¢ Future Farmers	2.45	3.15	4.20
☐ 1025	3¢ Trucking Industry	2.45	3.15	4.20
☐ 1026	3¢ Gen. G.S. Patton, Jr.	2.45	3.15	4.20
☐ 1027	3¢ New York City	2.45	3.15	4.20
☐ 1028	3¢ Gadsden Purchase	2.45	3.15	4.20
☐ 1029	3¢ Columbia University	2.45	3.15	4.20
☐ 1030	½¢ Franklin	2.45	3.15	4.20
☐ 1031	1¢ Washington	2.45	3.15	4.20
☐ 1031a	1¼¢ Palace	2.45	3.15	4.20
☐ 1032	1½¢ Mount Vernon	2.45	3.15	4.20
☐ 1033	2¢ Jefferson	2.45	3.15	4.20
☐ 1034	2½¢ Bunker Hill	2.45	3.15	4.20
☐ 1035	3¢ Statue of Liberty	2.45	3.15	4.20
☐ 1036	4¢ Lincoln	2.45	3.15	4.20
☐ 1037	4½¢ Hermitage	2.45	3.15	4.20
☐ 1038	5¢ Monroe	2.45	3.15	4.20
☐ 1039	6¢ Roosevelt	2.45	3.15	4.20
☐ 1040	7¢ Wilson	2.45	3.15	4.20
☐ 1041	8¢ Statue of Liberty	2.45	3.15	4.20
☐ 1042	8¢ Statue of Liberty	2.45	3.15	4.20
☐ 1042a	8¢ Pershing	2.35	3.15	4.00
☐ 1043	9¢ The Alamo	2.35	3.15	4.00
☐ 1044	10¢ Independence Hall	2.35	3.15	4.00
☐ 1045	12¢ Harrison	2.35	3.15	4.00
☐ 1046	15¢ John Jay	2.35	3.15	4.00
☐ 1046a	15¢ John Jay	36.00	3.15	4.00
☐ 1047	20¢ Monticello	2.35	3.15	4.00
☐ 1048	25¢ Paul Revere	2.35	3.15	4.00

Scott No.			Single	Block	Plate Block
☐ 1049	30¢	Robert Lee	2.40	3.20	4.10
☐ 1050	40¢	John Marshall	3.10	4.60	8.00
☐ 1051	50¢	Susan Anthony	7.10	9.20	15.00
☐ 1052	$1	Patrick Henry	14.00	22.00	32.00
☐ 1053	$5	Alexander Hamilton	84.00	148.00	208.00
☐ 1054	1¢	Washington	2.15	—	—
☐ 1055	2¢	Jefferson	2.15	—	—
☐ 1056	2½¢	Bunker Hill	2.15	—	—
☐ 1057	3¢	Statue of Liberty	2.35	—	—
☐ 1058	4¢	Lincoln	2.40	—	—
☐ 1059	4½¢	The Hermitage	2.90	—	—
☐ 1059A	25¢	Paul Revere	3.20	—	—
☐ 1059Ab	25¢	Tagged	17.00	—	—
☐ 1060	3¢	Nebraska Territory	2.15	2.90	3.90
☐ 1061	3¢	Kansas Territory	2.15	2.90	3.90
☐ 1062	3¢	George Eastman	2.15	2.90	3.90
☐ 1063	3¢	Lewis & Clark	2.15	2.90	3.90
☐ 1064	3¢	Pennsylvania Academy of the Fine Arts	2.15	2.90	3.90
☐ 1065	3¢	Land Grant Colleges	2.15	2.90	3.90
☐ 1066	8¢	Rotary International	2.15	2.90	3.90
☐ 1067	3¢	Armed Forces Reserve	2.15	2.90	3.90
☐ 1068	3¢	New Hampshire	2.15	2.90	3.90
☐ 1069	3¢	Soo Locks	2.15	2.90	3.90
☐ 1070	3¢	Atoms for Peace	2.15	2.90	3.90
☐ 1071	3¢	Fort Ticonderoga	2.15	2.90	3.90
☐ 1072	3¢	Andrew W. Mellon	2.15	2.90	3.90
☐ 1073	3¢	Benjamin Franklin	2.15	2.90	3.90
☐ 1074	3¢	Booker T. Washington	2.15	2.90	3.90
☐ 1075	3¢, 8¢	FIPEX Souvenir Sheet	13.00	2.90	3.90
☐ 1076	3¢	FIPEX	2.00	2.90	3.90
☐ 1077	3¢	Wildlife (Turkey)	2.00	2.90	3.90
☐ 1078	3¢	Wildlife (Antelope)	2.00	2.90	3.90
☐ 1079	3¢	Wildlife (Salmon)	2.00	2.90	3.90
☐ 1080	3¢	Pure Food and Drug Laws	2.00	2.90	3.90
☐ 1081	3¢	Wheatland	2.00	2.80	3.90
☐ 1082	3¢	Labor Day	2.00	2.80	3.90
☐ 1083	3¢	Nassau Hall	2.00	2.80	3.90
☐ 1084	3¢	Devils Tower	2.00	2.80	3.90
☐ 1085	3¢	Children	2.00	2.80	3.90
☐ 1086	3¢	Alexander Hamilton	2.00	2.80	3.90
☐ 1087	3¢	Polio	2.00	2.80	3.90
☐ 1088	3¢	Coast & Geodetic Survey	2.00	2.80	3.90
☐ 1089	3¢	Architects	2.00	2.80	3.90
☐ 1090	3¢	Steel Industry	2.00	2.80	3.90
☐ 1091	3¢	Naval Review	2.00	2.80	3.90
☐ 1092	3¢	Oklahoma Statehood	2.00	2.80	3.90
☐ 1093	3¢	School Teachers	2.00	2.80	3.90
☐ 1094	4¢	Flag	2.00	2.80	3.90

Scott No.		Single	Block	Plate Block
☐ 1095	3¢ Shipbuilding	1.90	2.70	3.80
☐ 1096	8¢ Ramon Magsaysay	1.90	2.70	3.80
☐ 1097	3¢ Lafayette Bicentenary	1.90	2.70	3.80
☐ 1098	3¢ Wildlife (Whooping Crane)	1.90	2.70	3.80
☐ 1099	3¢ Religious Freedom	1.90	2.70	3.80
☐ 1100	3¢ Gardening Horticulture	1.90	2.70	3.80
☐ 1104	3¢ Brussels Exhibition	1.90	2.70	3.80
☐ 1105	3¢ James Monroe	1.90	2.70	3.80
☐ 1106	3¢ Minnesota Statehood	1.90	2.70	3.80
☐ 1107	3¢ International Geophysical Year	1.90	2.70	3.80
☐ 1108	3¢ Gunston Hall	1.90	2.70	3.80
☐ 1109	3¢ Mackinac Bridge	1.90	2.70	3.80
☐ 1110	4¢ Simon Bolivar	1.90	2.70	3.80
☐ 1111	8¢ Simon Bolivar	1.90	2.70	3.80
☐ 1112	4¢ Atlantic Cable	1.90	2.70	3.80
☐ 1113	1¢ Lincoln Sesquicentennial	1.90	2.70	3.80
☐ 1114	3¢ Lincoln Sesquicentennial	1.90	2.70	3.80
☐ 1115	4¢ Lincoln-Douglas Debates	1.90	2.70	3.80
☐ 1116	4¢ Lincoln Sesquicentennial	1.90	2.70	3.80
☐ 1117	4¢ Lajos Kossuth	1.90	2.70	3.80
☐ 1118	8¢ Lajos Kossuth	1.90	2.70	3.80
☐ 1119	4¢ Freedom of Press	1.90	2.70	3.80
☐ 1120	4¢ Overland Mail	1.90	2.70	3.80
☐ 1121	4¢ Noah Webster	1.90	2.70	3.80
☐ 1122	4¢ Forest Conservation	1.90	2.70	3.80
☐ 1123	4¢ Fort Duquesne	1.90	2.70	3.80
☐ 1124	4¢ Oregon Statehood	1.90	2.70	3.80
☐ 1125	4¢ San Martin	1.90	2.70	3.80
☐ 1126	8¢ San Martin	1.90	2.70	3.80
☐ 1127	4¢ NATO	1.90	2.70	3.80
☐ 1128	4¢ Arctic Explorations	1.90	2.70	3.80
☐ 1129	8¢ World Trade	1.90	2.70	3.80
☐ 1130	4¢ Silver Centennial	1.90	2.70	3.80
☐ 1131	4¢ St. Lawrence Seaway	1.90	2.70	3.80
☐ 1132	4¢ Flag	1.90	2.65	3.80
☐ 1133	4¢ Soil Conservation	1.90	2.65	3.80
☐ 1134	4¢ Petroleum Industry	1.90	2.65	3.80
☐ 1135	4¢ Dental Health	1.90	2.65	3.80
☐ 1136	4¢ Reuter	1.90	2.65	3.80
☐ 1137	8¢ Reuter	1.90	2.65	3.80
☐ 1138	4¢ Dr. Ephraim McDowell	1.90	2.65	3.80
☐ 1139	4¢ Washington "Credo"	1.90	2.65	3.80
☐ 1140	4¢ Franklin "Credo"	1.90	2.65	3.80
☐ 1141	4¢ Jefferson "Credo"	1.90	2.65	3.80
☐ 1142	4¢ Frances Scott Key "Credo"	1.90	2.65	3.80
☐ 1143	4¢ Lincoln "Credo"	1.90	2.65	3.80
☐ 1144	4¢ Patrick Henry "Credo"	1.90	2.70	3.80
☐ 1145	4¢ Boy Scouts	1.90	2.65	3.80

Scott No.		Single	Block	Plate Block
☐ 1146	4¢ Olympic Winter Games	1.90	2.70	3.70
☐ 1147	4¢ Masaryk	1.90	2.70	3.70
☐ 1148	8¢ Masaryk	1.90	2.70	3.70
☐ 1149	4¢ World Refugee Year	1.90	2.70	3.70
☐ 1150	4¢ Water Conservation	1.90	2.70	3.70
☐ 1151	4¢ SEATO	1.90	2.70	3.70
☐ 1152	4¢ American Woman	1.90	2.70	3.70
☐ 1153	4¢ 50-Star Flag	1.90	2.70	3.70
☐ 1154	4¢ Pony Express Centennial	1.90	2.70	3.70
☐ 1155	4¢ Employ the Handicapped	1.90	2.70	3.70
☐ 1156	4¢ World Forestry Congress	1.90	2.70	3.70
☐ 1157	4¢ Mexican Independence	1.90	2.70	3.70
☐ 1158	4¢ U.S. Japan Treaty	1.90	2.70	3.70
☐ 1159	4¢ Paderewski	1.90	2.70	3.70
☐ 1160	8¢ Paderewski	1.90	2.70	3.70
☐ 1161	4¢ Robert A. Taft	1.90	2.70	3.70
☐ 1162	4¢ Wheels of Freedom	1.90	2.70	3.70
☐ 1163	4¢ Boys' Clubs	1.90	2.70	3.70
☐ 1164	4¢ Automated P.O.	1.90	2.70	3.70
☐ 1165	4¢ Mannerheim	1.90	2.70	3.70
☐ 1166	8¢ Mannerheim	1.90	2.70	3.70
☐ 1167	4¢ Camp Fire Girls	1.90	2.70	3.70
☐ 1168	4¢ Garibaldi	1.90	2.70	3.70
☐ 1169	8¢ Garibaldi	1.90	2.70	3.70
☐ 1170	4¢ Senator George	1.90	2.70	3.70
☐ 1171	4¢ Andrew Carnegie	1.90	2.70	3.70
☐ 1172	4¢ John Foster Dulles	1.90	2.70	3.70
☐ 1173	4¢ Echo I	1.90	2.70	3.70
☐ 1174	4¢ Gandhi	1.90	2.70	3.70
☐ 1175	8¢ Gandhi	1.90	2.70	3.70
☐ 1176	4¢ Range Conservation	1.90	2.70	3.70
☐ 1177	4¢ Horace Greeley	1.90	2.70	3.70
☐ 1178	4¢ Fort Sumter	1.90	2.70	3.70
☐ 1179	4¢ Battle of Shiloh	1.90	2.70	3.70
☐ 1180	5¢ Battle of Gettysburg	1.90	2.70	3.70
☐ 1181	5¢ Battle of Wilderness	1.90	2.70	3.70
☐ 1182	5¢ Appomattox	1.90	2.70	3.70
☐ 1183	4¢ Kansas Statehood	1.90	2.70	3.70
☐ 1184	4¢ Senator Norris	1.90	2.70	3.70
☐ 1185	4¢ Naval Aviation	1.90	2.70	3.70
☐ 1186	4¢ Workmen's Compensation	1.90	2.70	3.70
☐ 1187	4¢ Frederic Remington	1.90	2.70	3.70
☐ 1188	4¢ China Republic	1.90	2.70	3.70
☐ 1189	4¢ Naismith	1.90	2.70	3.70
☐ 1190	4¢ Nursing	1.90	2.70	3.70
☐ 1191	4¢ New Mexico Statehood	2.40	3.40	4.80
☐ 1192	4¢ Arizona Statehood	1.90	2.80	3.70
☐ 1193	4¢ Project Mercury	1.90	2.80	3.70

Scott No.			Single	Block	Plate Block
☐ 1194	4¢	Malaria Eradication	1.80	2.75	3.70
☐ 1195	4¢	Charles Evans Hughes	1.80	2.75	3.70
☐ 1196	4¢	Seattle World's Fair	1.80	2.75	3.70
☐ 1197	4¢	Louisiana Statehood	1.80	2.75	3.70
☐ 1198	4¢	Homestead Act	1.80	2.75	3.70
☐ 1199	4¢	Girl Scouts	1.80	2.75	3.70
☐ 1200	4¢	Brien McMahon	1.80	2.75	3.70
☐ 1201	4¢	Apprenticeship	1.80	2.75	3.70
☐ 1202	4¢	Sam Rayburn	1.80	2.75	3.70
☐ 1203	4¢	Dag Hammarskjold	1.80	2.75	3.70
☐ 1204	4¢	Hammarskjold "Error"	4.90	8.10	13.00
☐ 1205	4¢	Christmas	2.20	3.30	4.60
☐ 1206	4¢	Higher Education	1.50	2.70	3.80
☐ 1207	4¢	Winslow Homer	1.50	2.70	3.80
☐ 1208	4¢	Flag	1.50	2.70	3.80
☐ 1209	4¢	Jackson	1.50	2.70	3.80
☐ 1213	5¢	Washington	1.50	2.70	3.60
☐ 1225	1¢	Jackson (coil)	1.50	2.70	2.70
☐ 1229	5¢	Washington (coil)	1.50	2.70	2.70
☐ 1230	5¢	Carolina Charter	1.50	2.60	3.75
☐ 1231	5¢	Food for Peace	1.50	2.60	3.75
☐ 1232	5¢	West Virginia Statehood	1.50	2.60	3.75
☐ 1233	5¢	Emancipation Proclamation	1.50	2.60	3.75
☐ 1234	5¢	Alliance for Progress	1.50	2.60	3.75
☐ 1235	5¢	Cordell Hull	1.50	2.60	3.75
☐ 1236	5¢	Eleanor Roosevelt	1.50	2.60	3.75
☐ 1237	5¢	Science	1.50	2.60	3.75
☐ 1238	5¢	City Mail Delivery	1.50	2.60	3.75
☐ 1239	5¢	Red Cross	1.50	2.60	3.75
☐ 1240	5¢	Christmas	1.50	2.60	3.75
☐ 1241	5¢	Audubon	1.50	2.60	3.75
☐ 1242	5¢	Sam Houston	1.50	2.60	3.75
☐ 1243	5¢	Charles Russell	1.50	2.60	3.75
☐ 1244	5¢	N.Y. World's Fair	1.50	2.60	3.75
☐ 1245	5¢	John Muir	1.50	2.65	3.75
☐ 1246	5¢	John F. Kennedy	1.50	2.65	3.75
☐ 1247	5¢	New Jersey Tercentenary	1.50	2.65	3.75
☐ 1248	5¢	Nevada Statehood	1.50	2.65	3.75
☐ 1249	5¢	Register & Vote	1.50	2.65	3.75
☐ 1250	5¢	Shakespeare	1.50	2.65	3.75
☐ 1251	5¢	Drs. Mayo	1.50	2.65	3.75
☐ 1252	5¢	American Music	1.50	2.65	3.75
☐ 1253	5¢	Homemakers	1.50	2.65	3.75
☐ 1254–57	5¢	Christmas	—	4.70	7.25
☐ 1258	5¢	Verrazano-Narrows Bridge	1.40	2.50	3.50
☐ 1259	5¢	Fine Arts	1.40	2.50	3.50
☐ 1260	5¢	Amateur Radio	1.40	2.50	3.50
☐ 1261	5¢	Battle of New Orleans	1.40	2.50	3.50

Scott No.			Single	Block	Plate Block
☐ 1262	5¢	Physical Fitness	1.40	2.45	3.40
☐ 1263	5¢	Cancer Crusade	1.40	2.45	3.40
☐ 1264	5¢	Churchill	1.40	2.45	3.40
☐ 1265	5¢	Magna Carta	1.40	2.45	3.40
☐ 1266	5¢	Intl. Cooperation Year	1.40	2.45	3.40
☐ 1267	5¢	Salvation Army	1.40	2.45	3.40
☐ 1268	5¢	Dante	1.40	2.45	3.40
☐ 1269	5¢	Herbert Hoover	1.40	2.45	3.40
☐ 1270	5¢	Robert Fulton	1.40	2.45	3.40
☐ 1271	5¢	Florida Settlement	1.40	2.45	3.40
☐ 1272	5¢	Traffic Safety	1.40	2.45	3.40
☐ 1273	5¢	Copley	1.40	2.45	3.40
☐ 1274	11¢	Intl. Telecommunication Union	1.40	2.45	3.40
☐ 1275	5¢	Adlai Stevenson	1.40	2.45	3.40
☐ 1276	5¢	Christmas	1.40	2.45	3.40
☐ 1278	1¢	Jefferson	1.40	2.45	3.40
☐ 1279	1¼¢	Gallatin	—	2.45	3.40
☐ 1280	2¢	Wright	—	2.45	3.40
☐ 1281	3¢	Parkman	—	2.45	3.40
☐ 1282	4¢	Lincoln	1.40	2.45	3.40
☐ 1283	5¢	Washington	1.40	2.45	3.40
☐ 1283B	5¢	Washington	1.40	2.45	3.40
☐ 1284	6¢	Roosevelt	1.40	2.45	3.40
☐ 1285	8¢	Einstein	1.40	2.45	3.40
☐ 1286	10¢	Jackson	1.40	2.45	3.40
☐ 1286a	12¢	Ford	1.40	2.45	3.40
☐ 1287	13¢	Kennedy	1.40	2.45	3.40
☐ 1288	15¢	Holmes	1.40	2.45	3.40
☐ 1289	20¢	Marshall	1.40	2.45	3.40
☐ 1290	25¢	Douglas	1.40	2.45	3.40
☐ 1291	30¢	Dewey	2.50	3.70	4.70
☐ 1292	40¢	Paine	3.70	5.10	6.70
☐ 1293	50¢	Stone	3.90	5.70	9.10
☐ 1294	$1	O'Neill	7.10	13.00	21.00
☐ 1295	$5	Moore	62.00	100.00	135.00
☐ 1304	5¢	Washington (coil)	—	pr. 2.20	lp. 3.10
☐ 1305	6¢	Roosevelt (coil)	—	pr. 2.20	lp. 3.10
☐ 1305C	$1	O'Neill (coil)	—	pr. 11.00	lp. 12.00
☐ 1306	5¢	Migratory Bird Treaty	1.40	2.45	3.50
☐ 1307	5¢	Humane Treatment of Animals	1.40	2.45	3.50
☐ 1308	5¢	Indiana Statehood	1.40	2.45	3.50
☐ 1309	5¢	Circus	1.40	2.45	3.50
☐ 1310	5¢	SIPEX	1.40	2.45	3.50
☐ 1311	5¢	SIPEX	1.40	2.45	3.50
☐ 1312	5¢	Bill of Rights	1.40	2.45	3.50
☐ 1313	5¢	Polish Millenium	1.40	2.45	3.50
☐ 1314	5¢	National Park Service	1.40	2.45	3.50
☐ 1315	5¢	Marine Corps Reserve	1.40	2.45	3.50

Scott No.			Single	Block	Plate Block
☐ 1316	5¢	Genl. Fed. of Women's Clubs	1.40	2.50	3.45
☐ 1317	5¢	Johnny Appleseed	1.40	2.50	3.45
☐ 1318	5¢	Beautification of America	1.40	2.50	3.45
☐ 1319	5¢	Great River Road	1.40	2.50	3.45
☐ 1320	5¢	Savings Bonds	1.40	2.50	3.45
☐ 1321	5¢	Christmas	1.40	2.50	3.45
☐ 1322	5¢	Mary Cassatt	1.40	2.50	3.45
☐ 1323	5¢	National Grange	1.40	2.50	3.45
☐ 1324	5¢	Canada Centenary	1.40	2.50	3.45
☐ 1325	5¢	Erie Canal	1.40	2.50	3.45
☐ 1326	5¢	Search for Peace	1.40	2.50	3.45
☐ 1327	5¢	Thoreau	1.40	2.50	3.45
☐ 1328	5¢	Nebraska Statehood	1.40	2.50	3.45
☐ 1329	5¢	Voice of America	1.40	2.50	3.45
☐ 1330	5¢	Davy Crockett	1.40	2.50	3.45
☐ 1331– 1332	5¢	Space Accomplishments	13.50 pr.	19.00	24.00
☐ 1333	5¢	Urban Planning	1.40	2.45	3.50
☐ 1334	5¢	Finland Independence	1.40	2.45	3.50
☐ 1335	5¢	Thomas Eakins	1.40	2.45	3.50
☐ 1336	5¢	Christmas	1.40	2.45	3.50
☐ 1337	5¢	Mississippi Statehood	1.40	2.45	3.50
☐ 1338	6¢	Flag	1.40	2.45	3.50
☐ 1339	6¢	Illinois Statehood	1.40	2.45	3.50
☐ 1340	6¢	Hemis Fair '68	1.40	2.45	3.50
☐ 1341	$1	Airlift	11.00	16.00	21.00
☐ 1342	6¢	Youth-Elks	1.40	2.40	3.20
☐ 1343	6¢	Law and Order	1.40	2.40	3.20
☐ 1344	6¢	Register and Vote	1.40	2.40	3.20
☐ 1345– 1354	6¢	Historic Flag series of 10, all on one cover	14.00	—	—
☐ 1355	6¢	Disney	3.60	4.30	5.20
☐ 1356	6¢	Marquette	1.50	2.45	3.30
☐ 1357	6¢	Daniel Boone	1.50	2.45	3.30
☐ 1358	6¢	Arkansas River	1.50	2.45	3.30
☐ 1359	6¢	Leif Erikson	1.50	2.45	3.30
☐ 1360	6¢	Cherokee Strip	1.50	2.45	3.30
☐ 1361	6¢	John Trumbull	1.50	2.45	3.30
☐ 1362	6¢	Waterfowl Conservation	1.50	2.45	3.30
☐ 1363	6¢	Christmas	1.50	2.45	3.30
☐ 1364	6¢	American Indian	1.50	2.45	3.30
☐ 1365– 1368	6¢	Beautification of America	3.20	10.00	13.10
☐ 1369	6¢	American Legion	1.40	2.50	3.30
☐ 1370	6¢	Grandma Moses	1.40	2.50	3.30
☐ 1371	6¢	Apollo 8	3.00	4.20	6.10

NOTE: From number 1372 to date, most First Day Covers have a value of $1.25 for single stamps, $2.25 for blocks of four and $3 for plate blocks of four.

MEMBERSHIP IN THE ANA COULD BE YOUR BEST INVESTMENT THIS YEAR.

As a rare coin collector or hobbyist, you continually deal with a variety of questions. How can you know that the coin you're about to purchase is not counterfeit? How can you find the detailed, current information you need to build your collection? There is no authority to help you solve all these problems. Unless you belong to the American Numismatic Association.

Coin Certification and Grading. ANA experts examine rare coins for authenticity to help safeguard against counterfeiting and misrepresentation. ANA now offers the ANACS Grading Service—third party expert opinions as to the condition of U.S. coins submitted for examination, and will issue certificates of authenticity.

Library Service. The largest circulating numismatic library in the world is maintained by the ANA. Its sole purpose is to provide you with free access to invaluable information that can't be found anywhere else.

The Numismatist. The Association's fully-illustrated magazine, considered *the* outstanding publication devoted exclusively to all phases of numismatics, is mailed free to all members.

And there are more benefits available through the ANA. Like coin insurance, special seminars, free booklets and photographic services. You can't find benefits like these anywhere else. Don't you owe it to yourself to join today?

JOIN US!

Application for Membership

Check one: □ Reg. □ Jr. □ Assoc. □ Life □ Club

Check one: □ Mr. □ Mrs. □ Ms. □ Club

Name (please print and use first name)

Street

City

State   Zip Code

Birth Date   Occupation

ANA Bylaws require the publication of each application. If you DO NOT wish your STREET address published, please check this box. □

I herewith make application for membership in the American Numismatic Association, subject to the Bylaws of said Association. I also agree to abide by the Code of Ethics adopted by the Association.

Signature of Applicant   Date

Signature of Proposer (optional)   ANA No.

Signature of Parent or Guardian
(Must sign for Junior applicants)

To charge to your credit card, please complete the following:

Account No. (All Digits) □ MasterCard □ Visa

☐☐☐☐☐☐☐☐☐☐☐☐☐☐☐☐

☐☐☐☐

Exp. Date of Card / MasterCard Interbank No.

DUES

Regular (adult)—*U.S. only* .... $ 26*
Regular (adult)—*all other countries* 28*
Club—*any country* 30*
Junior (11-17 years old).............. 11
Associate (child or spouse of R or LM
   member living at member's address).. 4
Life (adult individual) 350
   *Installment, $60 with application,** plus
   $25 per month for 12 months*
Life (club) $1250

* Add $6 application fee, first year only
** Includes $10 bookkeeping fee, deducted from
   final payment if made within 90 days of application. Life Membership is not effective until
   full $350 fee is paid.

Nonmember annual subscription—*U.S. only* $28
Subscription—*all other countries* $33

Foreign applications must be accompanied by
U.S. funds drawn on a U.S. bank.

Send your application to:

American Numismatic Association
P.O. Box 2366
Colorado Springs, CO 80901

============ **FOR IMMEDIATE DELIVERY** ============

VISA & MASTER CARD CUSTOMERS

ORDER TOLL FREE!
1-800-638-6460

This number is for orders only; it is not tied into the customer service or business office. Customers not using charge cards must use mail for ordering since payment is required with the order—sorry, no C.O.D.'s.

OR SEND ORDERS TO

THE HOUSE OF COLLECTIBLES
201 East 50th Street
New York, New York 10022

———— **POSTAGE & HANDLING RATES** ————

First Book	$1.00
Each Additional Copy or Title	$0.50

Total from columns on order form. Quantity_____ $_____

☐ Check or money order enclosed $_____ (include postage and handling)

☐ Please charge $_____ to my: ☐ MASTERCARD ☐ VISA

Charge Card Customers Not Using Our Toll Free Number
Please Fill Out The Information Below

Account No. _____ Expiration Date_____
                  (All Digits)
Signature_____

NAME (please print)_____ PHONE_____

ADDRESS_____ APT. #_____

CITY_____ STATE_____ ZIP_____

☐══════ **FOR IMMEDIATE DELIVERY** ══════☐

VISA & MASTER CARD CUSTOMERS
ORDER TOLL FREE!
1-800-638-6460

This number is for orders only; it is not tied into the
customer service or business office. Customers not using
charge cards must use mail for ordering since payment is
required with the order—sorry, no C.O.D.'s.

OR SEND ORDERS TO

THE HOUSE OF COLLECTIBLES
201 East 50th Street
New York, New York 10022

—————— **POSTAGE & HANDLING RATES** ——————

First Book $1.00
Each Additional Copy or Title $0.50

Total from columns on order form. Quantity_____ $_____

☐ Check or money order enclosed $_____ (include postage and handling)

☐ Please charge $_____ to my: ☐ MASTERCARD ☐ VISA

Charge Card Customers Not Using Our Toll Free Number
Please Fill Out The Information Below

Account No. _____ (All Digits) _____ Expiration Date_____

Signature_____

NAME (please print)_____ PHONE_____

ADDRESS_____ APT. #_____

CITY_____ STATE_____ ZIP_____